Cass Turnbull's Guide to Pruning

MARIAN good luck!

Cass

Cass Turnbull's
Guide to
Pruning

What, When, Where & How to Prune for a More Beautiful Garden

by the founder of

PlantAmnesty

SASQUATCH BOOKS
SEATTLE

Printed in the United States of America

Published by Sasquatch Books

Distributed by Publishers Group West

10 09 08 07 06 05 04   6 5 4 3 2

Cover design: Kate Basart

Cover Illustration: Yan Nascimbene

Interior design and composition: Stewart A. Williams

Interior illustrations: Kate Allen

Production editor: Cassandra Mitchell

Copy editor: Julie Van Pelt

Proofreader: Alice Smith

Indexer: Michael Ferreira

Library of Congress Cataloging-in-Publication Data

Turnbull, Cass, 1951–

The Northwest pruning guide: what, when, where & how to prune for a beautiful garden/by Cass Turnbull.

     p. cm.

  Includes index.

  ISBN 1-57061-316-8

      1. Pruning—Northwest, Pacific. 2. Pruning. I. Title.

SB125.T83 2004

635.9'1542/09795—dc22

2003058974

Sasquatch Books

119 South Main Street, Suite 400

Seattle, WA 98104

206/467-4300

www.sasquatchbooks.com

custserv@sasquatchbooks.com

Contents

PART ONE THE BASICS

PART TWO THE PLANTS

Contents

Foreword

I first met Cass Turnbull many years ago at a conference for Women in Horticulture. After I spoke about my experiences as a writer, gardener, and single mom, she walked up to me and said, "I thought I wanted to be you when I grew up, but today I realized I'm already older than you." I still chuckle over that, and I think Cass has grown up to be Cass, which is an even better plan.

Cass is a remarkable person, a woman of vision and character capable of uniting people of all ages and persuasions into a cohesive action group that has created positive horticultural change. Not only is this an outstanding achievement, but she does this unifying with grace, wit, and sparkling humor. I suspect she learned long ago that you can get people to do just about anything if you can make them laugh first. It's a great lesson, one I've absorbed as well.

Cass is a passionate person with a serious commitment to plant rights, plant health, and, if such a thing exists, plant happiness. Cass cares what happens to trees—all trees, everywhere. Through her teaching, her programs, and her writing, she makes many other people realize how deeply *we* care as well.

It is a testimony to her persuasive powers that the thousands of people who have been positively influenced through her organization, PlantAmnesty, all regard her with respectful fondness approaching love. They come away from Cass's programs with a healthy respect and informed appreciation for trees that changes the way they plant, prune, feed, and water their woodies.

If you've ever been to a Cass Turnbull class, you'll never forget the lessons you learned there. If you can't make her classes, or want a deeper, fuller, more explicit understanding of how to prune plants for optimal health, this book is for you. It's a keeper, one you'll use over and over, share with friends, and pass on to your kids. In fact, if Cass has her way (which I bet she will), all kids will learn how to prune properly before they get out of high school.

So read this book, not just when you know you need it, but when you have time to ponder. This is great material, presented in a clear unfussy manner that's a pleasure to read. Savor Cass's words and thoughts at leisure and your plants will thank you. So will your kids, and their kids, and the generations to come who will love and appreciate the trees we plant, prune, and cherish wisely today.

—Ann Lovejoy / October, 2003

Acknowledgments

I must thank my wonderful illustrator, Kate Allen, for the many hours and years she has spent creating a kinder, gentler world for plants. I know that it is her pictures that will make it possible for the reader to master the mysterious art of pruning. I am equally grateful to Glen Grantham, the illustrator of my first book, *The Complete Guide to Landscape Design, Renovation and Maintenance*, for agreeing to let Kate redraw his illustrations in her hand for this book. Thanks also to Ciscoe Morris for his expert advice and writing in the clematis section of Chapter 10. Most of all, I thank my husband, John, for underwriting PlantAmnesty over these many years (without really consenting to it, I'm afraid) and for his short-deadline, free editing service, and his steadfast love and support.

Introduction

Thomas Jefferson said, "Though I am an old man, I am but a young gardener." I feel much the same. I've been a professional gardener for more than twenty years and I'm still learning how to prune, observing how each species responds over the course of years. I have taken many classes on pruning and have read many books, but it is only by combining such education with field experience that I have come to know how to prune. I started out wanting to control Nature, bending her to my will with loppers, pruners, and saw. I now believe, instead, that I've been trained by Nature, in that patient, silent way that she has. I've come to understand that I must obey her laws if I hope to achieve a modicum of success in pruning and gardening. And only by giving many classes have I learned how to communicate the skill of pruning to others. I think that it is this combination of field experience, academic training, and experience teaching others that uniquely qualifies me to explain pruning to the beginner, both homeowner and professional.

When I was first learning to prune, the books I read were of little help. They showed pictures of shrubs that looked so good I wouldn't have bothered pruning them. I found a lot of information about pruning situations I rarely encountered, like how to fan-prune a peach tree, and yet there was little about *my* most common pruning problems. For example, people always wanted me to prune the giant rhododendrons that were blocking their windows. The pruning books I read tended to say something utterly unhelpful like "requires little pruning." Also, most pruning guides told me that the purpose of pruning was to improve the bloom and health of shrubs. Although I care about these things, what I mostly needed to know was how to make plants smaller.

Nothing about pruning is obvious. In fact, most of it is downright counterintuitive. People try to prune plants the way they cut lumber. But that doesn't work if the goal is a smaller plant. Instead, the plants respond by going into a spasm of regrowth, locking the homeowner into a high-maintenance battle against water sprouts and suckers.

I suspect that soon after man emerged from his cave with the first cutting tool, he whacked a limb off a bush, and it felt good. Bad pruning (what I call *mal-pruning*) accounts for more than 80 percent of all the work done by homeowners and professionals alike. And this sad state of affairs has persisted for decades. It was as if I were a member in a small secret society of people who somehow knew how to prune. We were doomed to watch helplessly as the rest of the world crashed through the greenscape with tools of destruction in their well-intentioned mission to restore order to their yards. Needless to say, it troubled me that so many plants were being treated exactly opposite of how they should be. People wasted so much time and money, cutting in ways that would eventually make their plants unhealthy, unpretty, unmanageable, and costly to maintain. It was just crazy!

Then one day, as part of a self-actualization seminar, I brainstormed the end of mal-pruning. In my unbridled imagination the most common forms of mal-pruning—tree topping, shrub shearing, and overthinning—became the topic of newspaper articles and the evening TV news. In the future, everyone would know what a heading cut was, and everyone would know how to prune. Or if not, they would know whom to hire to prune their yards: professionals who really did know how to prune.

Why, there would have to be an organization. It would be called "PlantAmnesty," and its mission and first goal would be "to end the senseless torture and mutilation of trees and shrubs caused by mal-pruning." The name made me laugh. What started as something of a lark soon got away from me. Sixteen years later our nonprofit group had eight hundred members.

PlantAmnesty has three major goals, the first of which is *to alert the public to the crimes against Nature* being committed in their own backyards, mainly mal-pruning but other things as well. The problem is that the topic of pruning is so dull that most people don't pay much attention, or money, to see that it is done right. Our mock-militant name, the combination of humor and controversy, made the topic of pruning newsworthy, and what followed was media coverage occurring with amazing regularity. PlantAmnesty was featured on the evening news, in the local papers, and then in an Associated Press arti-cle published across the country. I was also interviewed regularly on the radio, both locally and on the CBC (Canadian Broadcasting Corporation) and even the ABC (Australian Broadcasting Corporation), thus raising the public's awareness of the problem. We made people laugh with the idea of "the Ugly Yard Contest," but at the same time we instilled a low-grade fear among individuals that they might be doing something wrong and might even wind up being featured on the evening news!

During my years as executive director, PlantAmnesty used other methods to alert people to common plant "abuses." We developed the popular slide show of pruning horrors, a "Hall of Shame" educational booth, and TV public service announcements. We employed a nasty letter writer, distributed "arrest warrants," instigated two mutilated tree protests, and lobbied various city and state governing bodies. On the lighter side, we entered local parades with the precision marching gardeners' drill team and float, or sometimes we entered as the walking forest. We had Father Weedo Sarducci attend our events with his confessional, giving absolution to all those who confessed their horticultural sins.

Actually, it was Weedo who told me that when Moses was talking to his burning bush (see Chapter 7, Mounding-Habit Shrubs) he was given an additional ten commandments for gardeners:

1. Thou shalt not shear thy bush.

2. Thou shalt not top thy tree.

3. Thou shalt not plant thy sun lover in the shade, nor thy shade lover in the sun.

Weeping willow

4. Thou shalt mulch.

5. Thou shalt not leave stubs.

6. Thou shalt not flush cut, neither shalt thou paint wounds.

7. Thou shalt not cover up the base of thy plant, or thy tree, or thy shrub. Neither with mulch, nor with soil, nor with any landscape material.

8. Thou shalt cut circling/girdling roots.

9. Thou shalt not compact the root zone of thy tree, nor trench near the trunk of thy tree.

10. Thou shalt not weed-whip the trunk of thy tree, nor bash it with thy mower, nor leave anything tied on thy tree or the branches of thy tree, as is done in the land of the philistines.

The second goal of PlantAmnesty is *to provide the solutions* to the problem of poor pruning. We released a video on pruning, and a book, created the good gardeners and arborists' referral service, staffed the pruning hot line, published pamphlets of pruning information and articles, published a list of local classes on pruning, and gave classes. We organized volunteer pruning work parties for trees and needy landscapes.

PlantAmnesty's third goal is *to engender respect for plants*, which we did through many of the activities mentioned above, as well as by inventing the Seattle Heritage Tree Program.

We raised money for our group with tours, grants, plant sales, auctions, and such. Membership dues provided the major funding for our good works. In return, members attended regular meetings of horticultural interest and free pruning classes, gained access to the "cyber library," and received an educational and amusing newsletter. The newsletter contained (along with the usual organization updates) "Tales of Hope and Tales of Horror," the adopt-a-plant column (a listing of free plants), how-to pruning articles, cartoons, and other articles of horticultural/arboricultural interest.

After starting PlantAmnesty and teaching many pruning classes, I realized that people don't want to read an entire book just to figure out what to do with their camellia bush. But most encyclopedia-type pruning books leave a lot to be desired, devoting only a sentence or two to each plant. So, in each issue of the PlantAmnesty newsletter, I explained how to prune a specific plant or group of plants. I found that I could say everything needed in two or three pages. Most of these species-specific "pruning tips" have finally been collected in one place—this book. Each piece is meant to stand by itself. You will find in-depth information on specific plants in a variety of circumstances. As it turns out, there is more than one right way to prune a forsythia, as there is more than one wrong way. This means that you will find a fair amount of repetition within the book. But you will also be free to read it one bit at a time, as needed, though I recommend first reading the general-information Chapters 1 through 6.

I have also included information about corrective pruning for previously mal-pruned plants and tips on how to "read" the responses of plants. This will equip you to learn how to prune other plants, and indeed, will enroll you in Nature's training course. You will find that the Goddess Flora is an easy mistress to please. She readily forgives your mistakes and generously rewards those who are willing to serve her.

PART ONE

The Basics

CHAPTER ONE

Basic Cuts

I f people understood plants' responses to basic cuts, they probably could figure out all the rest of pruning on their own. I wish it were taught in grade school along with how maple and oak leaves look. I suspect that people think that pruning plants must be the same as cutting hair. But it's not. If your hair worked like a plant, after a haircut your hair would grow 3 inches in a day or two (instead of a month) and the ends would be very, very bushy.

Kind pruning is not just a matter of the size of the cut, or even how the plant looks soon after pruning. The true test of success is "Are you retaining the long-term health and beauty of the plant?" Your pruning should succeed in getting you what you want, with minimal effort and without destroying the purpose of your tree or shrub (which in most cases is its natural beauty, or fruit production on fruiting trees).

Learning the kinds of cuts and how plants respond to them is the difficult part of learning to prune. It takes a little concentration, but once you understand it, you are more than halfway home. I often tell people that pruning is a skill like any other. You must pay attention and then practice. Learning to do a decent job of pruning takes more time and effort than learning to vacuum, but less than learning to play basketball. The sport of pruning takes about as much time as learning to play a decent game of ping-pong.

Pruning for beginners is often made more confusing by the fact that the experts disagree on the definitions of types of pruning cuts.

Below is the system I learned, and still prefer, for defining the types of basic pruning cuts.

PLANT TERMINOLOGY

Before learning about different pruning cuts, it helps to understand how plants grow. The theory behind a plant's mechanism for regrowth is called *apical dominance*. The end bud on any branch is called the *apical bud* (apex, the top) or *terminal bud* (terminal, the end). This bud releases a chemical called an *auxin* (like a hormone) that travels down the stem (via gravity) just below the bark and keeps all the *dormant* (sleeping) buds from growing. If the terminal bud is removed (i.e., with a heading cut) then dormant buds down below on the branch are released from apical dominance and are free to grow out (*break bud*). This is the plant's system of replacing damaged parts.

This brings me to more plant terminology. A shorthand way of saying "a bud or side branch" is to say *node*. (And, if you say "soil" instead of "dirt" and "shrubs" instead of "bushes," you are well on your way to speaking gardenese.) Knowing to cut to the node

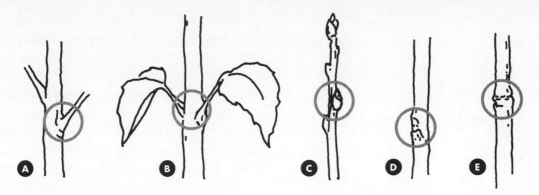

Figure 1.1 Types of nodes. Always cut to a node. A *node* is a place where a bud was or is. **A.** Branch node **B.** Leaf node **C.** Bud **D.** Leaf scar **E.** Bud scale scar

separates the pros from the amateurs in gardening. A node can also be a place where a leaf or branch used to be and where a dormant bud remains. Such a node will look like a bulge in the stem with a line or leaf scar where the leaf once was. If you cut to the node, a dormant bud will begin to grow out and form a new branch (see Figure 1.1).

Plants are categorized by their branching pattern into *alternate*, *opposite*, and *whorled* (see Figure 1.2).

The vast majority of plants are alternate in branching (with branches first to the left and then to the right). Opposite plants (with branches directly opposite one another) are harder to prune because it's difficult to

Figure 1.2 Branching patterns. **A.** Alternate **B.** Opposite **C.** Whorled

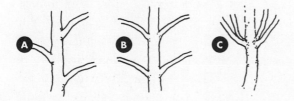

squeeze the tips of your hand pruners into the "V" to cut so as not to leave a stub to die back. A *stub* is the dead section of branch that occurred when the last person didn't cut to the node and so the branch died back. If buds or twigs are opposite each other, just cut off straight and as close to the paired side branches as you can (see Figure 1.3).

There's another reason why it's harder to direct the growth of opposite plants: Often the branch you chose because it was headed in the right direction (out from the center) is mirrored by one going the opposite (wrong) way. Do the best you can.

HEADING CUTS

Heading cuts are cuts that shorten branches, trunks, or twigs. There are two types of heading cuts, *nonselective* and *selective*.

Nonselective Heading

Nonselective heading means basically whacking back a branch to no place in particular. This sort of a cut is good for making things bushy, though not particularly good

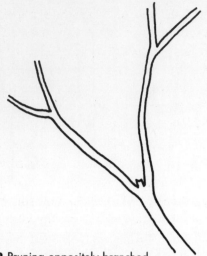

Figure 1.3 Pruning oppositely branched plants is difficult without leaving a small stub.

for general height reduction. It's the nonselective heading cut that gets most people into trouble (see Figure 1.4).

Wherever a cut is made, hidden dormant buds located directly below the cut end are stimulated into growing out into new branches. Furthermore, the shrub or tree speeds up its growth rate. The new growth on larger plants is most often skinny, unsightly, straight *water sprouts*. I call this the "Hydra effect," after the many-headed snake that Hercules battled. Every time Hercules cut off one of the snake's heads, two grew back in its place. People who cut back their tree or shrub in hopes of reducing its size are surprised to find that, by the end of the next year, the plant has grown back vigorously and thickly. Worst of all, for every one cut made, the pruner now has to make five or six new cuts. An exception is when you cut back into the older, barren wood of most conifers, such as junipers and firs. These conifers can't force new buds or regrow from barren wood! You are left looking at ugly brown branches for eternity. Oops!

Nonselective heading is also hard on a plant's health. All pruning cuts are an injury to a plant, but nonselective cuts are the hardest for a plant to take; and the bigger the cut, the harder it is for the plant to deal with it. In some pruning literature the nonselective heading cut is simply referred to as the "heading cut."

There are four types of nonselective heading cuts, based on the size of the cuts: topping, heading, tipping, and shearing. *Topping* is a term reserved for the large, nonselective heading of tree branches. *Heading*, or *heading-back*, refers to smaller cuts on trees or shrubs; heading can be either selective or nonselective. *Tipping*, or *tipping-back*, refers to very small cuts. *Shearing* refers to using

Figure 1.4 The *nonselective heading cut* creates bushiness. **A.** Removing tips **B.** stimulates dormant buds and **C.** results in rapid growth of water sprouts.

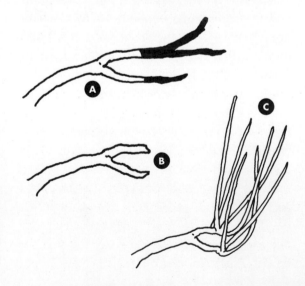

hedge shears (they look like a giant scissors) to cut back a plant uniformly.

Inappropriate Shearing

Shearing shrubs planted as a formal hedge, as the lower story of a Japanese formal garden, or as real topiary (plants sculpted into geometric shapes or animals) is perfectly all right. Unfortunately, most people, both professionals and homeowners, shear shrubs because they don't know how to selectively prune (see Selective Heading, below). One of the reasons I started PlantAmnesty was to stop what I call "inappropriate shearing" of shrubs. Shearing everything in sight is considered tacky by horticulturalists, but if it were simply a matter of taste, or if it were rare, I probably would have just ignored it. But I estimate that more than 90 percent of the work done on shrubs is exactly "inappropriate shearing," and although many garden writers have railed against it for, believe it or not, centuries, it persists throughout the world!

Aside from considerations of taste, there are other good reasons to avoid the use and misuse of shearing as a pruning technique:

Shearing is not a way to control size

Because shearing is nonselective heading, it will stimulate bushy regrowth, creating a twiggy outer shell on sheared plants. This layer of twigs shades out the interior, which then becomes leafless and full of dead leaves and deadwood. Meanwhile the outer shell becomes thicker and larger every year because, as it is sheared repeatedly, it must be cut a little farther out to retain its greenery. This dense, twiggy outer shell makes size reduction difficult because cutting back too far exposes that ugly dead zone inside the shrub. It is also physically difficult to cut through the thick twiggy mass. Although most plants will eventually green back up when they are pruned back into the dead zone, most needled evergreens, such as junipers, won't. Therefore, shearing is not a good way to control the size of a shrub. Selective pruning utilizing the selective heading cut (which I'll discuss later) ensures that there will be a green twig or branch to cut back to and can therefore be employed to reduce a shrub's size while retaining its natural look.

Only tough plants can take shearing

Shearing is also a drain on the health of plants. Selective pruners spend most of their time opening up the plant to let in more light and air and to reduce the buildup of deadwood and disease. Shearing plants creates the antithesis of a healthy environment, making shrubs more prone to insect attack, deadwood, and dieback. It adds a general stress on plants because the rapid, profuse growth promoted by repeated heading depletes their energy, and their resulting weakness and tender growth makes them more susceptible to injury from freeze or drought. This is why care must be taken to choose plants that are tough enough to take repeated shearing. Even then, the shearing must commence when the plants are young in order to avoid the sudden stress of shearing after they have reached maturity. Even with plants for which shearing is appropriate,

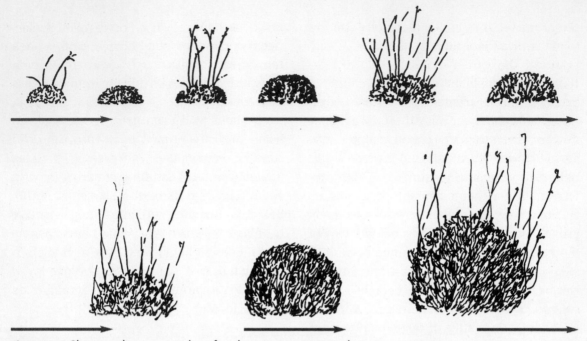

Figure 1.5 Shear madness: very tidy at first, but twice as messy in between prunings.

the good gardener will take time to reach inside and clean out the buildup of dead-wood and dead twigs.

Shearing is high maintenance

Another problem with shearing is that it is a high-maintenance chore. The new shoots (water sprouts) that result from heading cuts are thin and straight, and look quite wild. Heading cuts stimulate rapid regrowth, which soon destroys the tidy look that the first shearing created. Although shearing a plant may take little time, the tidy appearance vanishes very quickly, and shearing locks the practitioner into frequent reshear-ing (see Figure 1.5).

On the other hand, when a plant is selectively pruned, the new growth matches that which already exists and the plant ends up looking more natural (see Figure 1.6). The new growth continues at about the same rate as before, meaning that a selectively pruned plant doesn't look out of control quickly as one that has been sheared.

Shearing is a counter-productive form of pruning

I have even heard it compared to drug abuse—the first time through is very gratifying and very quick, but the unwary wielder of hedge shears will soon be locked into a high-mainte-nance habit. It will take more and more shear-ing to keep a plant looking its same tidy way, until one day the hapless homeowner will not be able to see out the window or open the door that's blocked by a giant ball or box. And eventually, the plant's health will begin to show signs of deterioration.

Shearing subverts a plant's natural beauty Aside from maintenance and health considerations, the gardener must also consider the purpose of plants when deciding how to prune them. Shearing often defeats the purpose of shrubbery, usually by cutting off the flowers, but other characteristics get subverted as well. True genius in landscaping is obtained by balancing theme and contrast. One of the elements of contrast is texture (for example, the fine leaves of a boxwood, the fluffy look of bridal wreath spiraea, or the bold, deep leaf of a viburnum). Shearing will eliminate contrast of texture, and everything will begin to look the same.

Shearing also does great violence to plants that have been chosen for their secondary characteristic of fine branch patterns. Such a plant is the star magnolia tree, which is valued for its flowers but is also valued for its beautiful branch patterns and fuzzy buds. Other shrubs and trees highly valued for their fine branch patterns are the doublefile viburnum, Harry Lauder's walking stick, Japanese maple, and eastern dogwood. Shearing ruins them. (See Chapter 9, Tree-Like Shrubs, and Chapter 11, Trees, for details on how to prune these plants.)

So, if you have a sheared hedge and you do rent a pair of power shears, restrain yourself from taking on the rest of the yard. Don't get carried away with shear madness.

Figure 1.6 *Selective heading* reduces size, allows a shrub to bloom and to retain its natural habit, and produces no ugly water sprouts between maintenance sessions. **A.** Original shrub **B.** Reduced with selective heading cuts (grab and snip) **C.** 1–3 years later **D.** Reduced with selective heading **E.** 2–5 more years **F.** Grab and snip again…and so on and so on….

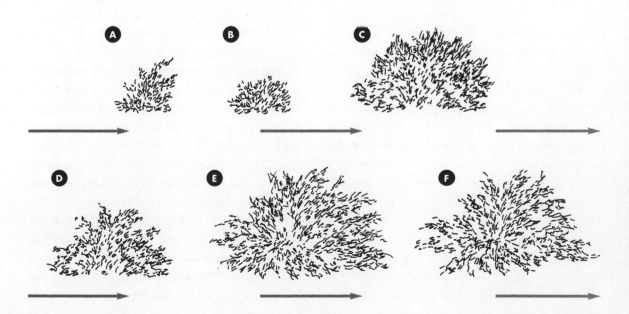

A Word About Tree Topping

Tree topping is the other major reason I started PlantAmnesty; it has been variously described as "vandalism for hire," "tree butchery," and a "disgrace to the tree service industry." It is estimated that 80 percent of the work done on trees, as a national average, is tree topping. In my opinion it constitutes a form of consumer fraud.

The large, nonselective heading cuts (topping cuts) cause rot (decay) to enter the tree trunk, much as gangrene follows a war wound. But there are no antibiotics for trees, and pruning paints have been shown to be ineffective in preventing the spread of decay in trees. Why do we care? Decay in trees shortens their lives and creates dangerous, weakened trunks. Topping also causes branches to die back, which is ugly, and at the same time, it stimulates water-sprout formation. These water sprouts are also ugly, but worse yet, they are weakly attached. Many years later, after they have become large, these new branches will be more prone to breakage than the original tree branches.

The perversity of tree topping is that it achieves none of the things people think it will. It makes a tree more dangerous, not safer, and it ruins the tree and the "water view" (since the topped tree rapidly reaches its original size again, except now it's ugly). Topping is not even a cheaper form of "pruning." It is paying to mutilate a tree on an ever increasing maintenance program (as water sprouts regrow exponentially in number every time they are cut off). Proper pruning of trees is actually done less and less frequently (not more and more often), though it does take more time on the original go-through than the few quick and dirty cuts of the tree topper.

The bottom line on tree pruning is that it should always maintain or improve the tree's natural beauty, health, and safety. Proper pruning will never increase maintenance by creating water sprouts or deadwood. Given that, you can prune a tree to solve a problem—such as creating access to a path, letting in more light, or decreasing limb breakage—or just to improve the looks of the tree itself.

Correct Uses of Nonselective Heading

Shearing is a correct way of pruning certain plants chosen to be topiary, formal hedges, or the lower story of Japanese gardens. In almost all cases the plants chosen for shearing have small leaves spaced closely together and are tough enough to take repeated shearing. The ubiquitous shearing of all other plants in the landscape into globes or cubes is not good pruning.

There are other correct uses of nonselective heading. A nonselective heading cut can be used to train young trees called "whips." Such young trees are sometimes cut to the ground to force regrowth of a straight new trunk. Sometimes the trunk of a sapling or whip is headed to force the branching that will become the tree's crown.

The nonselective heading cut is also used correctly on apple and pear trees to stiffen up young branches or to force production of fruit spurs. The ability of apple and pear trees to set up spurs distinguishes them from

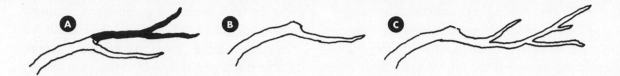

Figure 1.7 *Selective heading cut* **A.** Original branch **B.** Parent stem removed, leaving smaller side branch **C.** New growth continues through remaining existing branch.

other trees, and you can prune them differently because of it.

Selective Heading

Selective heading is the "right way" to shorten the branch of a tree or shrub. It reduces the amount of regrowth, looks more natural, and is easier on the health of the plant. Because of the Hydra effect, a combination of selective heading and thinning (see below) is the correct method for pruning the vast majority of shrubs and trees.

A *selective heading* cut—also called the reduction cut—reduces the length of a branch by cutting off one of two forks of a branch. The pruner selects the longest fork, follows it back to where it joins a shorter side branch, and cuts it off there. The side branch should be big enough to take over as the branch's end (see Figure 1.7).

How big a side branch is "big enough"? Well, it depends. The International Society of Arboriculture's Western Chapter Standards define it as "large enough to assume the terminal role." This means that the remaining fork will *not* respond by producing water sprouts (straight, skinny, ugly shoots that grow out at the site of a pruning cut). As an average, the remaining side branch should be at least half the diameter of the parent stem. Other authorities say that no more than a third of the foliage of the branch should be removed. "Big enough" is, however, a sliding scale, with many exceptions, based mostly on the requirements of the species in question. The questions to ask about any potential cut are "Will it rot the branch?", "Will it cause unsightly regrowth?", and "Will it eventually starve the branch, causing it to die?" If the answer to each question is no, cut away.

Selective Heading of Trees (Dropcrotching)

In general you could say that the bigger, older, and woodier a plant is, the harder heading cuts are for its health. Heading-back a privet, a spiraea, or a Japanese holly is no big deal. But when it comes to trees, we run into trouble.

No one knows why people often decide one day that their tree is too big. People don't declare all of a sudden that their dog, their house, or their kid is too big. But this subconscious assessment often leads to malpruning of the worst kind. Selective heading of trees (also called *dropcrotching, crown reduction,* or *de-horning*) is not as bad as topping, but it poses severe risks and is not the magic solution to the "too big" tree.

Dropcrotching is unsuccessful as an overall size control measure. After a *young, healthy* tree is pruned back, it increases its rate of growth. The remaining limbs elongate rapidly and very soon the tree is the size it was before. A tree that took five years to grow five feet taller will now grow five feet in a single year. Repeated dropcrotching will make the tree limbs leggier and the entire crown broader. But ten years later the tree will be the same height as its unpruned counterpart.

Very *large* dropcrotch cuts, or crown reduction, on very *old* trees may succeed in constraining size, but at an unacceptable cost to the health, safety, and longevity of the tree. The rot invades the main limbs, the tree expends valuable energy to deal with the wounds, and it may decline and die as a result. Even if the tree recovers, it will be more dangerous as a result. The lateral branches that take over as the main branches of the tree will likely be weaker and more prone to breakage even thirty years later.

When done, dropcrotching should probably be limited to a relatively few branches of a mature tree, say 2 percent of the total leaf area (for example, the branch hanging over the chimney or blocking the window). It should not be done for the sole purpose of trying to contain the size or height of a tree. Arborists estimate that an average tree's height can be reduced 5 to 10 percent without doing significant damage to the tree's health or natural beauty (depending on the tree's age, species, and health, of course). You would be hard pressed to find a tree (outside of a Japanese garden or a commercial orchard) that has been kept small by ongoing pruning. Trees are genetically programmed to reach a certain size, and unless you want to make it your life's work, you'd better plan on them getting to that size a lot sooner than you think. In places where trees are annually pruned for size control, using many small selective heading cuts (along the streets in Japan, for example, or where beech trees or hemlocks are used as hedges), you will find that the natural, characteristic branch pattern of the trees has been eliminated.

Dropcrotch pruning will always sadden an arborist who sees no good reason to cut other than the public's ever present arborphobia (fear of large trees) and the increasing obsession with water views. There would be no size reduction of trees in the best of all possible worlds.

Many people think that dropcrotching is an acceptable "heroic measure" to save certain special trees growing under powerlines. However, directional pruning, a sort of V-shaped pruning, has taken precedence for these situations (see "Pruning Trees for Powerlines" in Chapter 11, Trees). In this case pruning is used to redirect growth rather than to restrict the overall size of the tree.

Selective Heading of Shrubs and the Grab-and-Snip Method

With shrubs it's a different story. The smaller the leaves, the finer the branches, and the smaller the plant, the more you can use selective heading to tidy up the shrub and to reduce size within moderation. In general I would say that you can successfully make a shrub only a quarter smaller than it would be without pruning. If you do more (even using the correct selective heading cuts), it sends up water sprouts, looks funny, and/or grows back so fast that pruning is not worth the effort.

There is a decision-making process involved in pruning to reduce the size of a given shrub. It is not simply a matter of selectively heading-back every branch, as you might assume. Instead, you blur your eyes and stare at the offending shrub. Look for the branch that sticks up the highest or farthest into the walkway. Grab it with your left hand (assuming you're right-handed), then follow it down with your hand pruners into the interior of the shrub. Follow it down, down to where it meets a good-sized side branch that faces outward, and cut it off there. Or sometimes, if it is a wispy branch without internal side branches, you follow it down into the shrub and cut back to no place in particular, knowing that it will force buds to grow out at that point. Sure, it may "Hydra-back," but since the cut is located deep inside the shrub, the new growth will grow several months or perhaps a year before it reaches the surface; by that time it will have assumed a natural, pretty form, instead of sticking out awkwardly, as it would have had you made the cut closer to the surface.

After making the cut, toss the cut stem to the lawn. Repeat the process, always looking for the next-longest branch, not the next-closest one. In this way, the longest branches are removed. What remains are the unpruned branches that were already the size you want the shrub to be. (Figure 7.1 in Chapter 7 should help you visualize this.) By way of analogy, the difference between a shearing cut and a selective heading cut is like the difference between a blunt haircut and a shag haircut.

When you are done, the shrub retains its natural form, it is just smaller. And because many branches were not pruned at all, they still have their flower buds at the tips and the shrub will bloom no matter what season you prune.

"Selective pruning" means that you consciously select which branches to cut and which to leave in place, and that you have a clear idea of the purpose of the pruning session. "Selective pruning" is the name of real pruning, and PlantAmnesty's motto *Secare selecte* means "Prune selectively" (in Latin, of course).

THINNING

The *thinning* cut removes a branch (or twig) completely (see Figure 1.8). In other words, you cut a smaller, or "side," branch off of its larger, parent stem. Generally speaking, thinning cuts don't make plants smaller overall, they just reduce the bulk and clutter of the plant, making it sort of "see-through." Thinning off the lower, most interfering branches of a tree (called *skirting*, *limbing-up*, or *crown raising*) is more permanent and less harmful than crown reduction. Dr. Alex Shigo, the renowned research scientist known as the Isaac Newton of arboriculture, says in his lectures, "Trunk wood is different from branch wood." Trees are much better

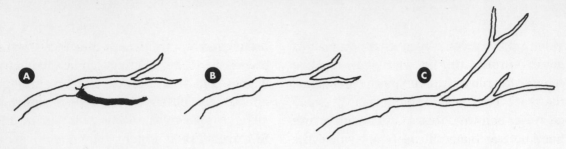

Figure 1.8 *Thinning cut* **A.** Original branch **B.** Smaller side branch removed **C.** Next season's growth is channeled into remaining limbs.

adapted to losing side branches than to having their major limbs or the *leader* (top part of the main trunk) cut in half.

Similarly, with many shrubs the correct approach is to take off the lower interfering branches that lie upon, or reach into, neighboring plants. You find the branch that stretches out most obtrusively into the pedestrian's way, follow it back to the main trunk, and cut it off there. General thinning throughout a plant, especially deadwooding, creates definition. It also increases air circulation, which is good for plant health. The plant just looks better (and, we assume, "feels" better). With those plants that resent being made smaller (being headed-back), we try to get what we want with thinning and raising.

Overthinning

As with so much in life, people get into trouble with "too much of a good thing." New pruners are apt to overthin. Once you can spot "wrong branches "(i.e., crossing, rubbing, wrong way, too straight, duplicating, etc.), you will be tempted to eradicate all the offenders. However, if you take out everything that is wrong, you are often left with a gutted plant or tree. Over-skirted plants look

top heavy, and in the case of trees, can be dangerous. Similarly, when all the internal branches are "skinned out" of a large tree, all the weight is dangerously concentrated at the ends of the scaffold branches. It is preferable to distribute the weight of foliage evenly throughout the tree. Overthinning the internal branches of a tree is called *lion's tailing*, and it should be avoided.

Correct Thinning

One consideration in thinning is aesthetics: An overthinned tree or shrub can look anorexic instead of artistic. Trees and shrubs vary in the degree to which they can be successfully thinned out. Here again the determining factors are "Will it water sprout?" and "Can this branch live if I remove this much foliage?" Most pines, for example, can't water-sprout back. They can also withstand an incredible amount of thinning before the overthinned branch in question dies (usually in a drought or freeze, or from sun scald some years later).

On the other end of the scale, some trees, such as ornamental cherries, plums, and crabapples, naturally have sort of a "messy" look and many crossing branches; but if you prune them too much (and it doesn't take much), they respond by producing a host of water sprouts. If the water sprouts are repeatedly removed every year thereafter, the tree's branches will rapidly age, crack, and eventually die. This is not to mention the incredible amounts of time and money that you are apt to waste by battling the mess of your own creation.

Most people want to prune to reduce the size of their plants, and you can moderately reduce many plants in size, always thinning as you do so. But let me add that most of what I do as a professional landscape renovator is prune out internal branches so that you can see into or through the plant. I also thin to break up the exterior solid-ball appearance of both old and young plants. This gives a shrub more character and definition. In addition, I prune to create definition between shrubs, so that instead of a mass of giant greenery jammed against the house, you can see three shrubs of different types, with room between them and the house. You will be able in some cases to see the soil beneath them.

It is not immediately apparent how following the rules (as often stated in pruning books: cutting off dead, crossing, and crowded branches) will result in a nicer, less oppressive looking shrub. So beginning gardeners will just have to follow the recipe with faith until they see the connection. When you make your cut on a shrub, do so just above a side branch or bud, slanting the way the bud is facing. Don't cut too close, but don't cut too far away. In the beginning,

don't agonize over which one is the right branch, just take your best shot and see how it goes. Then stand back and observe the effect on the plant's overall appearance.

SUMMARY

Pruning—especially heading—stimulates growth. Use thinning cuts. Avoid cutting ends or tips of branches to make things smaller; this technique often backfires.

Heading Cuts

Nonselective heading is good to stimulate bushiness. Examples: sheared hedges, chrysanthemums.

Selective heading is the cutting back to a side branch or bud. The remaining branch should be at least half the size of the one being removed. This reduces the plant size and is less likely to stimulate water sprouts or create dead wood.

Thinning Cuts

Thinning cuts remove branches to the point where they began as buds, or remove entire canes by cutting them off at the ground.

Thinning reduces the bulk and sometimes the height of shrubs (when the tallest canes are removed).

Thinning cuts are better for the health and good looks of plants, especially trees, than heading cuts.

Shrubs and trees vary in degree of thinning they can withstand. A pine tree will take a lot of thinning; a cherry tree resents even moderate thinning.

CHAPTER TWO

Selective Pruning Techniques

Selective pruning takes into account a plant's natural shape (habit) and characteristics. The kinds of cuts (heading or thinning), the total number of cuts (how much foliage is removed), and the size of the cuts should be matched to the specific plant. I call the combination of these factors a plant's "pruning budget." A large cut is harder on the plant (taking more of the pruning budget) than a smaller-diameter cut. A heading cut is harder on the plant's health (and therefore spends more of the budget) than a thinning cut. A nonselective heading cut is even harsher than a selective heading cut. And taking more foliage off a plant spends more of the pruning budget than taking off less.

THE PRUNING BUDGET

Some plants have a large pruning budget and others are very touchy. Too bad the budget isn't posted on the plant. It should be. Like the beeper at the do-it-yourself car wash, the plant should start beeping loudly as you are about to run out of allowable time. Instead, you continue pruning till it looks good to you now, by which time you may have unknowingly overpruned it. The plant waits until the next growing season and then explodes into water sprouts.

If your pruning budget is small (because the plant is, say, a deciduous viburnum), you may choose to spend it in any number of ways. You could make one medium selective heading cut and sixteen small thinning cuts. Or you might choose to make three large thinning cuts and a few smaller thinning cuts. Alternatively, you could do thirty small thinning cuts. It's up to you how you want to spend the budget, but you may not exceed your total budget allotment.

PLANT HABITS

When I gave my first lecture on pruning, I had to decide what to say. The principles of pruning are the same for every plant, but I knew that I approached a forsythia with a different mental attitude from the one with which I approached, say, a star magnolia. I concentrated on different kinds and sizes of branches. With the forsythia I spent most of my time sawing out large canes to the base; I didn't worry about its ability to recover. The magnolia, on the other hand, required dainty, thoughtful pruning that was more a matter of art. I realized that there were many plants that I pruned pretty much like forsythias and that I could tell how to approach most plants by simply observing their "habit" or natural shape.

This is how I came to divide plants into three broad categories. This classification is convenient, not scientific, but it will help you decide how to prune your shrubs by learning to read their habits. I have labeled these groups *mounding-habit*, *cane-growing*, and *tree-like*. This book is divided according to these habit categories and then by individual species within each group.

MATURE SIZE VS. ULTIMATE SIZE

The *mature size* of a plant is the size it will be in about ten years (give or take a few). It is what is listed on the plant tag that came with the plant from the nursery or what you found in your plant encyclopedia. It is just the average size of a given tree or shrub. The plant doesn't stop growing when it reaches its mature size; it slows down but continues growing to what I call the plant's *ultimate size*, roughly twice what is on the plant tag. Then it stops getting taller—although, like people, it may continue to get wider. It is good to know this fact of Nature, since I often hear people say odd things such as "My plant is out of control." It is, in fact, just growing up.

Over several years, I have tried to keep almost every plant I have encountered smaller with diligent pruning. My observation is this: You will be unable to keep a plant smaller than its mature size. The plant will just redouble its efforts, eventually exhausting you. Given that fact, you may have some success in moderating a mounding-habit or cane-growing shrub's size, keeping it in the mature size range with selective pruning. You don't need to let these types of shrubs grow to their ultimate size. However, it is best to let trees and most tree-like shrubs grow to their ultimate size. For these, thinning or removal of some of the lowest limbs may make them seem less oppressive or solve a perceived size problem.

Size Reduction and Root Mass

I have found that you can successfully reduce the size of a shrub by about one-quarter of what it would be without pruning. In the most obvious cases, you simply run out of green-leafed branches to cut back to; pruning such a shrub lower would mean reducing it to a jumble of barren branches. But even if there are still green-leaved branches to cut back to, you should not reduce the plant further than one-quarter of its current size. Plants will respond to size reduction based on their root mass. If you prune back too far, they simply grow back faster.

For example, some years ago a client asked me to reduce some Japanese holly shrubs (mounding-habit plants) so that the raised sprinklers could deliver irrigation over them, out to other shrubs. I easily accommodated her request, selectively reducing the size of the plants in a relatively short time. It took several years for them to get "too big" again. But every year it gets harder to achieve size reduction, as the plants gain in root mass. They regrow faster each year, and I must prune more and more frequently. The new growth no longer matches the old, but has begun to show the characteristic water-sprout look. And I know that, eventually, it will become impossible to keep the plants down.

REHABILITATIVE PRUNING

Given that most pruning is really mal-pruning, it is often necessary to restore plants to their original structure. I call such a process *rehabilitative pruning*. Whereas regular selective pruning (as an ongoing maintenance chore) goes quickly, rehabilitative pruning is quite time consuming. A plant may look better after just one long session, as in the case of, say "unshearing" a previously sheared azalea. But it may take years of patient work to return a previously topped tree to a decent form. On some occasions the plant in question will look worse, a lot worse, before it looks better.

The good news is that, given enough time, most trees and shrubs will reestablish their natural habits on their own. Our job is simply to assist them in doing so. Eventually, even water sprouts turn into thick, curved branches. Thinning and deadwooding will make mal-pruned plants look better as they recover, and simplifying tangled branch ends will move the process along.

RADICAL RENOVATION

I often tell my students that what the guy down the block did to his shrub is *plant butchery*. What I did is *radical renovation*. But at first the two can look much the same. Sometimes a previously mal-pruned shrub can be more quickly and effectively returned to its natural habit by cutting it to the ground or to a low, uneven framework. This is called *radical renovation*. It works best on the cane-growing category of shrubs and with somewhat lesser reliability on the mounding-habit shrubs. Even many tree-like shrubs

can withstand this treatment. It does look quite terrifying, though, and is a serious stress on the plant. But this practice is horticulturally accepted and is commonly referred to in many British garden books as "cutting back hard."

Occasionally, when it becomes necessary in the course of human events to radically reduce the size of plants, radical renovation is called upon. Such a practice is not to be entered into lightly or unadvisedly, but only when all other options have been exhausted. Radical renovation is done only once in a great many years to start a shrub over, giving it a second life. It is not done to keep a shrub small. This is an important distinction. And, like surgery, radical renovation is a calculated risk. Sometimes the plant dies. Most often it grows back and looks better than ever.

Timing is important. Pick the season with the longest period of benign, warm, wet weather so that the plant has the best chance at recovery. That usually means early spring. When most people radically renovate, they err on the side of not cutting back far enough. They wind up with the barren "legs" of a mature plant topped by the thick regrowth of a new crown. It looks bad. On broadleaf evergreen plants (like camellias and rhodies) I also recommend cutting all the branches back at once—not in thirds, as is often recommended. If you whack back a single branch that is then shaded by the remaining leafy stems, it is more likely to die than to break bud and grow back. In summary, radical renovation is a "sink or swim" proposition.

As a note of interest, some plants are cut to the ground annually as a regular mainte-

Figure 2.1 Victim of radical renovation **A.** Monday, Tuesday, Wednesday, Thursday . . . **B.** . . . Friday

nance procedure. This is then called either *stooling* when done to shrubs or *coppicing* when done to trees. The reason it is done is to accentuate some special feature of the plant. Red twig dogwood shrubs regrow with brighter red canes to add winter interest to a garden. Smoke bushes and paulownia trees will develop enormous leaves, adding interest to a mixed border. Though it isn't technically stooling, some people also cut hydrangeas and butterfly bushes (*Buddleia*) to the ground annually to get plants with even bigger blooms. In all cases, this kind of annual pruning is extremely high maintenance and is not to be confused with a way to keep other shrubs or trees small.

CHAPTER THREE

Suckers and Water Sprouts

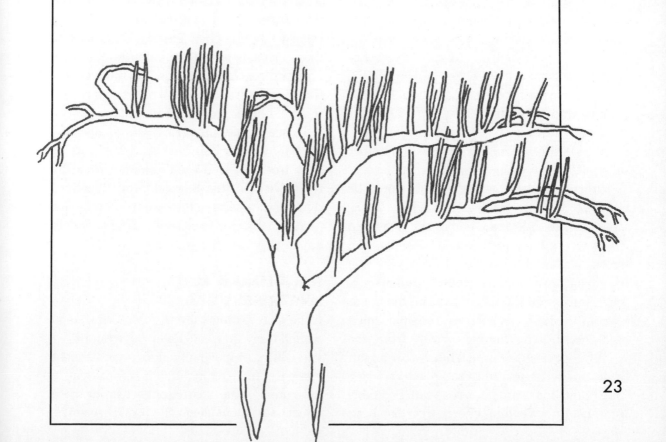

Many gardeners have picked up a bad habit of using the word "suckers" to indicate both suckers and water sprouts. Both terms refer to the rapidly growing, straight-up, skinny, ugly shoots found on trees and shrubs.

Water sprouts, however, occur on the crown or on the natural trunk and are usually a response to injury or mal-pruning (although a few plants grow water sprouts generally as a way of life, and natural new shoot growth occurring at the ends of branches can look like water sprouts on some young plants). Examples of injury include bashing the tree trunk with the lawn mower, topping, heading, overthinning, and *flush cutting*, which means cutting into the *branch collar* (the bulge of trunk wood at the base of a tree branch). In fact, the number of water sprouts on your tree or shrub is a pretty accurate reflection of too much or the wrong kind of pruning. This is bad news for many of you, I know. But it gets worse. Water sprouts exponentially increase in number every time you prune them off.

Other causes of water sprouts could be sudden, rapid freezing, as I have seen in the spring when side branches of budding plum trees freeze back to the scaffold limbs. And stress on an old tree, such as severe soil compaction, can cause water sprouts (properly, *epicormic shoots*) to form on the upper part of the limbs as a survival mechanism.

Suckers, true suckers, arise from the roots, rootstock, or on a trunk below a graft union. A *graft union* is the point at which one plant (for example, a rose with desirable blooms, or a weeping cherry tree) has been spliced (or grafted) to the rootstock or trunk of another vigorous, related-species plant. "Suckers" also refers to any other young shoots arising from the base of a shrub. Many naturally "suckering" shrubs, like quince or forsythia, can have old canes or branches cut to the ground and new suckers will arise as replacements.

Another important difference between water sprouts and suckers is how you deal with them. Water sprouts are best left to regrow into branches. True suckers—that is, those from below a graft union—must be removed regularly, forever. Naturally occurring suckers from a shrub's own roots can be removed or let grow as preferred.

I used to use the terms interchangeably, especially using "sucker" as a verb, as in "The tree suckered-back like mad when he topped it with the Sawsall." But I realized that in other parts of the country, people use "sucker" to refer exclusively to new shoots coming up from the ground.

HANDLING A FEW WATER SPROUTS

If the water sprouts are the result of a small wound—say, a Weed Eater™ "Whoops!"— you can try removing them all, and it might work. Cut them off in the summer (pruning in the summertime has a somewhat dwarfing effect). Cut them clear off; don't leave stubs.

Some people recommend ripping or snapping them off, sort of like pulling out your little sister's hair. But I have also heard that this doesn't work any better than cutting them off. Don't cut too close or wound the bark with your pruning tool either. Every once in a while a grounds crew member gets the idea that a whole cluster of water sprouts should be removed with one big slice. This causes major new damage to the plant (letting rot into the trunk of a tree, for example); and such cuts will only stimulate new water-sprout formation. You may care to rub off the buds as they reappear at the wound site with your thumbnail, thus catching them early and expending less effort.

Some people have reported moderate success using a product called Sucker Stopper that you spray on the cut ends. However, the product stops suckers for only about a year, and it is a chemical. The active ingredient (NAA, Ethyl 1-napthaleneacetate) damages new growth and should therefore be used only on wounds (pruning or otherwise) that are tiny, like the size of the base of a sucker. Don't spray the product on pruning cuts to prevent water sprouts as it will damage living tissue and interfere with wound closure.

HANDLING A LOT OF WATER SPROUTS

If you have many, many water sprouts on your tree or shrub, it won't work to take them all off. They will just keep returning, and always with some friends. They are, after all trying to replace that branch that was so rudely removed. They needed that branch and its leaves (solar collectors are how plants make food—you remember, photosynthesis). Since the plant can't regrow a nice big branch, it's regrowing many small ones (water sprouts) so that it won't starve. So what can you do if your tree is a mess of water sprouts? In some cases the kindest cut is the one to the ground level, then use a stump grinder. Like a car that's been in a crash, at some point many plants are considered a "total loss," aesthetically speaking.

However, I have been watching the progress of mal-pruned trees and shrubs for about sixteen years, and I can tell you that not only many but most trees and shrubs can recover given enough time. This is, I realize, more bad news for people who don't want to keep looking at a forest of ugly water sprouts. On trees, especially, you need to let water sprouts grow for several years. Usually about the time the water sprouts get to the height that the tree once was, they will stop growing straight up and will begin to curve again, fattening up, growing side branches, and becoming the new crown of the tree. The same thing applies to shrubs, except that they take less time to recover.

You can help hasten the process and make the afflicted plant look better for now by prompt removal of deadwood and by gradual reduction, over the years, of the number of water sprouts. At each cluster of sprouts, choose a few to cut off (usually the smallest and most crowded, and those headed too far down, too far up, or back toward the center). The ones you leave in place will help stop new ones from reappearing. Come back next year and get some more. Sneak up on them. Narrow the number of water sprouts down to the few that you have chosen to become replacement branches. If you remove too many too soon, you just get a spasm of water-sprout regrowth.

Patience is the greatest gardening lesson. In the end, should you develop an affinity for gardening, the forced delays (everything is on the five-year plan in gardening) will cease to be frustrating. Haven't you noticed how fast time is beginning to race by? Well, here's the way to slow it down.

Some plants are more prone to water-sprout growth than others. Heavily water-sprouting plants include ornamental cherry trees, ornamental plums, crabapples, witch hazels, deciduous viburnums, cotoneasters, dogwood trees, and magnolias. Prune these plants very lightly indeed, and avoid the heading cut. For moderately better success, in mild climates such as Seattle's, prune in the summer. If the plant begins to grow water sprouts (at the site of the cuts, the first growing season after pruning), do less, not more, next year.

As you now know, it is advantageous to let water sprouts grow unchecked for a year or two before doing anything except deadwooding. People often feel that they should jump on a water sprout right away, before it gets out of hand. Wrong! Let it grow. Let the plant regain what it needs. I realize this is all terribly counterintuitive, but there you have it.

TRUE SUCKERS
Occasionally suckers (true suckers) will appear from the roots of a plant or at the graft union. In this case you must remove all of the offending shoots. If you don't, the undesirable part of the tree or shrub can totally overtake the good part. Unfortunately you will probably have to remove suckers year, after year, after year. In the case of rootstock suckers—say, on a grafted rose— this means digging down to where they originate on the roots and cutting them off there. What a pain! If the suckers are from the base of a nongrafted plant, such as a lilac or a forsythia, you can let them grow up into trunks or canes. Some people use them as replacements for old canes that they prune out. Suckers are more common on younger plants and will eventually cease coming up on mature shrubs as long as the base remains shaded, healthy, and relatively unpruned.

STOPPING WATER SPROUTS AND SUCKERS
The only successful way to beat suckers and water sprouts is to not create them. Don't plant your tree too deep. Don't let plants suffer from drought, or compact the soil, or wound trees, or overprune or mal-prune. (You have already taken the first step in prevention: getting and reading this book on pruning.)

SUMMARY
Water sprouts are the straight-up, ugly, skinny shoots that occur on the limbs of a tree or shrub. They are usually the result of mal-pruning—either too much or the wrong way (flush cuts or heading cuts). The best way to get rid of them is to let them grow for several years until they turn back into branches. It won't work to cut them off. They just keep coming back with their friends.

True suckers (also straight-up, skinny, ugly shoots) from below a graft union on a trunk, or off the base of a tree, or from the rootstock of a grafted plant, must be removed every year. What a pain.

True suckers arising from a nongrafted plant can be removed or left alone to grow up into nice-looking replacement canes.

CHAPTER FOUR

Looking For Deadwood

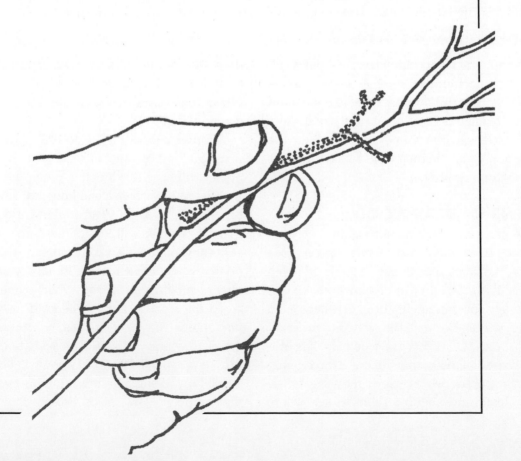

One of the great secrets of successful pruning, and the only overall rule, is "Prune out the deadwood" (it's also a favorite adage of politicians). Pruning out deadwood is called "deadwooding" by gardeners. Deadwood makes an amazing subconscious impact on the viewer: Before deadwooding the landscape seems messy and dirty, but after deadwooding it looks clean and healthy. I estimate that over 80 percent of my pruning work is simply pruning deadwood. You cannot hurt a plant by cutting out deadwood; there is no incorrect season for such pruning; deadwood cannot possibly grow new leaves or add any beauty. Equally important is pruning off any dead stubs you may find. These stubs also have a profound effect on the overall appearance of the plant.

Summer is a good time to prune out deadwood on deciduous plants; in the winter it is much more time consuming to sort out which branch is dead on shrubs like deciduous azaleas, viburnums, and lilacs. In the summer, you need only note which branches have no green leaves.

SIGNS OF DEADWOOD

New gardeners will have to train their eyes to see deadwood. I can't stop seeing it. I see it on houseplants; I see deadwood even when I'm driving 60 miles an hour on the freeway. You can tell if a branch is dead even in the winter, because the wood is a different color from the plant's live wood and it is brittle. Experienced gardeners are always gently bending branches to see if they are brittle and dead, and shaking them to see where they go. Sometimes merely tapping the branches with your pruners will snap them off; cotoneasters, for example, are easy to clean up this way.

Another clue is that dead branches have dead buds. Any time of year your healthy plants will have live-looking, plump buds on the tips of branches. Dead buds are smaller, browner, and, well, dead looking. Dead or dying branches will sometimes have coral spot fungi on them, sunken spots or wounds, or persistent dead leaves. Finally, you can always nick the bark with your pruners to see if the wood is alive or dead: If the layer just under the bark (called *cambium*) is green, the branch is still alive; if black or brown, it is dead. Eventually you will be able to tell how "dead" a branch is simply by looking at it.

HOW TO CUT BACK DEADWOOD

Many branches are in a state somewhere between totally alive and totally dead. When you cut back the suspected dead branch, you need to cut it back a little bit at a time until you find out where it is alive again (branches die from the tip back). Check the interior of the part of the branch you just cut off by looking at its cut end. If it's brown inside, it's dead. If it's light tan surrounded by green or all green, it's alive. When a branch becomes more dead than alive (when, say, it's died back by two-thirds), it's better to remove it entirely than to make a selective heading cut to the too-small remaining live-side branch.

It is not possible to prune deadwood at a distance—you are going to have to put on your grubbiest clothes, get on your hands and knees, and crawl into the shrub! Now sit there and stare at the branches. Spot the deadwood? Sometimes it helps to start from the bottom and work up, following one branch at a time. Don't just take the largest ones, get all the tiny twigs, too. Be patient, move slowly. If you are in a hurry, you will not see what is needed, and you will probably put your eye out, not to mention cutting off some nice live wood. Keep in mind that major cleanup needs to be done only once—the task will be only a minor job in coming years.

By now your underwear will be full of twigs and you should be feeling about as awful as your shrubs have been. But when you have finished, after, I estimate, between half an hour and two and a half hours per old shrub, then walk or crawl outside and see what you have unveiled. I promise a miraculous improvement in any shrub, if you prune out the deadwood before you do anything else. Most people ignore this part, and yet this *is* the real pruning.

Once you are done pruning out the deadwood, employ another great secret of professional gardeners: Use a fan rake to clean everything up. Raking out the leaves and pruning mess from under trees and plants invariably makes things look enormously better.

YOUR PLANTS WILL THANK YOU

When I was a novice gardener, I wondered what the big deal was about improving air circulation and the health of shrubs, which the professionals kept saying was the point of pruning. Your plants will love you for taking out the deadwood and raking up the dead leaves. (They'd do it themselves, but they can't move.) I have brought many plants back from death's door by pruning out the deadwood. Not only do they look infinitely better, but they grow better and are able to ward off disease better as well.

SUMMARY

Take out the deadwood. Do it first; do it always. Use your fan rake to remove debris. The signs of deadwood:

1. No leaves, or dead leaves, on dead branches.
2. Dead-looking buds.
3. Wood is a different color.
4. Branch or twig is brittle.
5. Cambium layer just under the bark is not green.

CHAPTER FIVE

Timing

33

Timing is a very simple matter. Just remember not to prune shrubs and trees that flower on the current season's wood till the first growing season after the winter solstice. Plants that bloom on last year's wood and lateral growth can be pruned any time in months that have thirty-one days except months with the letter R. Some trees will bleed if pruned in the spring or winter, but only if they are cambial tip-bearers or are in the family *Rosaceae*.

Just kidding! I have always been confused by timing, and I have been paying attention for several years now. But what I can tell you with utmost certainty is that *when* you prune isn't nearly important as you have been led to believe. *How* you prune is what counts. In beginners' pruning classes you are quite apt to hear such silly questions as "When is the best time to top my tree?" The answer, of course, is "Never."

People are fairly phobic about pruning and bloom time. There is almost a cult about timing. If you ask your garden columnist how to prune a forsythia, you are more apt to be told to wait to prune it until after it blooms, without much information on correct procedure. But if you are selectively pruning (as opposed to cutting it all back with heading cuts) the plant will still bloom. It will just be missing the flowers from the buds that you cut off. The casual observer of a camellia pruned at the "wrong" time will still see a shrub packed with lovely flowers on the now-more-graceful branches.

BLOOM TIME

Bloom-time considerations are only really important when you are considering radical renovations or any other wholesale heading-back, like stooling a butterfly bush (*Buddleia*) or cutting a clematis vine to the ground (as is often done), or shearing, which you probably shouldn't be doing to your flowering shrubs anyway. I will do my best to explain when to prune blooming plants. I'm probably oversimplifying, but here goes.

There are basically two kinds of plants: the ones that bloom in the spring, such as lilacs, rhododendrons, and forsythias, and the ones that bloom in the summer/fall, such as roses and cistus. How a spring bloomer works is that it wakes up in the spring with its flower buds already formed. It blooms. Then it grows for the summer. Then it sets flower buds and goes to sleep for the winter. Summer/fall bloomers wake up in the spring and grow for a while. Then they set flower buds and bloom. Then they go to sleep in the winter *without* setting flower buds.

Now if you were to cut back all the branches on a forsythia for some perverse reason and you did it in February just before it bloomed, it wouldn't. Bloom, that is. You just cut off all the flower buds. If you wait till after it blooms, and then cut the shrub to the ground, it regrows all summer, sets flower buds, goes to sleep, and blooms next spring. So you get flowers both this year and next.

With a summer/fall bloomer, you can head all the branches back in the spring and still have it bloom that year. Take, for example, a hybrid tea rose. We traditionally shorten all the canes way, way back in February. Then it wakes up, grows, sets up flower buds, and is blooming like crazy in June. Then it goes to sleep for the winter without flower buds (just the fruits, called rose hips) on the branches. In the spring it wakes up, grows, sets up flower buds, and blooms. Some summer/fall bloomers, like hybrid tea roses and cistus, will repeat-bloom if you prune them just after they bloom too. Others, like hydrangeas, continue to confuse me the more I read about them and the more people tell me what happens when they cut theirs to the ground.

That's the best I can do. If you selectively prune by removing some of a plant's branches, but leave many intact with their flower buds on them, then it doesn't matter when you prune them. I like to selectively prune forsythias *before* they bloom so that I can bring in the cut stems to force them in a flower vase. I like to selectively prune camellias while they are in bloom, and beautyberries (*Callicarpa*) too, so that I can use them in arrangements. If you prune a plant at the wrong time, you won't shock the plant into not blooming; there are just fewer blooms left on the plant—the ones you cut off. Knowing this, however, will not stop people from pouring out of the condo units to tell you that you are pruning the forsythia or the rhody at the wrong time. When this happens just turn to them and say, "I am selectively pruning it." For people who like timing rules or those who want to preserve the most blooms, I have made up a maxim: "Prune spring bloomers in the early summer, summer bloomers in the early spring." Another maxim that works is "Prune soon after the plant is through blooming." My favorite timing maxim is "Prune when the shears are sharp."

There are many things to know about timing that will help you make wise decisions, but thinking in terms of "a best time" to prune too often turns into a rule about "the only time" to prune. If you are selectively pruning in moderation, the best time to prune is any time. The following are some generalities on timing, along with a few nice-to-know specifics.

PRUNING BY SEASON

Springtime Generalities
This is the time when plants will grow back fastest and most vigorously. Spring pruning stimulates growth the most. Shoots are elongating. It is a kind time of year, weatherwise.

Springtime Specifics
Early spring (February–March) is a good time for radical reduction of shrubs—say, for example, your laurel hedge (it will grow out quickly, hiding the dead-looking twigs).

This is a good time for bud work (in the Northwest, we wait until spring to find plumping buds on hybrid tea roses to cut back to). You cut buds (called *candles*) on pines to achieve the Japanese cloud-pruned look and to control growth. You can score the bark just above plumping buds on rhododendron bark to force them to grow (see "My Rhody Is Too Big" in Chapter 9).

Some plants "bleed" if you prune before their leaves are out. This means that the sap flows out at a terrifying rate. It doesn't hurt the plants, we are told, but it will scare you. I remember cutting off a branch on a birch and it veritably squirted sap as if I had severed an artery! Therefore, avoid pruning dogwood trees, grapes, birches, maples, and walnuts in early spring.

Spring or early summer is a traditional time to prune rhodies and many other broadleaf evergreens.

Summertime Generalities

Summertime, especially hot, dry summertime, is very hard on the health of plants. So is heavy pruning, so go easy. Summertime pruning has a less stimulating effect on plant growth (some even say it has a dwarfing effect, but I think that overstates the case).

In August the Pacific Northwest is often in the throes of drought (referred to as "summer" by the locals). It is a terribly stressful time for plants, and if they have been hanging on to life in poor health, this is the time they will finally succumb to *permanent wilt*, which is a real technical term. If bark has been shaded all year is suddenly exposed to direct, 80-degree sun, bad things

happen. I generally ease up on the pruning in August. Deadwooding is always okay. And it does sort of depend on how hot the weather is in any given year. Was it Mark Twain who said the mildest winter he ever spent was a summer in Seattle?

Summertime Specifics

I do almost as much pruning in the summer as I do in the winter, but nothing drastic. Just after rhodies are through blooming they send up soft new vegetative shoots that are easy to snap off if you absolutely have to keep the plant from getting bigger. I do most of the rhody control work at this time. A little later in the year, about June or July, it becomes obvious to all my clients that everything is growing "out of control!" The tree branches that have dipped down under the weight of leaves are bipping dog walkers in the face. The Japanese holly has grown up over the sprinkler heads. The shrubs are too crowded. I like to wade in and restore order.

Also, summer is a great time to spot deadwood—dead branches have no leaves! On some shrubs it is especially difficult to distinguish deadwood in the winter, so I like to nip inside them in the summer and clip, clip, clip. The plants that come to mind as good summer deadwooding candidates are the deciduous azaleas, hydrangeas, a lot of the deciduous viburnums, and lilacs.

In the summer, prune those shrubs and trees that water-sprout easily (that is, if you have a choice in the matter). But don't fool yourself into thinking that this will stop them from water-sprouting if you *overprune*—and remember, it doesn't take much to overprune these plants. Briefly, they are dogwood trees, cherries, crabapples, plums, magnolias, plants related to witch hazels, and deciduous viburnums.

Summer is a good time to prune plants like cherry trees that are plagued by fungal-bacterial-canker diseases spread by rain, drizzle, fog, and mist. Summer is a good time to thin your apple and pear trees so that the fewer fruits will receive more sun and energy thus making bigger and better fruits. I like to prune Japanese maples, both upright and laceleaf, in June or July. That way their lovely branch structure can be enjoyed in the green season too.

Fall

September is a continuation of the drought summer, in my mind, and I avoid heavy pruning. More and more I am reluctant to do a lot of pruning in the fall. I'm not sure why, but I have a few ideas. If you shear or otherwise head-back the more tender shrubs, you might stimulate regrowth, which may subsequently freeze. Also, fungal diseases are all sporulating and looking for ways to attack plants. I think of plants as tired and worn out from all the summer work, or maybe that's me. But moderate pruning is always okay, especially thinning and deadwooding.

Winter Generalities

Winter is when all your deciduous plants are sound asleep and your evergreens are sort of dozing too. Winter is the traditional time to prune deciduous plants because they are safely dormant and because, now that the leaves are gone, you can see what's going on with the branches. And gardeners are finally through mowing and weeding and have the time to do major pruning. It's cold, so you can do major sawing and hauling without getting overheated. Winter pruning stimulates growth almost as much as spring. The evidence is just delayed until spring.

Winter Specifics

I am told that if temperatures drop much below freezing you might hurt brittle wood (and slowed-down cambium) on some trees and tree-like shrubs. Branch collars may suffer dieback if exposed. I'm not thoroughly convinced that these are dangers. It is true that radical reduction of tender plants may expose them to freezing.

IVY AND WISTERIA

If you are unfortunate enough to take care of a landscape with English ivy in it, and you need to minimize your maintenance time (and who doesn't?), the late summer/fall season is the most efficient time to peel off the tendrils that are climbing up the foundation, the brickwork, or the trunks of trees. Why? Because the ivy tendrils are still soft and relatively easy to scrape off with your hand pruners. If you let it go all winter, the tendrils/roots will harden off and really grab hold. Late summer is also better than spring for ivy work because if you cut ivy back in the spring it just grows back right away and you have to cut it over again.

Summer is the time that you will find yourself whacking back the new shoots (runners, whips) of wisteria vines too, just to keep them from overtaking the North American continent. You will be cutting the runners back every couple of weeks. But the most important thing to remember is to remove all the wisteria runners that have lashed themselves into nearby trees and wedged themselves under your shingles before winter. If you wait till next spring you will find that they have hardened off into unyielding tentacles. Then they can only be cut off, not pulled off—a very labor-intensive and frustrating job.

TREES

Because trees are a long-term investment in health care, good arborists may pay closer attention to specific requirements of certain trees than to the season for pruning. Generally speaking, arborists will avoid major pruning during the periods when a tree's leaves are expanding in the spring and when they are falling in the autumn. These are low energy times for the tree. Also, at some times in the spring, the bark fairly floats on sap and should not be "walked" on. Some trees have vulnerable times in their yearly cycles that make them susceptible to specific pest and disease organisms and therefore require additional timing considerations.

But, hey, that branch hanging over your car that hit Aunt Martha in the head? Saw away!

SUMMARY

People make too big a deal about timing. If you are pruning the right way, and in moderation, anytime is the right time to prune.

CHAPTER SIX

Pruning Tools

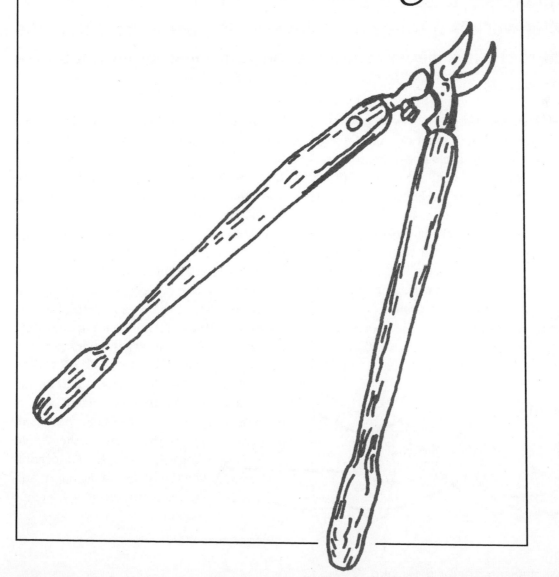

M

"an, the tool user" is a phrase that has stuck with me since junior high school. I usually quote this phrase when I'm trying to convince my husband to use something other than his hands as a hammer. It is certainly true that whenever you become engrossed in a project you are apt to resist taking the time to go search out the necessary tool. But it is an important lesson. It saves work in the not-too-long run, and saving work is intrinsically enjoyable. Furthermore, getting the right tool will save wear and tear on your most important tool—your hands.

HAND PRUNER

Occasionally, when I'm out on a garden consultation or doing a class demonstration, I borrow the homeowner's hand pruner (a.k.a. hand-shear or, if you are British or just well read, secateurs) to demonstrate a cut. These often turn out to be cheap tools that cut so poorly that I am tempted to give them the heave-ho into the bushes, right then and there. It's no wonder that many people give up trying to learn how to prune.

I remember my first pair of professional-quality hand pruners (see Figure 6.1). They were a red-handled Felco 2 that came in a

Figure 6.1 Hand pruner

leather holster, lay heavy in the hand, and were oh-so-sharp to the touch. Getting your first good hand pruner inspires much the same exultation you felt as a kid at Christmas. Felcos are definitely the Red Rider BB gun of the gardener's world.

Felco is the brand name of the most popular hand pruner. From time to time I try one of the many imitations. They look the same, but never seem to cut as well. I figure it must be the quality of the metal in the blade. I always go back. In all fairness, I should mention that other very good gardeners swear by Corona, Sanvik, and ARS. You might care to try them and let me know what you think. Originally I was impressed with the ratchet-type hand pruners because of the large cut they could effortlessly make. But eventually the blades splay apart, and I'm back to using my Felcos once again.

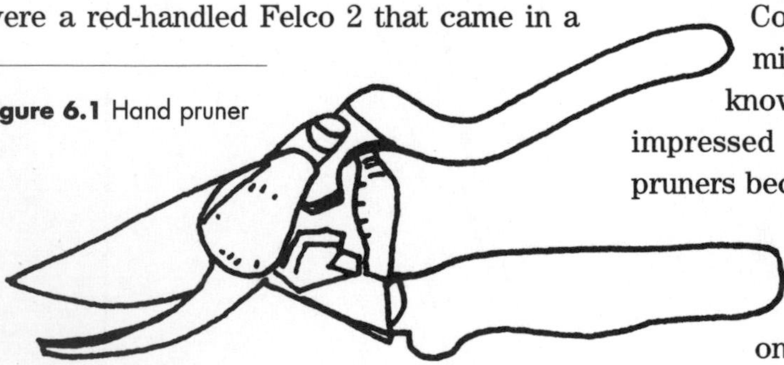

There are many other Felco models that are equally as good as Felco 2. You may find that you prefer a 6 or an 8. Some people like ones with smaller, straight blades—good for propagation work. Others prefer the pruners with a smaller grip because they are less damaging to their smaller hands. (This is no small matter for people in the business. Carpal tunnel syndrome, sometimes requiring surgery, is quite common.) For the same reason, Felco makes some models with a swivel handle. I never liked the looks of a moving handle. It just seems like one more thing to break, and I suspect it would get gunked up with dirt and pitch. But other gardeners have assured me that they are sturdy and of value.

In general it's hard to find one really good source for all the tools a gardener needs, and there is a lot of junk sold in hardware stores. The better nurseries usually carry a nice selection of good tools. Nationally, you can receive the A.M. Leonard wholesale catalog that has just about every landscaping tool on the market (call 1-800-543-8955 or visit *www.amleo.com*).

The topic of garden tools is subjective, and what works for one person may not work for another. I wouldn't want to get in an argument about which hand pruner is the best. But I can say the following: Most good pruners I know use the "bypass" type (that work like scissors; see Figure 6.2) rather than the "anvil" type (see Figure 6.3). You get a cleaner cut. Originally, I preferred the anvil type because it had more "umpf." But I now think of it as unprofessional and was slightly

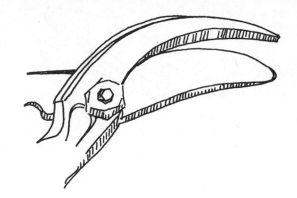

Figure 6.2 Bypass-type pruner

disappointed when Felco began offering an anvil-type pruner.

Anvil pruners always leave a tiny stub, and they purportedly crush, rather than cut, the stem. As you gain experience, you become more sensitive to the need for clean cuts. Like a chef or a surgeon, you fixate on getting ever sharper and more precise tools. Rather than searching for a small tool that can do a big job, you get a complete set of tools and keep them handy. Each one is specifically matched to a certain kind and size of job. When I worked for the Seattle Parks Department, we used to say "Get a bigger hammer." The two-pound hammer is still one of my favorite tools.

All parts of the Felco pruner, including the spring, the blade, and so forth, are replaceable. I rarely bother with parts, though. I can use the original pair for years, until the plastic coating wears off the handles. They hold up really well. And, I am ashamed to admit, I don't take very good care of them. I do give the blade a few licks with a file when I notice my pruning cuts are starting to tear. Other

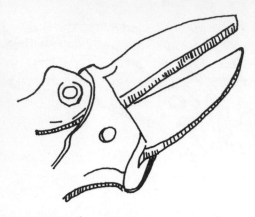

Figure 6.3 Anvil-type pruner

people, people of greater tool-care virtue than I, have more extensive regimes for sharpening and caring for pruning tools. Mine is pretty simple. After a rainy day of pruning and weeding I refrain from leaving them stored in the holster, or they get rusty. I take them inside and wash them off, scrubbing them in the sink. Then I spray them with WD-40 and store them open until dry.

In fact, when they are not inside my holster, my pruners are always open. This is because Felcos have a flaw. That little latch (supposed to keep the blades shut when not in use) loosens up and starts closing the pruners in between each and every cut. Very annoying! And there's no use trying to tighten it back up. I always just take the whole mechanism off and throw it away. The holster keeps the pruners shut when they're not in use, so I don't really need the latch anyway. And the spring-loaded tension of the open blades against the holster sides may even help the pruners stay inside the holster (say, for example, when I'm pruning upside-down). I think that Felco may have tried to fix the latch once, but it still fell open. Instead of fixing the problem, they just succeeded in making it so I couldn't unscrew the latch and get it off. Then I had to use a little piece of duct tape to keep it stuck open. It looked really professional, as you can imagine.

HOLSTER

Having a holster is essential. It keeps you from losing your very expensive pruners in a debris pile inside a shrub (for this reason, the hand-pruner handles are usually red). They make different kinds of holsters: One is sort of cone shaped, another is more U shaped to fit the different models of pruners. There is also one with a clip to attach to your pocket (good for women with hips), and the kind with slots that you thread your belt through. Having a holster means that you are always ready to act with quick-draw pruning whenever a stub is sighted. It's like having a pair of scissors with you at all times.

I use my pruners to stab open bags of soil, cut string-trimmer twine, and clean around sprinkler heads (more apologies to the people who take good care of their tools). On the Felco there is even a wire-cutting notch on the lower blade that you can use to cut free the odd strangled tree you might run across. And there are several uses for worn-out holsters.

Besides, having a leather holster makes you feel like a real cowgirl at the end of the day when you hang up it up (my husband, John, and I have His and Hers pegs for our belts). When you walk into a store or bank with it on, people immediately suspect that you are a person of some authority, like an electrician or a robber.

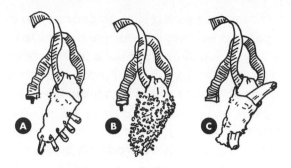

Figure 6.4 Uses for retired holsters **A.** Piercing object **B.** Chia Pet **C.** Lunch box

And, if perchance you find yourself waiting in a long line, you might even sidle up to the potted ficus to do a little absentminded deadwooding. I am so attached to my belt, holster, and pruners that I have been known to pack them up to take on vacation. Note that arborists don't have a separate holster for their hand pruners. I believe the pruner holster is built into their saw scabbard.

LOPPERS

I swear, the second most mispronounced word in gardening is "loppers" ("cotoneaster" is the first). People tend to rhyme it with "dopers." Actually it rhymes with "toppers." I prefer the Corona brand. And as with all pruning tools, it pays to buy the more expensive ones.

Figure 6.5 A person of authority

I like the wood-handled loppers because they are not as cold in your hands in the winter as the metal-handled ones (see Figure 6.6). Also, wood handles tend to break, not bend, when pushed too far, and it is much easier to discard, or repair, a broken-handled lopper; a bent-handled one tends to stay on board to annoy its users indefinitely. I know just how far I can push my wood-handled loppers, and I haven't broken a pair in years (and years).

When cutting up brush, I do sometimes brace one handle with my foot on the ground (hook side on the bottom, slip in the branch, and then push down, slowly, with both hands on the upper handle). The power of leverage is evident. It also always helps to make the cut at a slant (as anybody who cuts bamboo poles can tell you). At the risk of contradicting the "Get a bigger hammer" adage, I sometimes brace one handle against my breast bone and pull toward me with both hands to prune a large branch. This pruning technique can make for some interesting bruises.

Be prepared to shell out a little extra money for the loppers with a rubber lopper bumper at the hinge. (Go ahead, say "rubber lopper bumpers" five times, fast.) This cushions the blow to your hands when you're making repeated cuts. When I have not pruned for a while, cutting back a laurel hedge can ruin me for a week. Thank heaven I rarely do this. Like most professional gardeners, I got out of doing hedges as soon as I could. The last time I arborized and pruned 50 feet of laurel, I borrowed my husband's compound loppers. They really paid off. But in general, I avoid using heavy and/or complex tools,

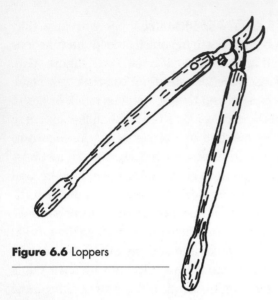

Figure 6.6 Loppers

preferring instead to get the next-sized "right" tool. When pruning, this means you trade the loppers in for a saw.

Pruning loppers, or lopping shears, are used for cuts from about ⅛ inch to 1 inch depending on the hardness of the wood. The long handles are good for extending your reach above your head or for reaching inside a thorny shrub. Loppers are also used to further reduce the size of pruned branches in order to fit them compactly into your truck. Finally, loppers are the tool of choice for cutting down a blackberry bush. You cut canes with it, you bash the bush bits down with it, and you also use it to fish out the cut brambles.

PRUNING SAW

The invention of the ARS-type, or trifaceted, blade and pruning saw practically put my loppers out of business. This revolutionary blade (also called Japanese style or trifaceted) cuts twice as fast as a similarly sized regular pruning saw. All the gardeners I know now carry a red, plastic-handled, folding Felco 60 in their back pockets (see Figure 6.7).

I used to have an old wood-handled folding saw, and it sufficed for years. But when I got my first ARS-type saw I found that it cut so fast that I rarely turned to my loppers. I would be clear across the yard before I noticed that I didn't have the loppers with me—I even made it home one day without them. And when I discovered that I had lost my loppers, I felt a twinge of pain just because we had been together for so long. It's not good to get emotionally attached to your tools.

In the beginning, I liked the bow saw—once again, because it seemed to have more power. But they are really no good for pruning. Bow saws are designed for cutting firewood. Pruning saws are crescent shaped with a narrow, pointed end so that they can fit into tight spaces. The bow of a bow saw often prevents you from making the proper-angled cut on a tree.

The idea behind the Felco 60 blade folding into the handle is, I assume, to protect your truck upholstery and yourself from inadvertent cuts. Once, when I was pruning inside an 8-foot shrub, I tossed a cut branch out to the

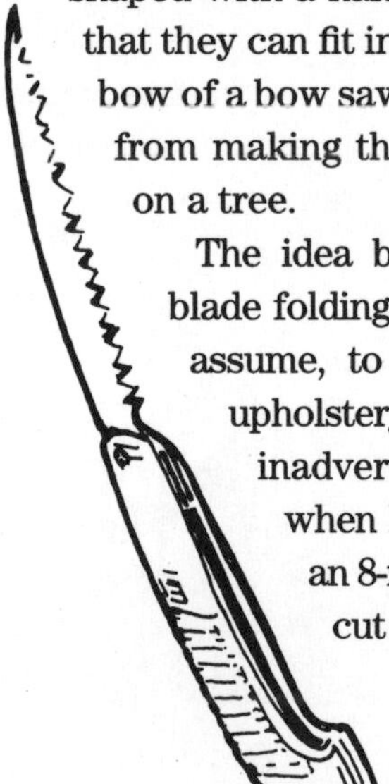

Figure 6.7 Folding pruning saw

lawn by throwing it up and out. Unfortunately, I still held my pruning saw open in the other hand and managed to make a significant pruning cut on my forearm. Just before the blood started to gush and the shock set in, I remember noting with some interest that the wound looked like an anatomical illustration showing the layers of skin.

Danger is everywhere, don't you know! A good way to cut off your finger is to reach around to the back side of the shrub in front of you with your hand pruners and prune it "backwards." The ARS-type pruning saws are frequently seen with the tips broken off: When new users try to force the blade through a branch, the tips snap off. I know someone who suffered an eye injury as a result. Like all pruning saws, the ARS ones cut on the pull stroke, which may account for some of the problem. I think the ARS-type saws have more slender blades than the old saws did, too. But really it's mostly a matter of learning how to finesse the cut, and only experience can teach you that. The saws with the broken tips still cut well, and you can always relegate them for use as root pruners, or "dirt saws" as my husband calls them.

Although I never think twice about using my loppers to cut roots, and I use my hand pruners to prune roots even though I know I shouldn't, I never let my good hand saws touch the dirt. The ARS-type blades cannot be sharpened, or at least not easily. The replacement blades are sold separately and are quick to install. Still, I guard the blade like a mother hen.

READY TO WORK

When preparing yourself to do a pruning job, suit up with all your tools. The Felco is in the holster, the loppers are slung over the shoulder, and the pruning saw is tucked in the back pocket. If it is raining out, the saw may be tucked into the rubber boot, since the rain gear has made the back pocket inaccessible. Then, as the size of the cut exceeds the limits of the tool, you can readily trade up.

I have taken to keeping an arborist's saw in a scabbard hanging from my tool belt. It looks pretty pretentious, I must admit, but comes in real handy for the larger cuts, if there aren't too many. Unlike the chain saw, it always starts on the first pull. You don't need to spend fifteen minutes filling it up with fuel and bar oil, or straightening out the new chain and putting it on. And it doesn't annoy the neighbors. The arborists' saw I use has the same tri-faceted blade as my little saw. It's called the "Turbo Cut." I guess that's sort of an arborist's joke. Which reminds me, how do you get a one-armed arborist out of a tree? Answer: Wave.

In conclusion, remember what Mr. Natural says: "Use the right tool for the job." You'll be glad you did.

SUMMARY

The starter kit for pruners includes Felco 2 hand pruners, a holster, a Felco 60 pruning saw, and a pair of good, wood-handled loppers with rubber lopper bumper. Buy only high-quality (expensive) pruning tools.

PART TWO

The Plants

CHAPTER SEVEN

Mounding-Habit Shrubs

Mounding-habit shrubs are basically the blobs of the plant world. They tend to be wider than tall, and most have small leaves or supple (soft, more herbaceous) branches. Examples are spiraea, evergreen azalea, choisya (Mexican orange), and escallonia. They are often used in mass plantings as opposed to being the featured plant (the specimen plant) of a garden area.

PRUNING MOUNDING-HABIT SHRUBS

Mounding-habit shrubs are the easiest shrubs to keep at a certain size, which means that (aside from the conifer shrubs of this type) they are better suited for placement under windows and next to walkways than other categories of shrubs. Mounding-habit shrubs have a generous pruning budget. You can generally remove a third of the shrub's leaf area without getting into trouble (see Chapter 2 for a discussion of "pruning budgets"). They are most often pruned to keep them tidy and relatively smaller using the grab and snip method (see Figure 7.1).

ABELIA *(Abelia)*

Abelias are nice mounding-habit plants with graceful arching stems and small leaves. They have profuse, small pink blooms late in the summer and fall, adding interest to the garden when most shrubs are just plain green. After blooming, the leaves and sepals remain with bronzy tints. If the winter

Mounding-Habit Shrubs

Abelia	*Abelia*
Aucuba	*Aucuba*
Barberry	*Berberis* (except *B. julianae*; see Chapter 8, Cane-Growing Shrubs)
Boxwood	*Buxus*
Box honeysuckle	*Lonicera nitida*
Broom	*Cytisus*
Burning bush	*Euonymus alata*
Ceanothus	*Ceanothus* (some species)
Cinquefoil	*Potentilla*
Escallonia	*Escallonia*
Evergreen azalea	*Rhododendron*
Evergreen euonymus	*Euonymus japonica*
Heath	*Erica*
Heather	*Calluna vulgaris*
Juniper	*Juniperus*
Japanese holly	*Ilex crenata*
Laurustinus	*Viburnum tinus*
Lavender	*Lavandula*
Mexican orange	*Choisya ternata*
Pernettya	*Pernettya mucronata*
Rockrose	*Cistus*
Snowberry	*Symphoricarpos*
Spiraea	*Spiraea*

Also see the list "Not One or the Other: In-Between Mounding-Habit, Cane-Growing, and Tree-Like Shrubs" at the end of Chapter 9.

Figure 7.1 For mounding-habit shrubs, use the grab-and-snip method, hiding cuts inside the plant. **A.** Before **B.** After: shorter and tidier but still natural looking

weather is not too cold—more than 20°F—an abelia will keep its leaves.

When I was first learning to prune as one of the grounds maintenance crew of the Seattle Parks Department, I remember going through one of the city parks with a senior horticulturist. When we got to the abelias I said, "I suppose these are okay to shear?" "NO!" was his adamant reply.

The Most Common Mistake

Abelias fit the criteria for plants that can take shearing: small leaves, evergreen, and tough. But shearing should be avoided on abelias, or on anything that is not planted as a formal hedge or topiary. It's not healthy and it's not in good taste.

The main reason I hate sheared shrubbery, though, is because of what happens next. Every place a cut is made, three shoots, wild and straight, leap up from the cut end. This is especially true for abelias. I call the long, arching branches "moon shots." My husband, John, calls such regrowth "the fright." Although shearing is fast and a real no-brainer,

it is self-defeating. The newly stimulated regrowth quickly destroys the neat and tidy sheared look. Therefore, in the not-so-long run, it is more expensive than selective pruning. The more you shear, the more moon shots you get, which need to be re-sheared, leading to a greater number of shoots, and on, and on. One is locked into a constant battle, and the plants look like heck half the time because of it.

General Maintenance Pruning

As with all shrubs, one can improve the looks of abelias by pruning out the deadwood and by cutting off a few of the lowest branches, especially ones touching the ground. Moderate height reduction can be achieved using the grab-and-snip method. Locating the longest branch first, you follow it down to a side branch and selectively head (snip) it off there. Repeat the process, always looking for the longest, most offending branch to prune next. In this way the shrub will be shorter, but natural looking.

Because abelias have small leaves, many people assume that the mature height of their shrub should be lower than it actually is. They think the shrub will be about 2 or 3 feet tall. Your average abelia *(A. grandiflora)* is 8 feet at maturity (as tall as the ceiling) and often more. The so-called smaller abelias (like *A. grandiflora* 'Edward Goucher') are 5 feet tall, which is not waist high, it is shoulder high. To prune in an attempt to keep a shrub, even a mounding-habit shrub, and especially a touchy abelia, smaller than its mature size is to ask for water-sprout trouble. So if you want an abelia that is smaller, pay close attention to the plant tag. 'Sherwoodii' and *A. grandiflora* 'Prostrata' are two cultivars that mature at less than 5 feet.

Avoiding Moon Shots

Abelias make water sprouts not only in response to shearing, but even when subjected to overly ambitious selective heading. This is especially true of young plants, which seem to naturally increase in size with those straight, ugly moon shots.

A common scenario is for the homeowner to purchase an abelia with a nice curved and arching branch structure. The plant looks great when it's first put into the ground. But the next spring it sends up these wild, stretched-out overachievers that ruin its good looks. The unsuspecting homeowner cuts off the offending shoots, which only results in a greater upsurge of them. Help!

So, how do you get rid of those long shoots? Well, you wait—maybe a couple of years. Eventually the plant sorts itself out.

The only abelias I know that don't have any of those long upshots are ones that nobody has been trying to keep small. One in particular that I have finally tamed is currently 7 feet tall. It looks great all the time and now needs very little pruning. You could never convince me to try to shorten it. I'm not looking for trouble.

Rehabilitative Pruning: How to Deal with the Mess

For those whose abelias have a really bad case of the fright, I have developed the following technique. It is utterly counterintuitive. Every fiber in your body will tell you that the solution is to cut off the moon shots and leave the prettier, curvaceous inner branches. But that won't work!

The goal of this rehabilitative pruning is not to make the plant prettier but to make it more uniform in appearance by modifying both the top (which is all straight branches) and the bottom (which has all pretty, curving branches). Then it will be less annoying to the viewer.

Step 1: *Thin up a portion of the skirt that touches the ground.* **Step 2:** *Take out some of the nicest curving branches from the lower portion.* (I know this is hard to do since these are often the prettiest.) **Step 3:** *Modify the top portion of mostly straight branches.* Remove a few of the longest, most upsetting branches, but leave the vast majority in place. You may head-back some branches to a promising bud, cut some off inside the shrub where they join a stem, and remove some stems at ground level (see Figure 7.2).

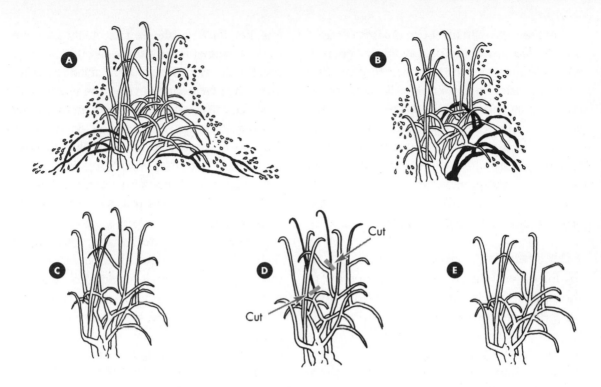

Figure 7.2 How to deal with a messy abelia **A.** Lift up the skirt. **B.** Cut out a few of the most arching (prettiest) branches, including interior, not just outward-facing, growth. **C.** Looking better! **D.** Deal with moon shots: Head some, remove some, leave many. **E.** Plant is more uniform, top and bottom.

In this fashion, the shrub becomes more uniform in appearance, and over time, as the shoots and branches age, they arch out and assume the characteristic pleasing habit of the plant. You cannot force branches to become more arching and beautiful. Only the aging process does that.

Radical Renovation

Cutting down a shrub, clear to the ground, to start it over is a radical step, but it is recommended for any abelia that has been sheared for numerous years. The plant will grow back remarkably fast, since it has the root system of a full-size plant. But the new growth will be unpleasantly straight for a year or more. When the shrub reaches its previous height, or even higher, the branches will begin to arch out, thicken up, and set more flower buds. If you choose this method, do it in the spring to lessen the chances of killing your shrub, and be sure you (and your neighbors) can stand the shock of seeing the initial results.

Summary

Abelias can be a bit difficult pruning-wise because when pruned for size control (either by shearing or even by selective heading) they respond with water sprouts. Even the normal new growth can be in the form of ugly, straight shoots. Therefore, avoid size control, and patiently wait for the plant to grow into graceful form. Be certain that the variety purchased has the desired mature size for the site. Other than that, abelias can be thinned, taking unwanted branches out at the base or to a parent stem. Deadwooding and removal of a few of the lower branches makes these shrubs look better. Abelias can be cut to the ground and regrown if necessary.

BOXWOOD *(Buxus)*

My husband, John, is the charter member of the S.O.B.s of America. That's an acronym for Stamp Out Boxwoods. John is a *complete* landscape maintenance gardener. That means he does lawns and hedges as well as the sort of bed maintenance that I do in my own separate but equal landscape business. Yes, he does do hedges, lots of them, including many boxwood hedges. And he hates them. I have done just enough to know why I don't do hedges anymore. It's tedious and frustrating, unless you like to shear. And we know that many people must *love* to shear, given what we see done to shrubs in yards everywhere. In such cases, a formal hedge or a sacrificial boxwood ball is just the thing to keep the industrious out of trouble.

Box Hedges

Boxwoods are good plants for hedges and topiaries because they have small leaves, grow slowly, and break bud if you have to cut into barren wood and want the plant to green back up. Even so, box hedges are higher maintenance than selectively pruned plants

and need to be sheared annually to keep them in shape. Really anal-retentive hedgers (isn't that a redundancy?) must also go through their hedges every few years, thinning the crowded branch ends and cleaning out the extensive collection of dead leaves that has accumulated within. This helps offset disease potential created by tight shearing. Another problem with a boxwood hedge is that if a piece flops out, it's hard to get it back in place.

Which leads me to another reason the S.O.B.s hate box hedges. By their very design these hedges make it impossible to rake leaves and other debris out of beds that are hemmed by the hedge itself. And if it is a rose bed, well, there you are—bending over in a cramped corner, trying to hand-rake leaves. It's uncomfortable and occasionally painful, as you can imagine. John also hates the commonly quoted admonition to clip hedges narrower at the top than the bottom. He says it is unnecessary, and he's probably right. But what can I say? People like how box hedges look. And gardens are there for looks, and gardeners are there for the sake of gardens.

I personally am not a member of the S.O.B. society; my philosophy is "No Bad Plants," just poorly situated or poorly used plants. Yet I know that someone will still accuse me of hating boxwoods and topiary. It's not true. In fact, at PlantAmnesty we once got a call from a representative of a local elementary school. As with most Seattle schools, the school grounds were utterly dull and empty as a result of years and years of budget cuts. What it did have was a boxwood hedge—a full 100 feet of 5-foot-tall, lumpy box hedge. PlantAmnesty volunteers sculpted it into a bookworm, with an open book to celebrate reading week. There's nothing wrong with topiary, if you do it right.

An Alternative to Boxwood

In the Northwest, boxwoods are slowly being replaced by Japanese holly (*Ilex crenata* 'Convexa'), which looks just like boxwood except that it stays a nice, glossy, dark green. Boxwood tends to turn various shades of icky yellow or gray for a variety of reasons: too much sun, too cold, not enough water, sheared at the wrong time of year, mites, scale, a nitrogen deficiency, dog damage, and so on.

Not only is Japanese holly the superior plant in color, but it is also easier to shear because its branches are stiff. Boxwood stems and leaves are very soft: They jam in hedge shears and drive gardeners crazy. And the tiny shorn leaves are equally frustrating, resisting cleanup like so much confetti on a wet wood floor.

Tools

John works on many box hedges of the 3-foot-and-under variety, including a real knot garden. A knot garden is a set of low, interwoven sheared hedges (often of different colors such as gray, green, and gold) used in a design that is reminiscent of macramé. It is a particularly interesting formal garden feature that is best viewed from an upper-story window.

For precision hedging John uses a special long-handled power hedge shear (the Maruyama brand). He claims it cuts his time

by two-thirds *and* that his lines are infinitely straighter since he stands back as he cuts. John recommends doing the top of the hedge first, and then the sides, because it's easier to get the sides perfectly square this way. However, listening to thirty-five minutes of power shearing, followed by a good blow down, is no treat, I can tell you. In Europe during the Age of Aristocracy, gardeners had to work at night so they wouldn't be seen—laborers look so uncouth, spoils the whole ambience of the garden, don't you know. But times have changed. Modern garden maintenance has all the auditory charm of *Saving Private Ryan*. Well, I guess that's what people deserve if they insist on formal box hedges and yards with no leaf out of place.

Timing

Correct timing is very important if you shear a box hedge. If it's too cold when you shear, or shortly thereafter, all the leaves turn gray. If it's too hot when you shear, or shortly thereafter, all the leaves turn gray. So the most opportune time is about a three-week window in April—which is, unfortunately, the busiest time of the year for gardeners.

The Natural Look

I think boxwoods are underutilized as a non-hedge plant. Their natural habit is billowing and fine leafed, making them the perfect counterpoint to the overabundance of really broad broadleaf evergreens (such as rhododendrons, camellias, and the like) in the Northwest. I especially like to see boxwoods planted in a little shade—the variegated form of *B. sempervirens*, 'Aureo-variegata', or the silver-edged form of true dwarf boxwood, *B. s.* 'Suffruticosa', will really brighten up a dark corner.

When keeping a plant in its natural form, it is imperative to accommodate its mature size. The mature size of an English or common boxwood *(B. sempervirens)* is 15 to 20 feet; the mature size of the true dwarf boxwood *(B. s.* 'Suffruticosa') is 4 to 5 feet, although it can be kept to about 2 feet with annual pruning. For even smaller places there are some incredibly cute super dwarfs, such as *B. s.* 'Rotundifolia' and *B. microphylla japonica* 'Compacta.' Consult your local nursery for more details.

Size Reduction

Given enough room to grow, boxwoods, like most plants, don't need pruning to look their best. Taking out dead twigs and branches is always in order. Any time is the right time. If and when boxwoods reach beyond the size of their allotted space, they are easy to reduce using the grab-and-snip method. First locate the branch that sticks out the most, that most interferes with the next shrub over, or the one that grows into the walkway. Grab the tip with one hand, and with your other hand (in which you hold a pair of Felco hand pruners) follow the branch to a place deep inside (say 6 inches or more on a 3-foot shrub). Cut it there. Most novice pruners don't go deep enough. If your pruners actually run up against a major side branch (clunk), this is an even better place to cut. Repeat the process. Between pruning cuts, scan the entire plant for the *worst* longest branch of all. Otherwise, you simply shear

Figure 7.3 You can prune boxwoods for a more natural look.

your plant one twig at a time. After a while you will find that your boxwood is miraculously shorter and tidier, but still loose and natural looking.

Thinning for Definition

Alternatively, a big old boxwood can be thinned out to make it open and airy, accentuating its branch structure (see Figure 7.3). You really can't get into too much trouble. If you thin "too much" it will easily break bud (growing numerous leaves on internal branches); the new growth looks just like the old growth and is not a mess of ugly water sprouts. The natural features of the plant will not be compromised, since boxwood is a dense, small-leaved plant to begin with. "Overthinning" the shrub may simply become an annual maintenance chore. And, if abandoned, the shrub will easily revert to its natural full form, none the worse.

To thin a shrub, you must physically open it up and look inside. Push branches gently aside and search for lateral branches (side branches) to cut. Work from the bottom up and the inside out, taking and leaving some branches, cutting both some large-ish and smaller branches.

Summary
Boxwoods can be sheared, thinned, selectively reduced in size, or renovated. If you shear, do it in April or all the leaves turn gray. Japanese holly makes a better hedge plant.

BURNING BUSH *(Euonymus alata)*
You may have a *Euonymus alata*, or you may have a lotta euonymuses, or both. In any case the burning bush is not to be confused with the smoke bush or smoke tree *(Cotinus coggygria)*. The burning bush is a deciduous shrub that is generally a big green globe. It grows easily 9 feet tall and 12 feet wide. The *E. a.* 'Compacta' version, sold more commonly to homeowners, still gets pretty dang big, around 5 feet by 6 feet. It used to be

pretty rare but lately it has been turning up in freeway plantings. You probably don't notice it until banks of them turn brilliant garnet red in the fall. I approve. (There is a spectacular planting of *E. alata* and Virginia creeper that turn color at the same time at the bridge entrance to the I-90 tunnel on the east side of Seattle, no doubt brightening the miserable commute of thousands.)

Because *E. alata* is now common on freeways, it is no longer considered good enough for many landscape owners. I think this is a mistake. Aside from its good fall color, *E. alata* has other attributes that make it a good choice for the garden. In my opinion, Northwest gardens are overwhelmingly composed of broadleaf evergreens (pieris, rhody, camellia), and the addition of deciduous shrubs helps create foliar contrast even in the summer. *E. alata* has a stiffish branch structure, with leaves that are arranged *opposite*, giving it a nice double-ranked textural quality.

Figure 7.4 Burning bush with corky ridges

Figure 7.5 Corky Ridges and the Burnin' Bush Boys

Subtle, I know, but there. New gardeners tend to pack their yards with all *choice* plants, forgetting that, in order for the star performer to show off, she needs a good chorus line. *E. alata* is one of those good chorus-line plants—tough as nails, always tidy, globe shaped, with its own moment in the spotlight during the fall. Sometimes the burning bush is called the winged euonymus because the twigs of the plant have corky ridges, interesting to note (figures 7.4 and 7.5). The shrub will color up better if planted in the sun.

Size Reduction

As you probably know from reading other sections of this book, shearing a burning bush, or any other plant not used as a formal hedge, is a no-no. Also, it doesn't pay to try to reduce a shrub by more than a quarter. It's just too much work. The harder you prune, the faster it grows.

That said, you can somewhat shorten and tidy your *E. alata* with selective pruning. Locate one of the branches that sticks out the farthest. Follow it inside the plant and prune it off, cutting to an internal side branch or sometimes just to a pair of leaves. Now scan the shrub to find the next worst branch that sticks out the farthest and repeat the process. Slowly work your way over the entire shrub—for example, pruning it to get it away from a walkway. Be sure to keep it sort of globe shaped, feathering it back from the walkway, instead of making one side a veritable straight wall of foliage. If it is up against a house or crammed next to another shrub, prune a bit where they interface. I

usually start at the bottom of a plant and prune it and the back side first. It just seems to work out better that way. I call it the "round-down" when fitting a shrub to a wall. I think of it as creating tunnels or shadows by pruning between plants that are too crowded.

The burning bush, unlike most of the mounding-habit plants, can also have all the remaining branches headed-back too. This is true because *E. alata* is not notable for flowers (which would be cut off with every branch headed). And, too, the regrowth is not an unpleasant looking hydra. The new growth, if the heading cut is moderate in size, will pretty well match the shrub's natural growth. The main point is to stagger your cuts at different heights.

Selective pruning, as opposed to shearing, also maintains the texture and natural character of the plant. And unlike shearing, selective pruning keeps some internal foliage green so that the size can be reduced (with shearing you can't cut into the outer twiggy shell without running into barren, ugly branches).

Thinning

You can also thin *E. alata* to make them more open and thereby show off their nice branch structure. If your shrub seems oppressively big, sometimes thinning will make it less imposing and more interesting. Spend most of your time at the base. Taking off a few of the lowermost limbs almost always lends some definition to a shrub. Then selectively thin off other branches—some small, some large—evenly throughout the shrub. I don't think of the burning bush as particularly sensitive or prone to the water-sprout response, so prune as much as you like. If you prune too much, it will regrow, but not with a billion ugly shoots that take years to turn into anything decent looking, as will happen with many other shrubs.

Radical Renovation

One of our PlantAmnesty members complained bitterly about the hack job done to the rows of *E. alata* in the median strip by a local mall. A similar hack job was done to scores of these shrubs along a main city arterial, cutting the plants to about a foot off the ground. Actually, both these instances were the correct use of the radical renovation technique, where oversized shrubs are started over by cutting them nearly to the ground. In one growing season the plants in these two places put on an average of a foot of new growth. One planting grew much faster than the other. I think it had to do with the time of year. I wish I had been taking notes.

The mistake most people make when they decide to do hard pruning is that they don't go down far enough. They cut the plant to the size they want it to be, trying to be nice. Unfortunately, with the heading cut, growth starts at the cut and goes up. And when a plant is pruned hard, it grows up very fast, much faster than its previous growth rate. So the very next year the shrub is too big again. By cutting very, very low, you allow room for the new growth to shoot up. And it gives the plant some time to reestablish its natural shape. If the new shoots grow rapidly and long, you may want to whack (shear, cut) it all again at the 2- or 3-foot level to create more internal bushiness. Be aware that radical renovation is not a maintenance procedure to keep a shrub smaller than it is programmed to be. It can be done once every fifteen years or so if there is a good reason. Usually this reason is that the plant has been horribly pruned for many, many years.

If you don't have automatic irrigation, do radical renovation in the early spring. It is also advisable to give the plant extra water in the summer. Hard pruning is tough on a plant, and so is summer drought. The two together can kill a shrub, even one as tough as *E. alata*.

Design Solutions

I know of another mass planting of *E. alata*, again along a major arterial, that recently got a quasi-renovation. The crews just whacked them back to fit the bed. Wrong! Whenever possible, it is better to adjust the site to the growing plants, not the other way around. It turns out to be too much work to stop plants from growing by pruning. In fact, it is a study in the law of diminishing returns. Here was the perfect opportunity to just remove the narrow strip of lawn. Really, who wants to mow a four-foot strip of lawn between the bed and the street, dragging mowers across three lanes of angry, smelly traffic every week? Similarly, at the mall described above, they could have just removed the bordering planting of low-growing holly (*Ilex crenata* 'Mariesii'). Many of the low shrubs had died because of car exhaust or a broken sprinkler system.

Instead, the crew chose to renovate the burning bushes and replant the hollies. That was okay, but they could have taken the other tack.

A clever landscape designer does not depend on pruning to keep a yard looking good. He or she uses several design tricks so that the young yard looks good, and later as the yard matures, lower-story plants can be removed or beds enlarged so that it ages gracefully and with minimal maintenance.

Summary

A burning bush may be pruned to make it somewhat shorter using the selective heading technique. Stagger the cuts to retain the plant's interesting texture. Or the shrub can be thinned for definition. It is a good candidate for radical renovation. Placed in the correct location it—like most plants—requires no pruning.

EVERGREEN AZALEA *(Rhododendron)*

What is the difference between azaleas and rhododendrons? Well, any horticulture student can tell you that all azaleas are a subset of rhododendrons. We tend to think of azaleas as smaller shrubs, but in truth, many true rhodies are quite small (*R. impeditum*, for example), and azaleas can be big, especially the deciduous ones (like the royal azalea, *R. schlippenbachii*). But evergreen azaleas (as opposed to deciduous azaleas) are the small-leaved, mounding-habit, low-growing shrubs most people think of when you say "azalea."

A Useful Plant

Many horticulturists dismiss the evergreen azalea as being too common and uninterest-ing to be a "choice" plant. I think they are common because they are very, very useful plants. Unlike the vast majority of shrubs, evergreen azaleas remain "small," providing the much needed lower story in our gardens. I find that most shrubs mature in the 7- to 10-foot range, overwhelming the average yard. I recommend that people plant 50 percent of their gardens in shrubs, perennials, and groundcovers that are less than 5 feet tall. Azaleas fit the bill.

Furthermore, they are evergreen, naturally tidy looking, have nice flowers, and many even have reddish tints to their foliage in the fall and winter. Azaleas take sun and part shade. If watered correctly they live in loam or clay. Best of all, they transplant like a dream. When renovating old yards I often enlarge the beds and transplant all the sword ferns and azaleas to make the new lower story. It's sort of like rearranging the furniture. And lastly, evergreen azaleas are agreeable to all sorts of pruning.

No Pruning

As with all shrubs, if it's not broken don't fix it. If your azaleas look good and are doing their job, just leave them alone. Plants don't always need to be pruned.

The Most Common Mistake

People usually err by shearing shrubs into balls. Evergreen azaleas are no exception. On the one hand, evergreen azaleas fit the criteria of good plants to use in formal settings, such as true formal Japanese gardens, where they can be sheared as individual plants or in masses. They have small, closely spaced evergreen leaves, they break bud everywhere down each stem, and they can put up with constant shearing. This is high maintenance, however, requiring frequent shearings to keep the plant looking tidy. And with shearing, timing is important. To preserve flowers, shearing must be timed soon after the plants are through blooming. If you shear at the wrong time, evergreen azaleas won't bloom, and if you shear at the right time, you increase the number of flowers. I almost lost it when I heard that for the first time. (That's one reason I like selective pruning. No matter what time of year you prune, there will be plenty of flowers left. Don't let anyone tell you differently.)

Although evergreen azaleas can take it, shearing them in most gardens is the hallmark of bad taste. It just shows the world that you don't know how to selectively prune, to "enhance the natural shape," as gardening books say. I remember consulting in a yard where all the azaleas had been sheared into separate balls. When they bloomed, all in different colors—white, pink, orange, carmine, and deep purple—it looked like a giant gumball machine had spilled. Luckily, evergreen azaleas are the easiest of all the shrubs to convert back into their natural form. My friend Tina calls it "ball busting." In print we call it rehabilitative pruning.

Deadwood

Deadwood is pretty obvious in evergreen azaleas—there are no live leaves at the tips. The dead twigs inside azaleas are so brittle that you can brush, or "crunch," them out with your hands (your *gloved* hands, that is). Such a course makes the biggest difference in the shortest amount of time (see Figure 7.6).

You are supposed to go back and carefully cut the dead stubs cleanly from where you "crunched" off the deadwood. But sometimes you can save that for when there is more time. Whenever I see stubs left from a unknown previous gardener's hectic deadwood job, I feel a kinship that transcends time and space.

A grade-A deadwood job leaves no stubs. You should be able to run your bare hands

Figure 7.6 Deadwooding azaleas **A.** Collected dead leaves and dead twigs **B.** After deadwooding

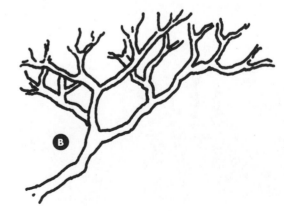

down the stems and feel bumps (nodes), but no sharp edges. I sometimes tell new gardeners that they should be able to pass through their shrubbery with a knitted sweater on, and not have it catch.

Puppy-Dog Tails

Evergreen azaleas often have a few branches that stick out strangely beyond the rest. Northwest garden columnist Marianne Binetti calls them puppy-dog tails; I call them stick-ups. We both allow that people may want to remove them. To do so, use the grab-and-snip method: Follow the offending branch down to a place inside the shrub and cut it off where it meets a side branch or a parent stem (see Figure 7.7).

The most common mistake is to just cut a branch off at the shrub's perimeter. This is nonselective heading, or mal-pruning, and it will just stimulate the dormant buds situated directly below the cut. Those buds will spring into action, growing out rapidly into a whorl of ugly, straight shoots, or water sprouts. On the other hand, cutting back to a side branch (selective heading) reduces or eliminates the water-sprout rebound effect.

There are other plants that are prone to growing stick-ups (or puppy-dog tails). They are enkianthus, evergreen huckleberry, deciduous azaleas, and Pacific wax myrtle. The stick-ups are these plants' natural way of increasing in size. This is true for evergreen azaleas too. You are ill advised to eliminate all of them in an effort to tidy the mounding outline of the shrub. This tends to stimulate even more stick-ups over time, even if you are pruning selectively, as the plant struggles to increase its size. So, as a general rule, I prune only a few of the most offending branches (look for the worst first). The goal of pruning is not absolute control. Pruning can only make a plant better, not perfect.

Size Reduction

If your azalea has gotten too large, use the same grab-and-snip technique described for puppy-dog tails above to make it smaller. Always locate the branch that sticks out too far and follow it back inside the plant. Cut where it meets up with a side branch, the larger the side branch the better (see Figure 7.8). Then look for the next *worst* branch of the entire shrub that sticks out too far. Don't go for the next *closest* branch that sticks out.

Be aware that most novices err by concentrating on the top portion of the plant. The part of the azalea that actually prevents people from walking past it or that crowds nearby shrubs is often the *lower* part. Check out those branches. In fact, I think taking off a few of the lowest branches almost always

Figure 7.7 Cut puppy-dog tails off at a point deep inside the shrub.

Don't cut here

Don't cut here

Leave as is

Yes, cut here

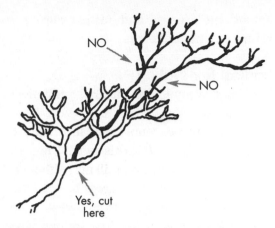

Figure 7.8 To make evergreen azaleas smaller, selectively cut out the tallest branches.

makes azaleas look better. Remove any aggressive groundcovers trying to swallow them up. Only the most diminutive plants can be used around azaleas, say the smaller sedums/sempervivums. Tear out ivy and periwinkle. They shouldn't be anywhere near these shrubs.

Thinning

Evergreen azaleas have a very nice branch structure, which can be better featured by thinning. Thinning out means pruning off smaller side branches throughout the shrub. Generally you should do more thinning where a number of branches meet up, thus simplifying the cluster. Also prune out some of the worst branches that cross and rub others, drag on the ground, wander too far, or clog up the interior. It doesn't matter much which ones you choose. Just follow a side branch back to its parent stem and prune it there. Generally speaking, you prune to "open up the center," leaving branches that

head up and out, while removing some (not all) of the ones that cross, rub, wander, and head back through the center. Simplifying crowded branching inside the plant will allow dead leaves to drop through to the ground rather than collecting like a bird's nest.

Although this sort of pruning does improve the health of plants, it's mainly done to improve the looks of them. It makes evergreen azaleas look airy and delicate. Don't worry about pruning too much (except during a drought). It's okay if you get a little overzealous on these particular plants. Azaleas readily break bud (grow back from barren or headed branches) just about everywhere. And the new growth is attractive, not a billion ugly water sprouts.

Rehabilitative Pruning

To turn a sheared evergreen azalea back into its natural form, you prune the same as you

Figure 7.9 Simplify branches by cutting out the crowded center.

would thin (described above), only there will be a great deal more of it to do. Be patient. You could easily spend twenty minutes deadwooding and thinning the first time through. You need to crawl around, behind, and inside the plant, gently pulling branches apart or reaching in from the bottom up to get to the multitude of black, dead, brittle twigs that clog the interior. While you're in there, drag out the huge piles of dead, composting leaves that have been collecting on limbs and at the base. Use your hands. After that, a tidy-up prune will only be needed every two to four years and it will only take a minute or two.

When a shrub has been sheared into a box or globe, it pays to spend more time at the base of the plant, pruning off the lower branches to break up the geometric look (see Figure 7.10). By cutting off as much as the lower third you will return the azalea to its more characteristic chevron form. Up top, where thickly branched hydras interlock, look for the worst parts and prune them out, fearlessly cutting them off with selective heading or thinning cuts. Evergreen azaleas are very resilient and are among the easiest and fastest shrubs to return to a natural form.

Radical Renovation

I see part of my job as pushing the limits of pruning. Although reluctant to do it, I have used the radical renovation technique on evergreen azaleas. It works well. They survive and regrow in good form. (Although I must warn you that they grow back to their previous size quite quickly, in a year or so.) Since radical renovation is a serious stress on most shrubs, it shouldn't be done but once every ten or fifteen years. Which brings up the question, Why do it? I usually renovate as a quick way to return a shrub to its natural form if it has been mal-pruned.

Radical renovation is the cutting back (way, way back) of a shrub to a low, uneven framework, leaving 2 to 7 inches of horribly headed branches to regrow. Timing is important. Pick the season with the longest period of benign, warm, wet weather so the plant has the best chance at recovery. That usually means early spring.

Figure 7.10 Rehabilitating a "boxed" azalea **A.** Before: Concentrate on lower branches, looking for a more natural chevron shape. **B.** After: Remaining growth has been directed to renew natural form.

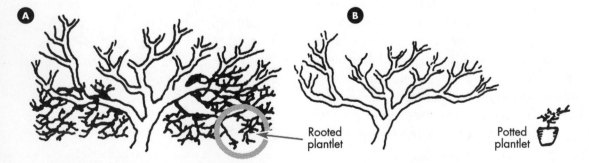

Rooted plantlet

Potted plantlet

Summary

Azaleas are easy to prune and can be pruned many ways. They can be selectively pruned to reduce size, they can be thinned, and they can be radically renovated. They are also quite easy to transplant. Always take out the deadwood and some lower branches to make these shrubs look better.

HEATH/HEATHER, LAVENDER, ROCKROSE, AND BROOM

(Erica/Calluna, Lavandula, Cistus, and Cytisus)

The most common pruning transgression is not tree topping. Though topping may be the worst of the horticultural sins, the most *common* one is the inappropriate shearing of shrubs. People, nationwide, seem to share a deep-seated, unconscious drive to make their bushes into green boxes, balls, buns, and corn dogs. None of this is good pruning and, aside from being tacky, it also gets people into horticultural hot water.

PlantAmnesty's general advice is: *If it isn't planted as a formal hedge, don't shear it!* That's a pretty simple rule. Unfortunately, exceptions do exist. All the plants listed here can benefit from regular shearing.

Horticulturists use shearing to keep certain rangy plants *more compact and tidy.* These plants are the brooms (*Cytisus* spp.), lavender (*Lavandula* spp.) and other silver plants, heaths (*Erica* spp.), heathers *(Calluna vulgaris)*, and rockrose (*Cistus* spp.). When using hedge shears to keep these plants compact, timing is important. If you shear right before they bloom, you will cut off all the buds, and so the plants won't bloom. That's just common sense. One of the main reasons I like selective pruning is because it can be done anytime without eliminating the flower show.

Heaths and Heathers

The problem with heaths and heathers is that their old flowers fall off, leaving barren stems. If the plants are not sheared (shortly after blooming) they may eventually develop ugly barren centers. An annual light shearing is all that is needed. Don't wait. Do it now before the plants get too old and woody. When cut too far into old brown, barren branches, a plant may not break bud and green back up. If you have inherited a mature yard, it may be necessary to severely prune an old neglected heather. It will either regenerate, or die. Probably the latter. An exception is the tree heath *Erica arborea*, which purportedly responds well to radical renovation (and I have witnessed it).

Shearing is done to prevent "bald spots," but selective pruning can also be used to alleviate overcrowding and sprawling. In this situation, "undercut" the heathers that are running into each other or out into the walkway. To do this, simply lift up the top and cut off handfuls of the lower branches as far back as is practicable. Then drop the top back down. I rarely think of my job as making plants smaller with pruning, but rather as refereeing between them (see Figures 7.11 and 7.12).

Lavender and Other Silver Plants

Gray- or silver-leaved plants like lavender, senecio, and artemisia have always intimi-

Figure 7.11 Pruning as refereeing **A.** Two heathers compete. **B.** Two heathers relax.

dated me, since some books warn that hard pruning can kill them. I think that this must apply only to old plants, since I have pruned numerous young lavenders and some *Senecio greyi* by cutting way, way back to barren twigs (1 to 4 inches above the ground) early in the spring (at the express instructions of my client). They came back great in time to bloom and look super for the season (see Figure 7.13).

Okay, one died. But it had been overcome by a nearby plant to begin with. In any case, when you do radical pruning, do it in the early spring, and stick to younger plants or to smaller-diameter branches on older plants. If you do light, tidy-up pruning (a.k.a. light shearing), do so just after the plants are through blooming.

Kate Allen, Seattle gardener and this book's illustrator, says that there is an art to timing when cutting back *Artemisia* 'Powis Castle' (see Figure 7.14). You should cut it back early enough and far enough, in the spring, so that it stays compact. Otherwise it sprawls and develops that telltale deadish spot in the middle. But don't prune too much, or too soon, or it suffers a total setback, becoming a gray smudge the rest of the year. Ah, the trials and tribulations of the perennial gardener! Just as with fertilizing, when pruning, one is admonished not to do too much, too little, or the wrong kind, or to do it too soon or too late!

I suspect that a lot of these plants that become old, woody, and scraggly are meant to just be replaced every ten years or so. When you whack the plant back hard one spring, and it dies, that will be your cue to remove and replace. The same goes for all those giant tree-mallows (*Lavatera*). Cut them hard, to a foot or three off the ground every year. Some year one might die from this. Then get a new one, or something you like better.

Figure 7.12 "Heather Tending," from a tea service ca. 18th century, origin unknown. Note how the heather is being lifted up and clipped from beneath. The movement of the branches is reminiscent of waves breaking on rocky shores. The tarp is, of course, from the plastique period.

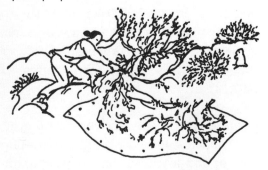

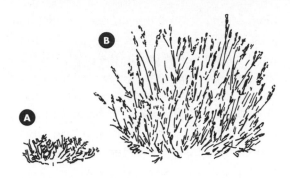

Figure 7.13 Lavender **A.** After spring pruning…
B. come summer's delights.

Rockrose

I am increasingly fond of the rockrose, since it blooms in the summer and it actually likes living on hot, dry banks, making it a logical alternative to junipers. In most years it's evergreen. I was heartbroken to hear that, like many others in this pruning category, it may not reliably return if cut back hard (meaning that it's cut to a few inches from the ground or cut deep into older, thicker branches). If rockrose would regenerate easily, it would be the perfect choice for play areas and traffic circles. So if you have information to the contrary, be sure to write. Like other drought-tolerant sun lovers, rockrose is apt to freeze to death in a hard winter in the Northwest. Its main drawback, however, seems to be its somewhat rangy habit.

(New gardeners of course, want all things from all plants—not just a tidy habit, but attractive blooms, fast growth to full size yet easily made smaller, and evergreen. As you become more sophisticated horticulturally, you begin to appreciate the diversification and specialization in the plant world. Then the game becomes one of "mix and match," a game that is infinitely more fun.)

The rockrose's rangy habit can be modified somewhat by heavy shearing early on in its life (in the nursery they shear hard in the spring, delaying bloom) and by annual lighter shearing later in its life, timed after bloom. This is not to say that cistus cannot be selectively pruned using the grab-and-snip method as an alternative. As I said, I like selective pruning because you can do it any time of the year and still have plenty of flowers.

As with heathers, I find most of my time is spent undercutting rockrose where it has flopped onto some nearby desirable plant. By the way, Seattle gardening expert Ciscoe Morris says that he has used mass plantings of rockrose to effectively smother horsetail. Please make a note of it.

It pays to know the limits of each plant. At a recent slide show, an audience member confessed that she had given up selectively pruning her rockrose and had resorted to heavy-handed hedge shearing. Eventually, I explained, such methods would also fail her.

Figure 7.14 Left unpruned, *Artemisia* 'Powis Castle' quite happily flops out and roots, assuming the position of a doughnut or an octopus with silver pom-poms.

The reason was that she had overplanted the shrubs along her driveway to begin with. I have noticed people have an almost universal habit of mentally downsizing plants. Although the plant tag clearly states that the shrub will get *4 to 5 feet high and as wide*, the purchaser crowds them into a *3-foot strip*. Five years later, the holler is heard, "They're out of control!" What did they think was going to happen? The shrubs won't stop when they have reached the size you wanted. And neither wishing nor pruning can make it so.

Broom

Another family of plants that are correctly sheared as a maintenance procedure (or so I read) are the brooms. Christopher Brickell, in his famous book *Pruning: Roses, Deciduous Shrubs, Evergreens, Hedges, Wall Shrubs, Fruit Bushes and Trees and Deciduous Trees*, actually shows someone taking scissors to a broom's outer perimeter. As with lavender, this presumably removes the untidy spent blooms and encourages a more compact form. But like most pruning, it will not stop a plant from reaching its mature height, though it may take it longer to get there. I would avoid heavy pruning of brooms, as with the similar plants I have mentioned. If the plants are young, they may readily resprout, although I fear older plants will simply die if all the green is removed.

Brooms, like many of these plants, like the sun but lack the architectural structure for people to regard them as "choice." But hey, they are evergreen and tough, and they can be used effectively in mass plantings. I

have often admired our city's freeway plantings. At 55 miles an hour and over (or more likely under, these days), the plants that are too large or too coarse for the average back yard find their highest and best uses. I especially like the contrast of the mass planting of deodar cedars against fields of 'Moonlight' broom (apologies to hay-fever victims). I think the broom is especially well suited for slowing the cars that are involved in freeway accidents without stopping them cold.

A Final Word of Caution

Just because the above plants can be sheared does not mean that they must be sheared. I find that this assumption is commonly made by students of pruning. "Can" becomes "should." "Might be harmful" becomes "always is harmful." A well-planned landscape needs very little pruning. I believe that the natural habit of plants is their best habit. One person's "rangy" could be another person's "freestyle texture." If plants could talk, I'm sure that their only request would be for deadwooding and removal of the occasional crossing/rubbing branch. With the exception of heathers mentioned above, these plants don't *need* to be pruned. If the shrubs in your yard look good, then let them be and enjoy the time off. Maybe you could use the time to do some weeding—which, unfortunately, *always*, should be done.

Summary

Heaths, heathers, lavender, rockrose, and broom can be sheared to keep them tidy and compact. Shear lightly soon after blooming. Take care not to cut deeply into old, barren wood, as these plants in particular might not grow back. Undercutting, by removing the lowest, sprawling branches, may solve a crowding problem. Hard pruning is a kill-or-cure method (more likely kill) that can be used to renovate an old, leggy plant.

JUNIPER *(Juniperus)*

I think junipers are an overly maligned group of plants and I'm not afraid to say so. If the truth be known, I'm even fond of Pfitzers (*Juniperis chinensis* 'Pfitzeriana'). They remind me of the way waves are shown in Japanese paintings.

Every once in a while you run across a phrase or passage that changes the way you think forever. In a 1988 article printed in the *Ornamentals Northwest* newsletter ("Some Practical Tips on Pruning Shrubs"), Tom Cook eloquently wrote about the problems of inappropriate shearing of shrubs. Here is what he said about junipers: "Junipers by nature are irregular in growth and come in a multitude of colors and forms. Pruned naturally, they retain this delightful variation. Sheared, they all look like boxes or pompons. Advocates of natural pruning have been known to get physically ill while walking in a neighborhood where junipers have been sheared."

It wasn't until reading that passage that I realized that junipers could be "delightful." Many people's dislike of certain plants is based on the fact that the ones they have known were ill suited to the site, or mistreated and sick. Why hate junipers just because they are overplanted and malpruned? In truth, they are wonderfully tough,

sun-loving, drought-resistant (and even shade-tolerant) plants. Junipers come in shapes, sizes, and textures to match any taste or place, from the tidy, flat J. horizontalis 'Blue Rug' to the wild and crazy 'Hollywood'. They have it all.

Prune, Don't Shear

I'm not sure that junipers should put in the mounding-habit category. Many are pruned using the grab-and-snip method, yet they are still relatively to difficult to reduce in size. The low-growing ones are used in mass plantings, and they are the ones I address here.

The first thing to know is what *not* to do. And that means don't shear them. You'll just trade in a "too-big" mass of textured junipers for "a too-big but now smooth" mass of junipers. Once junipers have been sheared, all hope of any size reduction whatsoever is eliminated. The green internal branches (ones that you could have cut back to) get shaded out and die. You are left with a thin green outer shell on a plant that gets a bit bigger every year.

The Dead Zone

Like many conifers (things that remind you of Christmas trees), junipers, are difficult to adjust with pruning. A common mistake is to bluntly cut back the row of juniper tams (*J. sabina* 'Tamariscifolia') that extends too far over the sidewalk (see Figure 7.15). The uninformed pruner will saw the plants off straight to the sidewalk's edge, cutting deeply into the barren branches. These branches, now devoid of any green needles, are unable to break bud and regrow within. You will be

Figure 7.15 Wrong way: Don't bluntly cut juniper, even next to a walkway. Such cuts reveal ugly stems—the dead zone. **A.** Before **B**. After blunt cut.

left staring at an ugly brown stripe for a long, long time, maybe forever. (Dr. Ray Maleike of Washington State University calls it the *dead zone*.) If one radically cuts back a laurel hedge, it will assuredly resprout everywhere and be just fine come spring. But this doesn't work on most conifers (with the notable exception of yews).

The Lowest Limbs

When the juniper (e.g., *J. horizontalis* or *J. sabina* 'Tamariscifolia') extends over the sidewalk, the best strategy is to lift up the top (holding it back awkwardly with your ankle or leg) and cut off the lowest limbs (see Figure 7.16). Then drop the top back down. Voilà! The juniper no longer extends so far over the walkway, but miraculously it still looks natural. This process is sort of the opposite of sweeping things under the rug.

The same technique is used to help ameliorate the generally oppressed and invaded feeling you get as the junipers begin to crowd the other plants and trees in the landscape. By incorporating a little empty space between the juniper masses and other objects—tree trunks, lamp posts, the build-

ing—you can make the landscape seem more under control. You do this by removing the lowest juniper limbs as described above. On the other end, you can help by limbing up trees and shrubs a bit farther above the masses of low-growing junipers. Often this is not a perfectly satisfactory solution, but remember your options are limited by the plants' inability to take heavy pruning. "Better" may be all that you can do, aside from replanting the entire area with shrubs that will be "too small" for quite a while.

As for oceans of Pfitzers, use the same lower limb removal technique to get them away from walkways and such. In addition, a good pruner can effectively remove some of the most interfering branches up above. Here again, use selective pruning (hiding the cuts down inside the plant), rather than just whacking back the branches. Strive to retain the characteristic pointy "waves" instead of turning the shrub into an uninteresting ball. Before cutting, grab the intended victim and move it aside. Ask yourself, "By cutting this branch off, will I expose ugly, barren-looking branches?" If not, cut away. This works best for eliminating the branch that prevents you

Figure 7.16 Right way: Do lift up top branches, cut off lowest ones, then drop the top back down.

from walking out to the garage. I rarely try to keep an entire mass planting lower by doing this. It's just too much work. Besides, the best-looking junipers are the ones that are left alone but kept weeded (yes, you need to put the loppers down, crawl inside the plant, and weed out that grass).

Rehabilitative Pruning

A previously sheared or headed mass of Pfitzers can be made to look better by selectively eliminating branches and encouraging more of the natural chevron shape. In this case, pruning is used to accentuate texture. It creates shadows. In a sense it is the opposite of shearing. The mass of junipers might still be too big, but now it will at least be more interesting looking.

Grab-and-Snip

What about the juniper tams or other low-growing junipers that are encroaching on both sides of the entryway? If you don't do something they will soon close off access completely. Use the time-honored grab-and-snip method to keep on top of the problem. Every year locate the branchlets that extend the farthest out and snip them off, hopefully hiding the cuts beneath other greenery. If such a cut is not possible, try to cut back to a bit of green that faces forward. Be sure to selectively prune the shrub all the way back at a slant so that the entire plant stays looking natural.

Deadwood Torture

What hope is there for people who have unwittingly exposed the dead zone or for those whose artistic pom-pom or K-Mart bonsai didn't quite come out looking right? (See Figure 7.17.) Well, as in so many cases, the best solution to the pruning "oops" is thorough, meticulous deadwooding. And with a juniper this can be a lengthy and very painful experience. Every tiny, yucky, dead twig must be individually cut off at the parent stem. A good, sharp pair of high-quality hand pruners is essential. I have spent a lot of time helping mal-pruned junipers look better, and I always dream of inventing the "Lady Juniper"—a limb shaver for just this purpose. The tiny needles on junipers always prick your skin and sneak into your underwear. You develop a juniper rash that stings,

Figure 7.17 Avoid shearing junipers: no K-Mart bonsais.

and it will sting again when the shower water hits it later. To make matters worse, why do you always seems to be pruning junipers in either 80-degree weather or pouring rain?

But try to remember that after an hour or two of patient deadwood removal, you will be gratified to see that those horrible plants look "almost human" again. And note: You will not have to do it again next year. Unlike "bad" pruning, "good" pruning stays done a long time.

Removal

Occasionally, previously mal-pruned junipers are so ugly that a more attractive solution is to remove them entirely. Junipers are relatively easy to dig out with a mattock, loppers, and a shovel. Old (or I guess I should say experienced) gardeners keep a chain in their truck for the specific purpose of murdering junipers. You attach one end of the chain to the truck bumper and use the other end as a

"choker" around the plant. Then drive off slowly. It works amazingly well.

Oh dear, there I go again, telling people how to kill plants. Not only should we prune selectively *(Secare selecte)*, we should also kill selectively *(Necare selecte)*. The Plant Amnesty creed reads: "We promise that when we take what we want from nature, we will do so selectively and with respect. Always we will preserve the health and integrity of the whole, be it a plant, a rain forest, or our planet." Good advice for a troubled yard and a troubled world.

Summary

Junipers, like most conifers, are difficult to prune. This is because the barren portions of the branches can't produce new greenery (break bud) once the exterior green has been removed (headed-back). Never expose those ugly, barren internal branches. If you do, your next step is to deadwood like crazy. Or take the whole plant out. What little can be done to help an overgrown planting involves removal of the lowest limbs, and/or selective heading (grab-and-snip) or thinning off the worst, most interfering branches. Always hide the cut beneath some natural-looking greenery.

SPIRAEA *(Spiraea)*

My first gardening mentor, a woman named Andrea, once said to me, "If you don't know what a shrub is, it's probably a spiraea or a viburnum." This is sort of a horticulturist's joke, and one of some truth too. She said it because both genera have a huge number of plants in them.

The spiraeas all have a mounding habit and are tough, deciduous flowering shrubs. They take sun or part shade, survive in a wide range of soils, and take all sorts of abuse and neglect. Some bloom in the spring, others in the summer or fall. Their sizes range from 2 feet to 8 feet tall and as wide. One of my favorites is *S. trilobata* 'Swan Lake', which the *Sunset Western Garden Book* says "is like a smaller bridal wreath spiraea [and] gives a massive show of tiny white flowers in May and June." It is dainty and feathery and looks like sweet spring to me. The other spiraea I particularly like is a summer/fall bloomer and is a variety of *S. japonica* named 'Anthony Waterer'. It, too, is a fluffy little bun. *Sunset* describes it as having "flat-topped, bright carmine flower clusters and maroon-tinged foliage." Now there are some with golden foliage. I planted a group of them around some taller purple barberries (*Berberis thunbergii* 'Atropurpurea') and a purple smoke bush (*Cotinus coggygria* 'Purpureus') and together they look stupendous! If I do say so myself.

I think the spireas are best used in groups or as a ring at the border of a more distant bed, since their winter branches aren't particularly pleasant looking.

General Pruning

As with most of the plants in the mounding-habit category, the grab-and-snip method works well to tidy spiraeas and reduce size within moderation. There are limits to size reduction that don't result in a wild upsurge of new growth. In general, you should be able to successfully reduce a spiraea's height by about a quarter. And know that, no matter how dutifully or determinedly you prune, eventually you will be unable to keep the spiraea smaller than the size listed for it on the plant tag. "Eventually" means after it has been in the ground about ten years.

But, as stated above, moderate pruning is fine. As you follow the offending branch with your hand pruners, reaching down deep inside the shrub, you may find that there are no likely lateral (side) branches to which you can cut back. Take heart! You can just cut to no place in particular—snip. The branches on most spireas are so slender that cutting to a bud will do, and there are dormant buds hidden all along the stems. Yes, it might hydra back, but since you cut low, it will take a while for it to get "too tall" again. And, by the time the new growth reaches the surface of the shrub, it will have branched gracefully and put on flowers, instead of being an ugly straight shoot. Or maybe it will just die back and become deadwood for some future pruning session. In any case, by making a low cut, you will have bought some time before it gets "too big" again. You will have retained the shrub's natural texture and flowers no matter when you prune.

While you are inside, look for chunky, too-stiff-looking, older branches. Prune them out to the ground level. And, as always, remove deadwood, weeds, and litter.

Bloom Time

Spiraeas and most flowering shrubs don't really need to be pruned in order to flower, as many have been led to believe. But you may have a very tired old bush and the flowers may be getting puny and few. If the reason for this isn't too much shade or not enough water, you might want (and be able) to force some new growth. New shoots will come up from the base of the plant if you cut some of the branches down to the ground, pruning it more like a cane-grower (see Chapter 8). The new growth may start out thin and straight, but by the end of this year or the next, it should become graceful, arching, flowering branches.

If you are selectively pruning, you can do so any time of the year. If the shrub is blooming, you can use the cut flowers in a vase. The shrub that remains will still be full of flowers. Really, timing matters only if you are shearing (which you shouldn't do anyway) or if you cut the entire shrub to the ground.

If you are still compelled by the notion of right-time pruning, know that you will get *maximum* flowers by pruning the spring bloomers soon after they are done flowering, and the summer/fall bloomers soon after

they are through flowering or even in the early spring.

Rehabilitative Pruning

A spiraea looks horrible when sheared, developing dead bits and losing its flowers, and, in the winter, you can see what looks like rats' nests of leaves and debris collecting inside. The sheared branch-ends soon begin to look like the snarled hair of a feral child. Rehabilitative pruning for previously sheared spiraeas may require that the pruner remove a third of the "split ends" for three years in a row, always hiding the cuts inside the plant. If possible, cut back to a side branch and choose branches that grow outward from the center of the shrub.

Radical Renovation

If you have a nasty mal-pruned spiraea, and you are bold, you can just cut the entire shrub to the ground or an inch above, all at once. If you do so, do it in the spring. In a

Figure 7.18 Radical renovation of a spiraea **A.** Freshly cut to the ground **B.** 1 year later **C.** 2 years later

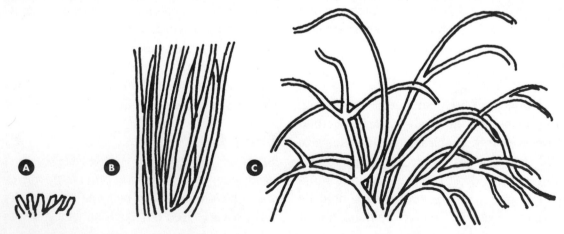

year or two the shrub will regrow and be just fine (see Figure 7.18).

Radical renovation of this sort is a serious stress on a shrub's health, so be sure it is well cared for otherwise. By this I mean it should have enough sun, and enough water, both the year before and the year after renovation. And please refrain from pruning this way as a regular maintenance procedure. Plants don't need to be pruned to look and do their best. Spiraeas are no exception.

Summary

Spiraeas are easy to prune, though they don't need to be pruned to bloom and look their best. You can lower and tidy your shrub using the grab-and-snip method. Remove deadwood. Prune off the branches hanging onto the ground. If it has been mal-pruned (sheared), restore the natural habit by thinning out crowded branches over three years (rehabilitative pruning), or cut the entire shrub to the ground (radical renovation). If you are selective pruning, it doesn't matter when you prune. If you like timing rules: Prune spring bloomers in the early summer. Prune summer bloomers in the early spring (February–March). If you are going to cut your shrub to the ground, do that in the spring.

CHAPTER EIGHT

Cane-Growing Shrubs

hrubs with the habit I call cane-growing are made up of branches that arise from the ground (canes). Canes do not divide many times as do tree branches, nor do they taper. These shrubs tend to be taller than they are wide, with a vertical or vase-shaped habit. They are planted for the show of flowers (like forsythia or hybrid roses) or to add a foliage effect (Oregon grape, bamboo). The deciduous stems of some cane-growers are an interesting color, brightening the dull days of winter. Examples are the red twig dogwood *(Cornus stolonifera)* and *(Kerria japonica)*, which features bright green stems as well as cheery yellow flowers in the spring.

PRUNING CANE-GROWERS

These plants are very tough indeed, having a huge pruning budget, up to 100 percent! This is because they readily renew themselves by sending up new replacement canes from ground level. Often these plants are pruned by cutting out entire canes at the ground level or 1 to 3 inches above (see Figure 8.1).

Figure 8.1 Prune cane-growers by removing selected canes at the ground.

But they can be pruned other ways too. Some can be limbed up so that they look like a little tree. Others can be made less oppressive by thinning out crossing/rubbing and wrong-way branches. Deadwooding is always in order. New pruners are encouraged to practice on cane-growers because if you overprune you will be quickly forgiven as the plant reestablishes a nice form in only one year.

BAMBOO, HEAVENLY BAMBOO, KERRIA, OREGON GRAPE, AND JULIAN'S BARBERRY

(Family *Poaceae/Gramineae, Nandina domestica, Mahonia aquifolium, and Berberis julianae)*

What all these plants have in common is a very vertical habit, even more so than others in the cane-grower category. This makes them useful to put in places requiring tall, skinny plants (along fences and walkways),

Cane-Growing Shrubs

Bamboo	*Family Poaceae (Gramineae)*
Butterfly bush	*Buddleia*
Fatsia	*Fatsia japonica*
Forsythia	*Forsythia*
Heavenly bamboo	*Nandina domestica*
Hydrangea	*Hydrangea*

Julian's barberry	*Berberis julianae*
Kerria	*Kerria japonica*
Red twig dogwood	*Cornus stolonifera*
Rose	*Rosa*
Oregon grape	*Mahonia aquifolium*

Also see the list "Not One or the Other: In-Between Mounding-Habit, Cane-Growing, and Tree-Like Shrubs" at the end of Chapter 9.

and they add valuable contrast in *form* for your landscape. *Contrast*, not flowers, is the stuff of great gardens. I think we tend to overplant shrubs with the rounded form, like rhododendrons, Japanese laceleaf maples, and evergreen azaleas. Some examples of contrasting forms would be horizontal (witch hazel), spiked (yucca), and vertical (bamboo). Other ways to add contrast are to vary plantings in terms of height, foliage, and color.

Bamboo

I think the bamboos (of which there are more species than you can shake a shoot at) are among the most beautiful plants in the world. Add to that that they are practically indestructible and virtually care free. And each cane grows to its ultimate height in one year. The different species grow to different heights, ranging from 2-foot ground covers to 60-foot so-called "timber bamboo."

Bamboo would be a perfect urban plant, especially the perfect screen or hedge, except for that little problem of invasiveness. Professional gardeners all have their favorite bamboo horror stories. I've heard "It's coming through the fireplace!", "It's coming through the refrigerator!", and "It's coming from the other side of the street, under the road!" The

bamboos are divided into "running" and "clumping" forms, with the clumping ones preferred for obvious reasons. I have heard that sometimes the runners don't run, and the clumpers will occasionally decide to run for some unknown reason. I have seen old stands of bamboo successfully contained in plastic pots set in the ground or with bamboo barrier or concrete borders. In other places I have seen all these methods fail. Bamboo is also extremely hard to cut, dig up, and prevent from regrowing from little bits left behind in the soil.

This isn't to say don't plant it.

Heavenly Bamboo

Nandina domestica is called heavenly bamboo, but it's not a real bamboo. I have seen some nandinas spread moderately, but it has never ruined anybody's garden or life, or their neighbor's garden or life. It is the perfect plant for the most difficult spot in the yard, which is that tight place by the front door bordered by the house, the stairs, and the walkway. And it's not likely to grow up to block the window.

People want a plant for this high-profile spot to be evergreen, tidy, and interesting. Enter *N. domestica* 'Compacta'. It looks like a bamboo. It has lacy leaves that are pinkish when they emerge and pick up purple and bronze tints in the fall. Each cane is topped with a nice white burble flower thing, followed by nifty little red berries. In most years the plant stays green all winter. It takes sun and part shade. And it has a cute story that goes as follows: In Japan the man of the household comes home and tells his troubles to the nandina instead of taking them out on his wife, before he goes inside. Hence the species name, *domestica*, as in domestic harmony. This is the other reason they are often seen planted at the front door of the gardener's home.

Kerria

Kerria japonica, like the tall bamboos, will fan out at the top, looking quite graceful. It is made up of many thin canes and spreads underground, becoming a shrub about 8 feet tall and 6 feet wide. It blooms with many small yellow or orange flowers in early spring, and adds interest to the winter garden with its bright green stems. One of my favorite spring plantings is a "yellow garden," with many different kinds of daffodils, forsythia, kerria, some gold-leafed aucuba, and spurge *(Euphorbia cyparissias)*.

Oregon Grape

Mahonia aquifolium is a good foliage plant, adding textural contrast as well as the benefit of its vertical habit. The leaves are reminiscent of holly with their spines. They are rather large leaves, shiny or leathery, that appear all up and down the 1- to 2-inch-diameter stems. The multistemmed shrub is

spreading, and grows 5 to 10 feet tall but can be kept to 5 feet with pruning. Oregon grape is good for a tough evergreen screen or an informal hedge, for contrast, and the foliage is nice to clip and use in vase arrangements. It grows in sun or part shade and is a tough plant, although serious drought or total shade will bring on a bad case of powdery mildew.

Julian's Barberry

Julian's barberry *(Berberis julianae)* is even thornier than Oregon grape, so it is often planted as a barrier. But it is also as tough as all the other barberries, which is very tough—taking poor soil, compacted soil, sun, part shade, and various kinds of abuse and neglect. The plants are not unpretty, having the vertical canes for variety in form; they grow to 6 feet unpruned, and have leathery, dark green leaves that turn reddish in the fall.

Pruning Mistakes

The only mistake I see people make on these plants is to crop off the tops evenly. This destroys their natural beauty. Kerria and bamboos that grow more than 6 feet tall look their best as tall, fountain-shaped plants. Nandina, Julian's barberry, and Oregon grape are even more vertical and should be evenly foliated all up and down the stem, not left showing bare legs. Shearing or tipping-back will cause this unwanted legginess to occur over time. Nandina, however, just tends to get that way, with ugly, dead "pegs" (the bit that once held a leaflet) persisting on the barren, lower stems and the foliage gathered at the top.

Believe it or not, bamboo is used as a hedge in formal Japanese gardens (and in those cases can be sheared), and Oregon grape takes well to being used as a sheared formal screen (though some would argue). However, the indiscriminate shearing of these plants is a form of mal-pruning. Deb Stenoin, an early PlantActivist and creator of the "screaming tree" logo, joined up when she witnessed a gardener shear her favorite stand of bamboo "into a refrigerator." My local bank just sheared its newly planted nandinas into a series of tidy little balls, reminiscent of a broken rack of billiard balls. When sheared, all these plants lose their nice foliar effect and develop an outer shell of green that keeps getting larger with no chance for size reduction.

General Pruning

Generally you thin out cane-growers by pruning some of the canes out, cutting them off at the ground. Assume the classic pruning position, which is on your knees, end up.

Use loppers, a crescent-shaped pruning saw, or a hand pruner. Cut the canes to the ground and them pull them down and out. This is not a delicate operation, though the closer you cut to the ground, the nicer it will look (especially with the bamboo).

How much should you take out? A bamboo expert of my acquaintance says that you can't really overthin bamboo. In fact, she recommends removing up to 50 percent of the canes. To that I would add that I clip off some of the side leaflets (to further accentuate the lines), removing somewhat more of them from the base than from farther up.

Figure 8.2 Assume the pruning position.

With the other plants in this category, I follow the same technique, although to a somewhat lesser degree. It always pays to stand back periodically and ask yourself if things are still looking better, or whether it's time to quit while you're ahead.

And remember—plants don't necessarily need to be pruned. If your plant looks good and isn't bothering anybody or anything, just leave it alone and take the credit for being a great gardener.

Counter Creeping Plants

Bamboo, kerria, and Oregon grape can all start creeping out if they aren't corralled periodically (see Figure 8.3). New homeowners sometimes find kerria canes everywhere, entwining in numerous other plants. Don't be timid. If the plant is not where you want it, just dig it up and throw it away! Use a

Figure 8.3 Bamboo can creep along at an alarming rate!

spade and loppers (with a mattock if necessary), and dig up all of it or just parts, if it's simply gotten too wide. If you are an experienced, clever gardener, you pot it up and donate it to a friend or to the plant sale. Don't worry, you will not damage the remaining plant. Some people are tempted to use the herbicide Roundup on the spreading roots, but it is not recommended since it is a translocated poison and can potentially kill off the parent plant. It has been used with success on the emerging shoots of unwanted bamboo to prevent its spread. Because of the aggressive nature of the beast, the owners of bamboo are often willing to take the risk.

Stop the Flopping

Bamboo is a very useful plant for tight quarters or narrow places, but it is known to flop into the path of foot traffic after a rain, after thinning, or all on its own. It can be easily tied into place or back to the wall with clear fishing line. You don't need to worry about girdling it. Unlike a tree trunk or other shrub stem, which gets fatter every year, a bamboo cane never increases in girth. (It's really a

grass, you know.) It comes out of the ground the same size as it will always be, and reaches its ultimate height in one year.

Nandina gets floppy when it gets leggy and top-heavy. Cut out the canes that fall over, reach up too tall, or brush against the house. Saw them off at ground level. Pretty simple stuff. Use the same technique for the others.

Cover Up Their Knees

Nandina and previously sheared Oregon grape can become leggy. This is easily remedied with the "shotgun" method of pruning (see Figure 8.4). Cut some canes to the ground, but head others back to force new growth inside. Follow the cane down with your eyes, looking inside the plant, to locate a likely node to cut back to. (A node is a place where a leaf was or is, and where a dormant bud remains. It will usually look like a bulge with a line in the stem.) Cut just above the line (see Figure 8.5). New growth will commence exactly at that place and grow up from there (see Figure 8.6).

Leave several canes (the best-looking ones, or the shorter ones under the window) unpruned. In this manner you are planning for the future. You cycle out old, mottled, floppy, too tall, or otherwise unwanted canes. You cycle in new canes that grow up from the base, or that flush out with fresh, healthy new growth from the heading cuts you made.

Radical Renovation

What if you or a previous owner made the mistake of shearing these plants into boxes

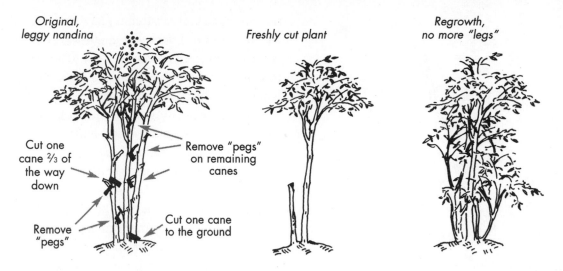

Original, leggy nandina

Cut one cane ⅔ of the way down

Remove "pegs" on remaining canes

Remove "pegs"

Cut one cane to the ground

Freshly cut plant

Regrowth, no more "legs"

Figure 8.4 The shotgun method

or balls? No problem. These plants respond well to radical renovation. That means, you cut the entire plant down to the ground (bamboo, kerria) or at least to a low, uneven framework (barberry, Oregon grape). If the plant was under stress already, and you renovate it during a drought or a freeze, I suppose you could conceivably kill it. But especially here in the Pacific Northwest, where the difference between the summer and the winter is the temperature of the drizzle, casualties are rare.

A few years ago, a television film crew was coming to my house to shoot a little footage. I noticed with some concern how crummy my nandinas looked since the freeze had hit them. I panicked and cut them to the ground lest the crew think me a less-than-perfect gardener. By the end of the growing season, the plants were 3 feet tall

again and looking great! My advice to new gardeners with regard to radical renovation is: only for healthy plants; do it in the early spring; water well for a year; no fertilizer during the recovery period.

Summary

The plants in this group are easy to prune and can take a lot of pruning. Cut unwanted canes (too tall, too floppy, or too many) to the ground and remove them. Also thin some side branches or leaflets. Julian's barberry and Oregon grape can be kept short, hiding many cuts deep inside the plant and heading the rest to the desired height. Kerria and bamboo should be left unheaded (not shortened) or they won't look right. All can be pruned hard, renovated by cutting to the ground or a low framework. If these plants spread, dig up unwanted canes and throw them away.

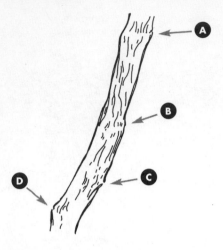

Figure 8.5 Make cuts at points **A**, **B**, **C**, or **D**—just above nodes.

FORSYTHIA *(Forsythia)*

I guess we all cut our pruner's teeth on forsythias. Like many plants in the cane-grower category, these shrubs are planted mostly for their flowers. Their yellow blooms come out in March, before their leaves emerge. After the long, drab, gray winter, the sight of these bright yellow explosions lifts our spirits. In addition, they have a reasonably nice fall coloring, which many people tend to forget.

The Most Common Mistakes

A thing people never seem to grasp is that all plants, including forsythias, have a height and width that is genetically programmed into them, and pruning really can't keep them under a certain size (for any reasonable time). For most forsythias, that size is 7 to 10 feet tall and about as wide.

When you buy a plant at the nursery, it's just a fraction of its adult size. You imagine the shrub will grow to about 5 feet tall and 4

feet wide, so you put it in a place that such a shrub would fit. Eventually, quite soon in fact, it doesn't. Fit, that is. Then I'm apt to hear, "It's too big, it's out of control, it's gone crazy," when actually it's just grown up.

The initial reaction is to cut back the so-called overgrown shrub (and make it into a tidy globe too). Next year this results in an upsurge of straight, ugly, even-wilder shoots arising from the end of each cut tip (the common result of nonselective heading). If you know something about pruning, you might selectively head-back branches to nice laterals (side branches) or remove a quarter to a third of the canes (cutting them to the ground) each year. You will maintain the natural fan, fountain, or vase shape of a forsythia and stop it from continuing up to 12 to 15 feet tall and 18 feet wide. But you will not, trust me, be able to keep a mature plant under 8 feet tall. It's just too much work. The harder you prune, the faster it grows. In the end, you will do what you should have done in the first place: Transplant it to a location where it has room to live as a grown-up.

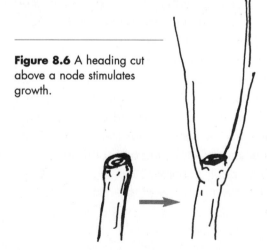

Figure 8.6 A heading cut above a node stimulates growth.

Figure 8.7 Forsythias: They get big.

The Trouble with Forsythias

Forsythias, almost as much so as quinces, have a disturbing branch pattern. It's a mess. This untidy appearance leads to mal-pruning done in an effort to smooth out the perimeter into a globe. The winter aspect is then a jumble of crossing twigs shaped into a ball, followed the next season with a ton of ugly new shoots as described above. Not much of an improvement, I'd say, and certainly too much work.

Not all shrubs have a great winter structure like a witch hazel, or a tidy perimeter like a rhody. Forsythias are sort of the Isadora Duncans of the plant world. They want to be wild and free. Judicious thinning will relieve some of the crossing, crowded branches, but not all. A forsythia is just one of those plants it doesn't pay to look at too closely. At its best, a forsythia's form looks like a vase of large, arching feathers.

The other problem is that, like blackberries, forsythias tip-root. When the canes dip over from their own weight and the tips touch the ground, they will sprout roots and begin a new shrub. In this manner a single shrub can eventually colonize a whole hillside, or run through many neighboring shrubs (see Figure 8.8).

When you prune, it is advisable to cut out, or cut back, these canes and rip up the wandering rooted shrublets. You corral the plant back to the original shrub. Don't worry about using shovels, loppers, or a mattock to get them out. You won't hurt what's left.

Traditional Pruning

The traditional method of pruning a forsythia is to cut canes (with loppers or saw) out at the base. The limit is generally set at a third of the total shrub, although you can, in fact, cut an entire multicaned shrub down (as in stooling or radical renovation) and it will all be back in twelve months. Alternatively, when you cut out just some of the biggest, tallest canes (as fat as 2 or more inches) you are left with a smaller plant. You are also renewing growth, as new shoots will arise from the ground or the low stubs where you cut. These new shoots are very thin, very

Figure 8.8 Forsythias tip-root. **A**. Unconnect the dots (before). **B**. Unconnect the dots (after).

straight, and very rapidly growing, with few flowers and long spaces between the nodes. Eventually they arch over, put on side branches, and add flowers, becoming the new replacement canes. Sometimes a cut cane just dies, becoming deadwood for some future gardener to remove. As in a volleyball game, you are rotating the players. You remove old canes, which usually stimulates some new growth that will become new canes.

Not only does removing tall canes result in a somewhat smaller plant, it also thins the shrub out, making it seem less cluttered to the observer. (Most pruning, you know, is done to keep the plant owner calm, not to help the plants themselves.) To begin pruning your forsythia, you first stare into your shrub (most easily done in the winter when the leaves are off). Follow several canes from the tip down to the base. Your job is to locate a few of the very worst crossing/rubbing, and wrong-way (meaning they start on the outside and head back though the center and out the other side) canes and cut them off at or near the ground (for example, at 3 inches). Sometimes the selected victim is so wrapped around other canes that you must cut it in several places and take it out in pieces. Pull the canes down slowly, using the weight of your body to tug them out. Or sometimes you can toss them up and out of a very overgrown shrub. Mind your eyes!

"The Position"

Approach the overgrown forsythia on hands and knees, cutting out perimeter canes lying on the ground, and thus forcing the shrub to flow upward like a fountain. Cut out old, dead, stubbed-off canes at the base (see Figure 9.9). You'll know they are dead because they won't have any side branches growing off of them. Mostly they are so old as to be punky and you can just yank them out with your hand. Sometimes I simply step on an old dead stub and lean into it. It just snaps out. (In the tree-care business, the removal of dead limbs is sometimes referred to as "Oregon boot pruning.") Continue pruning by working your way up and out, moving in a roughly spiral fashion. Take out deadwood and some crossing/rubbing branches. Take out a few canes that crowd up the center, sometimes sawing with just the tip of your blade.

Spend a lot of time moving around getting into position for the best cut. Crawl outside

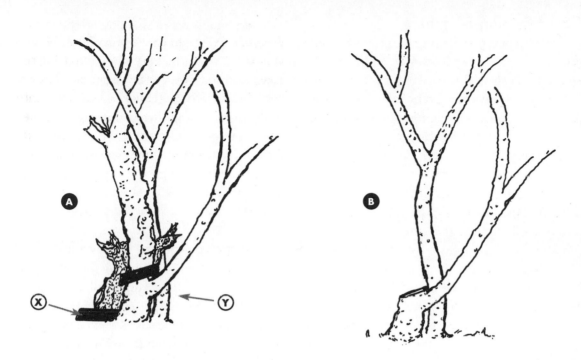

Figure 8.9 A. Before: Remove dead, spongelike wood (x). Cut back heavy growth to a fresh renewal branch near the base (y). **B.** After: Air, light, and space encourage fresh growth.

the shrub and walk around it every so often to judge your progress and plan your next avenue of attack. Why? One, you may see how much things are improving already and be encouraged to continue, or two, you may see that things are getting very thin on one side and decide to move to the other before you overthin the entire shrub. Remember, you never can get it to look perfect from all sides, so *quit while you're ahead.*

In point of fact, almost all branches in a forsythia are rubbing and crossing. This generally discourages the new pruner. Often he or she just gives up, cuts off the top, and goes back inside the house to fix a nice hot cup of cocoa. But remember, the job is not to *eliminate* wrong branches, but to *reduce the number* of them. It doesn't even really matter which ones you choose. You could blindfold yourself, throw six darts into the forsythia, cut out the darted branches, and it would miraculously look a lot better. So don't worry about which cane is the right one, just make yourself cut, and keep moving around. There is nothing that you can do to a mature forsythia (heading or overthinning) that you can't get back. So be brave. As an old client of mine says, "Prune with vigor." Forsythias are really, really tough, and can always renew themselves with new canes.

Cass's Pruning Technique

I have no trouble accepting the size of plants. When customers say they want a plant made *smaller*, I hear that they want it made *better looking*. I remove the branches lying on the ground. I thin out crossing/rubbing branches by cutting to a lateral branch, to a main stem, or to the ground. I look for stubs, stubs, stubs, and crowded branch ends where the poor shrub has been previously headed. I use the thinning cut to "simplify" these crowded, mal-pruned areas (see Figure 8.10).

I don't really spend a lot of time cutting canes to the ground. I'm just as likely to limb a plant up a bit to make it look more perky, and to cut off the worst rambling canes that head into nearby shrubs, touch the house, or look like they might poke someone in the eye. I spend a lot of time creating definition (or empty spaces between plants), so that plants seem to fit together better.

And know that selective pruning is just a series of choices—there are several correct ways to thin a forsythia (see Figures 8.11).

I very much recall working on the yard of a certain great old gal. Among other chores, she asked that I make the forsythia smaller. It was a fright of regrowth from the previous "cutting back" job. I tried to avoid the task, doing other needed work in the garden. But she pointed me back at it. So I screwed up my courage, went in, and mucked about, not trying to make it smaller, just better. Later she said, "Now, see how much better it looks?"

Stooling and Radical Renovation

An entire system of managing forsythias and other deciduous flowering shrubs is found in several pruning guides and in old British garden books. These sources recommend that the entire plant be cut down or to a low framework called a "stool." This is to be done every year after the shrubs are through blooming, which allows these tough plants time to regrow, set buds, and bloom for the next year. I figure it worked well in olden days because labor was cheap, and it was

Figure 8.10 To simplify crowded branch ends, **A.** remove two outer stems, or **B.** remove the center stem. Either choice is correct.

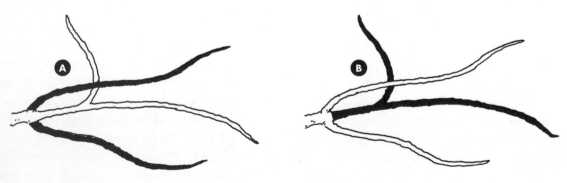

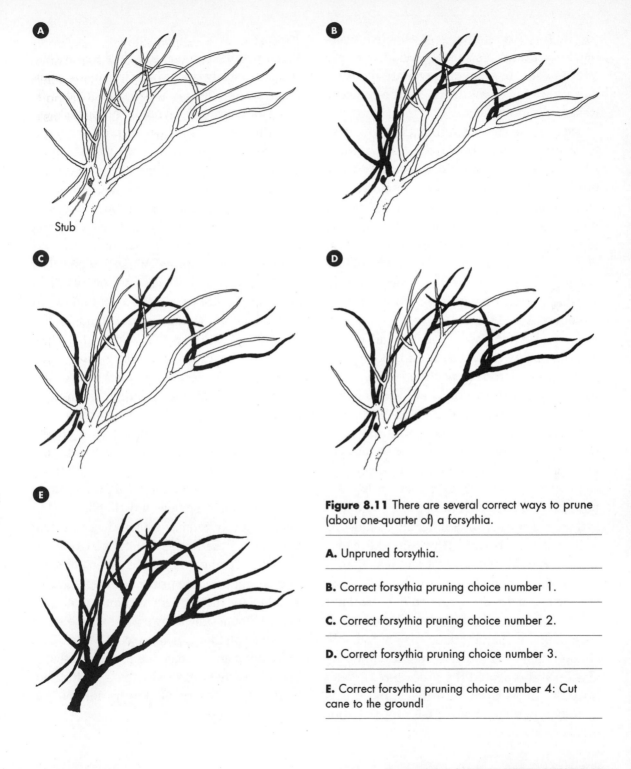

Stub

Figure 8.11 There are several correct ways to prune (about one-quarter of) a forsythia.

A. Unpruned forsythia.

B. Correct forsythia pruning choice number 1.

C. Correct forsythia pruning choice number 2.

D. Correct forsythia pruning choice number 3.

E. Correct forsythia pruning choice number 4: Cut cane to the ground!

too difficult to explain real selective pruning. I don't think it's such a good idea in very hot climates, or when done before the plant is thoroughly established (three years?). Besides, it looks mean.

I sometimes cut a shrub to the ground, or to a low, uneven framework, as a *radical renovation* procedure. It is a short cut (ha, ha) to rehabilitative pruning for a previously mal-pruned plant, but is *not* done as a yearly maintenance chore. The other common way to renovate a mal-pruned forsythia or other cane-grower is to cut one-quarter of the canes to the ground for three years in a row, at which point new growth will have completely replaced the old.

I recall a lady who had had all of her deciduous flowering shrubs had "boxed" for years. They got too big again and she couldn't figure out what to do. They were far too dense for the one-third method. Instead, I renovated every other shrub to a low (less than 2 feet), uneven framework of headed-off canes. This was done to encourage regrowth at uneven heights, which is more natural looking. The next spring the forsythia was up and blooming and almost as tall as it was before. However, the canes were very stiff and straight and less than ¼ inch in diameter. Over the following years, the canes fattened up, arched over, and put on side branches and more blooms, thus regaining the characteristic vase or fountain shape. Then I cut down the other half of the shrubs and repeated the procedure. I could have cut them all down at once, but this is usually too great a leap of faith for the average homeowner.

Timing

When people ask *how* to prune a forsythia, they are usually treated to a lecture on *when* to prune it. The pruner is admonished to prune only when the plant is through blooming. This really is only necessary if the stooling method is used, and it's just common sense. If you cut the entire shrub to the ground just before bloom time, it doesn't bloom because it's not there. But if you wait until it's through blooming, it has all spring and summer to regrow, set up buds, and bloom the next spring. When I renovate a shrub (which occurs only once every fifteen years in the life of a shrub), I often do so *before* bloom time. So the homeowner misses their flowers for a year, big deal. Heck, they're already in shock because I cut the whole thing to the ground! I prune early because it gives me a larger window of opportunity and it gives the shrub a few more weeks of warm (warm to a shrub) growing weather in which to recuperate from surgery.

But for general thinning and pruning done as regular maintenance, any time is good in my opinion. Winter is a nice time to prune because all the leaves are off and you can see what's going on in there. Spring or summer is a nice time to prune because it's nicer weather for the gardener. Thinning out just before bloom time allows you to force some branches indoors in a vase of water. The great thing about selective pruning is that it doesn't really matter when you do it, there will still be plenty of flowers left on the remaining canes.

Pronunciation

I had an interesting conversation with a British arborist over a mug of Guinness. He said he was tired of getting the "you poor, ignorant laborer" look every time he pronounced forsythia "fors-EYE-thia." He insisted that this was the correct pronunciation as the plant was named after a man called Forsythe from his country, as in "the Forsythe Saga." He's probably right, but I doubt that gardeners around here will take up that pronunciation anytime soon. After all, it took us so long to master Latin as we know it. Consider the fact that the correct pronunciation for *Pinus* (the genus of pine trees) is "PEE-noos." Our reputations would be shot.

Anyway, good luck with your forsythia and remember, "Prune with vigor!"

Summary

Forsythias are extremely tough. They can withstand any amount or kind of pruning. But don't shear them or just whack them back. It won't work.

Stare at your shrub.

Prune out the deadwood.

If you want to reduce size, cut out some big old canes, sawing them off at the ground or an inch or two above. Take out some of the tallest ones every year. Let some suckers grow back into replacement canes.

If you just want it to look better, limb it up by cutting off the branches lying on the ground, and remove a few of the worst crossing/rubbing branches. Prune to open the center a bit. Prune out the few of the worst canes that start at the outside of the shrub and then grow back into the center and out the other side (Mr. Wrong Way). Thin and selectively

---

Figure 8.12 Country Western forsythia: ♪ *That achey, breaky, rooty weepy* ♪... **A.** "I ache and need a break!" **B.** High as an elephant's eye **C.** Find the $52 saw in the prunings "hay stack."

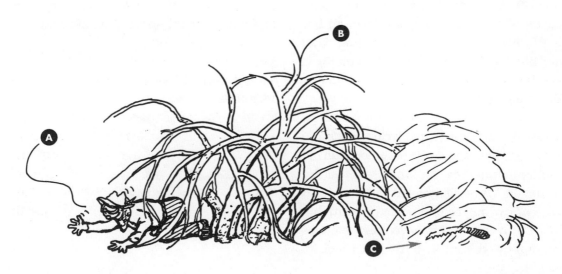

head-back some of the most troubling branches up top. Simplify crowded branch ends that have been previously headed.

If need be, an established, multicaned forsythia can be radically renovated in the spring.

HYDRANGEA *(Hydrangea)*

A year or two after I caught the gardening bug, I entered a phase akin to being a teenager. I spoke with the authority of a garden expert and expressed strong opinions on just about everything, including the worthiness of any given plant. Hydrangeas, as well as many of the deciduous flowering shrubs, I quickly dismissed as "little-old-lady plants." Now, some fifteen years later, they are among my favorites. I wonder what all this means?

I like hydrangeas because they bloom at a time other than spring, because they bloom in part shade, because they're tough, because of their old-fashioned colors and old-fashioned lace flowers, and because the blooms change color as they fade. And because of these things I now own all but one of the shrubs described below. Like many plant lovers, my yard is becoming a collection of desirables—what I used to call a "little-old-lady" garden.

Garden and Lace-Cap Hydrangeas

The garden hydrangea *(H. macrophylla)* is the one most people think of when you say "hydrangea." It is also called the mop-head or bigleaf hydrangea and is the one with big balls for flowers. I have never been particularly impressed with it, but when I met its lace-cap cousin—all understated and fabulously blue—I fell in love. Although it is the same species *(H. macrophylla)*, the lace-cap form is almost like a different plant. It looks more natural to me, so much so that I will use it in a woodland border. Like other hydrangeas, it blooms later in the summer and hangs on to its fading blooms into the fall, which is nice.

Prune the lace-cap like the regular garden hydrangea, which is to say—not much (see Figure 8.13). Many of the best looking hydrangeas aren't pruned at all. So once again, if it's not broken, don't fix it. Generally speaking, garden hydrangeas and lace-caps can be made to look "better" by following the rules of selective pruning: First, take out the deadwood. (Be careful. With hydrangeas, the canes often look hollow and dead when they are not—check the cambium to see if it's tan, not live green, before eliminating.) Take out a few of the worst crossing/rubbing canes, especially those that are too crowded in the center. Cut off canes lying on the ground, growing out too far, or touching the house. This will make the shrub more attractive.

Figure 8.13 Pruning garden and lace-cap hydrangeas

Where to Cut

When pruning, canes can be cut to the ground or to a promising side branch, node, or bud down inside the shrub.

Size Reduction

I have never successfully made a hydrangea shorter using the grab-and-snip method (as used for mounding-habit shrubs), or by cutting out a few of the tallest canes every year (the method used for cane-growers). And believe me, I've tried. The next growing season the shrub zooms up to its previous size, except now all the branches are weak and floppy.

For years, however, I have read and heard that hydrangeas can be managed by annually cutting them down to a low framework. That would be 3 inches to a foot above the ground. Whenever this sort of hard pruning is done, you will also get much larger blooms and larger leaves. The shrub grows back into a 2- or 3-foot (somewhat floppy) globe. Many people have told me that shrubs cut to the ground in April are blooming by the end of summer. Other people say that their shrubs didn't bloom the first year after hard pruning. I am at a loss to explain these conflicting reports. But I do know that in two years, three at the most, the hydrangea shrub pruned in this manner will be the same size as before, except it will be floppy. I therefore don't use this method; besides, it's too frightening looking and too much work. You are welcome to try cutting to 8 inches from the ground if you like, because hydrangeas are tough and you won't hurt them in doing so.

And if you know the answer to the puzzle, be sure to let me know.

Transplanting

The good news is that hydrangeas are easy to transplant and rarely die as a result. If the plant is too large for its current location, transplanting is a much wiser choice than pruning for size control. It is best done in the dormant season, but a hydrangea will survive when moved in other seasons, too. If you move your hydrangea in the summer, the leaves will wilt and look horrible, but if it is watered well, it has a very good chance of recovering. Because hydrangeas are so tough, you can even cut a shrub to a low framework and then move it, if that makes things easier for you. Remember to water it immediately and a lot next year. In fact, you should know that hydrangeas really want a lot of water. Is that the reason for their name?

Deadheading

Should you deadhead hydrangeas? In the late fall, people are tempted to cut off the fading flower heads to make the shrubs look cleaner. Some gardeners claim that removing the faded blooms will prevent snow from collecting on them and causing limb breakage. In parts of the country with colder climates, it is recommended that you leave the flowers on to protect the buds beneath from frost damage. Then in the early spring (when the danger of frost is past, but new growth hasn't started, perhaps February), these cold-climate gardeners will cut off the old flowers. When doing so, look for the four or five pairs of plump buds just beneath the old flower (see Figure 8.14).

If you cut back to the lowest, or second-lowest, set of these plump buds, the shrub will have flowers this year, and they may even be larger flowers. This is not a necessary thing to do, but a tip for those people who desire the most from their shrubbery.

Oakleaf Hydrangea

When I encounter a landscape that has had all the mature shrubs tied back, I take it as a sign that the previous gardener didn't know how to prune. And I suppose I'm thankful that they used tying, as opposed to whacking, in trying to restore order. The damage is less severe with tying—except, of course, where the ties have been left on too long and the shrubs have become girdled.

The only plant I am known to tie up is the oakleaf hydrangea (*H. quercifolia*), because it is a particularly floppy shrub. I don't want to cut it to the ground as some books advise. I love this plant. The new leaves on the tips emerge in the spring like two tiny pressed shirts, crisp and white. The fully emerged leaves, which look like large oak leaves, turn lovely scarlet in the fall. (The oakleaf should

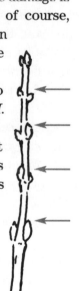

Figure 8.14 Hydrangea pruning: In early spring, cut back to any of the four topmost pairs of buds.

be planted in more sun than the other hydrangeas to encourage this fall color.) The late-summer flowers are like an old lace flounce on a blouse. They're a creamy white that fades to pink.

In the winter, the shrub looks like heck, as do all the hydrangeas after the first frost. Then all the leaves hang down—limp, slimy, and brown. But I'm not spending much time in the backyard in the winter, which is why it is a wise idea to locate hydrangeas there. I do try to nip out once a year and retie the oakleaf, so it doesn't get girdled. It is also okay to thin off or head-back a few unwanted branches at any time of the year.

Climbing Hydrangea

The only really well-behaved vine I know is the hydrangea vine (*H. anomala petiolaris*). And I like to say the words out loud too—hydrangea vine. The hydrangea vine has little suction-cup dealies on its "aerial roots," which means it can climb up structures like walls or tree trunks without a trellis. In fact it needs a solid surface, as opposed to a wire or wooden trellis, to climb on. The vine has white, lace-cap–type blooms, and the winter branches are presentable, unlike those of some other deciduous vines I could mention.

What's to know about the hydrangea vine is that it can be a bit slow to get established on the wall or tree trunk, failing to get a good grab for the first few years. And the young leaves and those closest to the ground always seem to look a little moth eaten. I don't know what's getting them, but I ignore it.

If you have to prune an old vine (say it's all piled up on itself growing on top of a wall for twenty years and is getting dangerously overextended), take heart. It, like all the hydrangeas, can take a lot of pruning, including heading. You will just lose the blooms on the parts you cut off, and only for a year. So it's best to stagger your work over a few years.

Peegee Hydrangea

In the late summer both my husband and I are apt to call out "peegee alert" when driving together in the same car. The peegees (*H. paniculata* 'Grandiflora'), grown as either a small tree (25 feet) or an enormous shrub (15 by 15 feet), burst on the scene with their giant white to pink, cone-shaped flowers covering the entire bush. I have never taken care of a peegee myself, but the books say that it can be pruned hard (to a few inches from the ground) every year. If done in the late winter or early spring, it will bloom that summer/fall. Personally, I wouldn't bother doing that as a regular maintenance chore. But I might consider it if my blooms became too small over the course of many years.

Summary

Hydrangeas don't need to be pruned to bloom and look good. But hydrangeas resprout easily from the base and from heading cuts and therefore *take* a lot of pruning, including cutting them to the ground or a foot above. Unfortunately, *moderate* size reduction on garden hydrangeas and lacecaps is doomed to failure (they grow right back, except floppy). All hydrangeas are extremely easy to transplant. Some thinning, deadwooding, and removal of unwanted canes can help many plants look better. Dead-heading (taking off dead flower heads) is not necessary, but it makes the shrub look nicer.

HYBRID TEA ROSES *(Rosa)*

"They've butchered our roses!" exclaimed the woman on the phone. She was calling to report this crime to PlantAmnesty. "There was nothing wrong with them. The grounds crew just came through and hacked them down to a foot off the ground. My God, there's not a leaf left on them!" At the time I was the official answer person for the PlantAmnesty hotline and referral service. I did my best to calm her, saying, "Correct rose pruning can look very severe." And I followed up with some illustrated literature.

It's true. To the novice, the annual pruning of hybrid tea–type roses (the kind most people have) can look quite frightening. Half of the canes are removed at the base and then those that are left get reduced in height to 2 feet or so. One rosarian I know teaches his students a chant: "You can't kill a rose by pruning it, you can't kill a rose by pruning it." Novice pruners repeat it to give themselves courage.

The Most Common Mistakes

Underpruning

This is not to say that a rose can't be malpruned. But the most common mistake, I believe, is not pruning "teas" sufficiently. Often a homeowner moves into a house with a yard wherein lives a towering 8-foot rose bush. Its canes are as thick around as your aunt's ankles. The new owner, not knowing what else to do, props a trellis under it and maintains it at that height. Which brings me to the reason we prune hybrid teas so heavily. I have concluded that it is to keep them down where we can pick and enjoy the flowers. If left unpruned, who knows at what great height a tea could top out? To restore an overgrown tea, cut half of those giant canes to the bottom, in hopes of stimulating new cane growth from buds on the graft union (looks like a bulge at ground level just above the roots). Lightly tip-back the remainder.

The heavy, annual thinning and pruning commonly done to teas results in fewer but larger roses, too. Let's face it, cut flowers for the vase is the reason to have teas. They have little to offer in the way of form for the landscape. And in the winter they are just a jumble of straight sticks. Therefore I think they look best segregated into their own bed with an edging of lavender or something else to give it a feeling of tidy formality. Some expert gardeners I know have incorporated tea roses into mixed borders with excellent results. I have not had such luck. Whenever I try to plant them closely with perennials, they succumb to black spot and die a horrible and prolonged death. Often I find solitary rose bushes scattered about in the gardens I visit. They look as out of place as a pink chiffon prom dress at the pizza parlor.

Overpruning

On the other hand, people who have been pruning roses for a few years are often tempted to prune too hard. A famous treatise on the topic surmises that people do this just because they can get away with it. Until, of course they finally starve the poor plant to death. Or so claims the author, a rosarian from Portland, Oregon (the "Rose City"). By "too hard" I mean that canes are cut down to three or four buds from the ground. That's about 2 to 3 inches tall. Yikes! Such pruning, I am told, produces long stems and enormous flowers. Thus it is justified for growing show roses (in conjunction with *disbudding*, which is the removal of young buds to force more growth into the remaining flowers). For the rest of us mere mortals it is best to prune back the average rose bush to 2 or 3 feet tall. I am sorry to report that some variation exists in the preferred height even among hybrid teas.

It's Not a Tea Rose

Sometimes people move into a yard with a neglected landscape. The original tea rose suffered dieback in a drought or freeze. The rootstock survived and now grows out wildly, with long arching canes that defy tea-type pruning. These canes are often put on a fan-shaped trellis as well. Although rootstock roses, which are usually red-flowered, are not unpretty, the homeowner should feel no guilt over tearing out the usurper and replacing it with something better suited to the site.

Other times people fail to realize that what they have are actually climbers or shrub roses. These are pruned differently from teas. Some are labor intensive, others can be practically ignored.

I have a great little book on rose varieties. It has wonderful drawings and descriptions. It includes pruning and other cultural information and the occasional historical tidbit.

It's out of print, but you might still be able to find a copy at the library or a used bookstore Its title is *Roses*, by Kenneth A. Beckett, published in 1984 by the Garden Library, Ballantine.

The Unfinished Job

The only other mistake I see is when people don't take the time to finish their pruning job. They leave dead canes, and bits of dead canes and twigs. Some cut to the correct height but not to an out-facing bud, or they leave too many canes in the bush. Not that you need to be overly concerned. A recent field test showed that pruning a rose hedge with power hedge shears produced as good an effect as careful hand pruning. Of course, I couldn't recommend hedge shearing roses (around here they would become black-spot magnets), so don't quote me.

Other Roses

For those who like to incorporate roses into a larger bed design, know that there are many wonderful kinds (wonderfully confusing in number and variety). These include hedge roses, bush roses, shrub roses, climbers, and ramblers. Oh, and let us not forget pillars, species, antiques, and miniatures. And pompoms. And standard roses (roses trained to look like lollipops in a pot). The topic of the ancestry and breeding of roses can itself fill several volumes. I like the older shrub-type roses because of their history. And many have better scent, rose hips, and other desirable traits. I am not alone in finding shrub-type roses interesting. They are presently enjoying renewed popularity nationwide. Breeders have created many "new" old roses that combine the best of all worlds, meaning scent, repeat bloom, smaller size, and disease resistance.

February, by the way, is the traditional time to buy roses, *bare root* (sold in a baggie with no dirt on the roots), either in the store or through the catalogs. Roses are harder to find in the summer, though nowadays some nurseries carry them potted up. But then the plants are more expensive.

Old shrub roses are tough, and some can be care free—your basic glorified blackberry bushes, to my way of thinking. But many are very large, and space must be provided. The largest rose in the world is in China and goes on for several acres. Climbers and ramblers and pillars can be low maintenance if run through a tree, as the Brits have taught us to do. I thought my neighbor had a blackberry vine growing out of the top of his 20-foot Port Orford cedar until it turned into a waterfall of red roses in midsummer. Delightful!

But climbers can be high maintenance too, since most are forced to grow on a wall, fence, arbor, or trellis. Still, nothing is quite so evocative as the sight of a rose spilling over a wall or an archway. Certainly it is worth the constant tying and snipping required to keep them from becoming a menace to foot traffic. What other plant blooms after spring, and blooms and blooms and blooms? And smells so sweet? I suspect that it is the wedding of classic beauty with the danger of thorns that makes pruning roses so enjoyable. Regarde la femme fatale!

Tools

Be prepared. Wear tight-fitting leather gloves (hard to find, I know). Also wear a long-sleeved shirt, not a sweater. Have a sharp pair of bypass pruners, loppers, and a pruning saw. Gardeners tend to use the new ARS-type of folding saws. They are easily carried in the back pocket, and fit into tight spaces between canes.

Deadwood

Deadwood removal is first. This means mostly sawing out dead canes and stubs (see Figure 8.15).

The stubs, which are many and rather large, can be found close to the graft union. Take your time and saw each and every dead cane or stub off carefully and completely.

Old Canes

Remove sick canes and big old canes. How can you tell if canes are sick? Usually they

---

Figure 8.15 Hybrid tea pruning: Saw out dead stubs and canes.

are the older, thicker canes, but not always. The bark on "unhealthy" canes is mottled and blackish. The perfect, healthy cane (rarely seen in real life) is about as thick as your thumb and the outer bark is a clear, unblemished green.

Unthrifty Canes

Canes die from the tip down, as a result of freeze or drought. If the cane you are looking at fills an otherwise empty spot, you may want to keep it but shorten it to healthy, or at least healthier, tissue. To find out where that point is, cut a bit off the top and look at the cut end. The pith of an unhealthy cane is black, or partially black and brown. As you continue cutting back the cane, the wood usually becomes a more clear, tan color. Then you finish off by cutting to the nearest side branch or bud facing outward.

Completely remove canes that are *too skinny*, cutting them off where they meet the graft union. One recommendation is to prune out canes that are smaller than a pencil.

Remove Rootstock Suckers

Cut or tear off all suckers. Many roses are sort of spliced (grafted) to the roots of a tougher plant. Suckers are canes that arise from any portion *below* the graft union. These suspicious canes have different-colored bark, have different leaves, and grow in a different form. If the cane originates from the graft union itself, it is probably okay. If the cane originates from the roots, dig down to where it meets the parent root. Twist and pull (yank, actually) it off. If you simply cut a sucker off at ground level, you will get twice as many growing at the same place next year.

Crossers/Rubbers

Remove canes that cross or rub others and some that fill up the center. The perfect rose bush, should such a thing exist, would have five or six clear, green canes, each as thick as a thumb, radiating evenly from the center (see Figure 8.16).

In reality, you do the best with what is available. Sometimes all the canes are weak and spindly. Sometimes the only decent-sized cane that exists goes horribly the wrong way. Sometimes all you have are crusty, mottled, and huge canes. Just do the best you can. Keep in mind, it's no big deal. For all the disease, dieback, and death found in roses, they are tough, tough plants. A rose's strategy for survival is to constantly renew itself by sending up replacement canes every year.

Cut Everything Back

Shorten the canes that remain. How much? One rule of thumb is to cut no shorter than half a cane's original height. I like to prune most teas to about 1 to 2 feet. Some people like them shorter, some like them taller. The thinner the cane, the shorter it is pruned. The fatter the cane, the higher you cut (see Figure 8.17).

Where to Cut

Cut to an out-facing bud, generally speaking. In the late winter/early spring these are easier to spot as they begin to plump up. They are about the size of pencil tips (see Figure

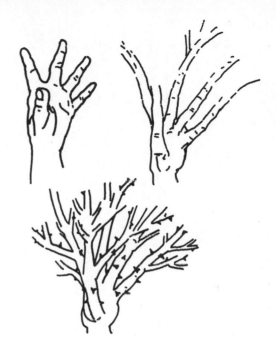

Figure 8.16 The perfect rose bush would have five or six clear, green canes as thick as a thumb and radiating evenly from the center.

8.18). Some books call them eyes, since they look like eyes. Teeny-weeny eyes.

In February, one is apt to find gardeners out in the rose beds on their knees with one hand down, practically standing on their heads, peering at the canes, their faces perilously close to thorns. They are trying to locate the optimum buds. Invariably, the bud at the right height is in the wrong place—that is, it faces into the center. As you prune, the height of some canes will be a little too high or too low. It's a balancing act. Sometimes the buds are a bit to one side or another. It's even okay to have a few that fill the inside.

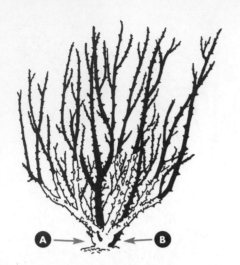

Figure 8.17 Hybrid tea pruning **A**. Graft union **B**. Sucker

When you cut, the bud just below will be stimulated into growing out. It grows out the same way the bud is facing. You can anticipate how your rose bush will look by imagining the shoots growing out. Later, if two little shoots grow out from the bud, snap out one with your fingers.

Make the cut at a slant, channeling the growth energy the same way the bud is headed. Don't cut too close, or the bud will die. Don't cut too far away, or the cane will die back to the bud and leave an ugly stub. Actually (should I put it in print?) I find that I tend to cut a bit high on roses. Don't ask me why, except that I know other rose pruners who do so as well. One arborist took me to task for "leaving stubs." "But it's a rose!" I pleaded my case.

Why Prune?

All this thinning opens up the rose bush, allowing for increased light and air circula-tion. This is more important on roses than on many other plants because roses are perpetually plagued by a host of fungal and bacterial diseases. Open pruning helps, but rarely cures. Roses, like cherry trees, are sort of the sick kids of the plant world. The homeowner is well advised to put up with a certain number of cruddy leaves. And the first criterion for buying a new rose is whether or not it shows good disease resistance.

What Next?

If you find evidence of a nasty bug called a cane borer (little holes) you may want to *seal the cuts*. There are commercial products for this, though a dab of clear nail polish or Elmer's glue works well, I am told. By the end of summer your rose bush will be an astounding 5 feet tall and full again.

Deadheading

Once the rose starts blooming, it is common to deadhead throughout the rest of the summer season. This means that every few weeks, you prune off the dead (spent) flowers before they turn into seeds (rose hips). This causes the shrub to continue to produce. (Really, you are preventing the bush

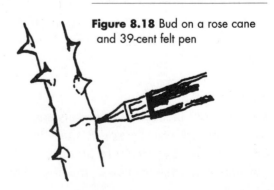

Figure 8.18 Bud on a rose cane and 39-cent felt pen

Figure 8.19 Cut canes back to either **A.** a bud or **B.** a leaflet, which will **C.** result in a new shoot and bloom.

from having babies. And so she has to keep putting on that fancy red dress to go out and try again. Poor girl!)

The general rule is to cut to a lower set of leaves with a bud in the *axil* (the place where the stem of a leaf joins the cane) facing out. We are always told to cut to a set of five leaves rather than to the other three-leaf kind (see Figures 8.20 and 8.21). The "fiver" produces flowers, not so the other kind. My husband tested this by pruning one rose bed to "fivers" and the other to "three-ers." The five-leaf bed bloomed more, although the other did still produce flowers.

Fall

Around August or September many folks let the rose finish up by ceasing to deadhead. The rose sets up hips. The theory is that, by finishing its life cycle, the rose bush will slow down and toughen up *(harden off)* for winter. This means that the rose will be less likely to freeze.

Winter

Around December or January, if and when the rose bushes go dormant, I often shorten the shrubs some. The excuse I give is to prevent "wind rock," which actually occurs in some parts of the country. But really, I do it because the roses are too tall and untidy, flapping around with dead leaves impaled on their thorns.

Spring

The major pruning is done in the late winter or early spring (gardeners in other parts of the country prune in fall or winter). In Seattle's

February, most gardeners are in a state of chronic angst, wondering whether or not they should prune the roses. Especially in a warm winter the roses have already started to bud out and grow. I should market Sleep-Eze for roses.

The general rule is to wait until *George Washington's birthday* to prune. Famous media horticulturist Ciscoe Morris insists on waiting until March. If you prune too soon, the plants are stimulated into growing right then. If we have a late freeze, that tender new growth is apt to (shall I say it?) get nipped in the bud. Worse yet, the plant might freeze to the ground. The temperatures need to get down into the teens and twenties before I worry. And if a plant dies, I see it as a wonderful opportunity to go buy a new disease-resistant variety.

Now you too can start worrying and watching your roses. You can wait to prune till later, but once the new shoots are expanding, it is difficult to prune without knocking them off. And too, you'll feel guilty cutting off all that nice new growth. I doubt

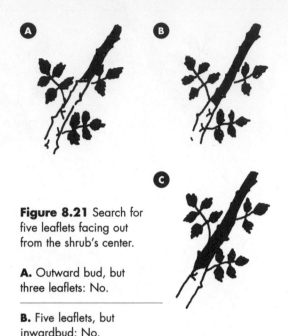

Figure 8.21 Search for five leaflets facing out from the shrub's center.

A. Outward bud, but three leaflets: No.

B. Five leaflets, but inwardbud: No.

C. Outward bud and five leaflets; Yes! Cut here.

that it hurts the roses much. After all, you will recall, you can't kill a rose by pruning it.

Summary

Prune your roses in late February. Cut out some of the too-big/old canes, some of the too-little or sick canes, and ones in the center. And deadwood, of course. Then shorten the three to six canes that are left to about a foot or so above the ground. A different rule of thumb is to reduce the rose to one-half its original height. Cut canes to an out-facing bud. It's a little pink thing about the size of a pencil tip.

Figure 8.20 A. Three-leaf Peace Rose **B.** Five-leaf Peace Rose

CHAPTER NINE

Tree-Like Shrubs

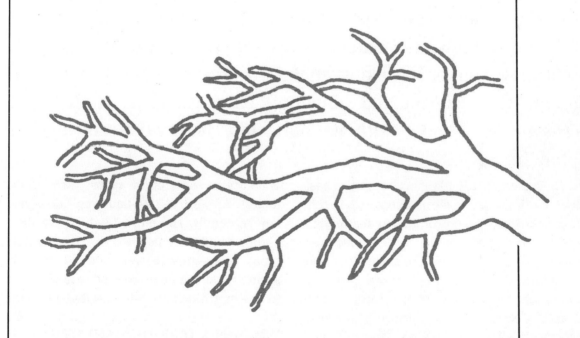

Tree-like shrubs are the Cadillacs of the shrub world. I call them "tree-like" not because they are huge or because they have a single trunk. They aren't, and they don't. I call them tree-like because they have a complex branch structure that divides many times, like a tree's branch. Examples are rhododendrons, camellias, witch hazels, and pieris. The branches of tree-like shrubs are stiffer (woodier) than those of plants such as, say, choisya (Mexican orange), which has softer (more herbaceous) wood. The complex, woodier branch structure is sort of the high cheekbones of shrubs. It makes these plants seem more elegant and tidier to the viewer than, say, a forsythia or a spiraea. And if the shrubs are deciduous, the fine branch pattern is an attractive feature in the winter. Examples are the barren curlicue branches of Harry Lauder's walking stick (*Corylus avellana* 'Contorta'), hung with catkins like dangling earrings, and witch hazel (*Hamamelis* spp.), with its horizontal and artistically angled branches.

Because the tree-like shrubs are the best looking of the three shrub categories in this book, they are often prominently featured in landscapes. They make good "specimen plants"—the ones chosen to stand alone and be admired. I feel that they are currently being overused in the new, suburban "McMansion" developments springing up everywhere. If all the plants are "special" they detract from each other. Tree-likes can be used in groupings, but great care must be given to spacing requirements. They are best allowed to grow as high and as wide as they want (size restriction ruins their good looks). An all–tree-like landscape does not age gracefully. Therefore I believe tree-like shrubs should be combined with other shrub types (cane-growers and mounding-habit shrubs) that can be more readily moderated in size and which provide valuable contrast.

PRUNING TREE-LIKE SHRUBS

It is their articulate branch structure that makes these plants more difficult to prune than mounding-habit shrubs or cane-growers. Their pruning budget tends to be small,

Tree-Like Shrubs

TREE-LIKES THAT TAKE MODERATE THINNING

Deciduous azalea	*Rhododendron*
Enkianthus	*Enkianthus*
Fothergilla	*Fothergilla*
Huckleberry	*Vaccinium*
Lilac	*Syringa* (or can be pruned like a cane-grower; see Chapter 8)
Mountain laurel	*Kalmia latifolia*
Pacific Wax Myrtle	*Myrica californica*

TREE-LIKES THAT WATER-SPROUT READILY SO THIN LIGHTLY

Beautyberry	*Callicarpa*
Cotoneaster	*Cotoneaster*
Doublefile viburnum	*Viburnum plicatum tomentosum*
Filbert	*Corylus*
Persian parrotia	*Parrotia persica*
Star magnolia	*Magnolia stellata*
Mountain laurel	*Kalmia latifolia*
Viburnum bodnantense	*Viburnum bodnantense*
Winter hazel	*Corylopsis*
Wintersweet	*Chimonanthus praecox*
Witch hazel	*Hamamelis*

TREE-LIKES THAT TAKE MORE THINNING

Andromeda	*Pieris*
Camellia	*Camellia*
English laurel	*Prunus laurocerasus*
Photinia	*Photinia fraseri*
Pine	*Pinus*
Portuguese laurel	*Prunus lusitanica*
Rhododendron	*Rhododendron*
Strawberry tree	*Arbutus unedo*
Thread cypress	*Chamaecyparis pisifera 'Filifera'*

TREE-LIKES TOUGH ENOUGH FOR SHEARING

English holly	*Ilex aquifolium*
English laurel	*Prunus laurocerasus*
Firethorn	*Pyracantha*
Photinia	*Photinia x fraseri*
Portuguese laurel	*Prunus lusitanica*
Privet (evergreen and deciduous)	*Ligustrum*
Sweet bay	*Laurus nobilis*
Yew	*Taxus*

Also see the list "Not One or the Other: In Between Mounding-Habit, Cane-Growing, and Tree-Like Shrubs" at the end of this chapter.

so size reduction is discouraged, and one should use mostly thinning cuts. Overpruning or heading is apt to stimulate water-sprout production or otherwise undermine branch structures and diminish the good looks of these plants. Pruning these plants is often done to create definition or to show off the inner beauty of deciduous shrubs in the winter. Most of the work is simply deadwooding. The pruner looks for crossing/rubbing branches, duplicating branches, and diseased wood. At the end of the job every space is filled, but with fewer branches. This is the art of thinning (see Figure 9.1).

Generally the pruner works from the bottom up, and the inside out, frequently getting out of the plant to judge the progress. There are no "right" branches to prune, only a series of choices. It is normal to keep a running conversation in your head: "Should I prune this branch or will it leave a big hole? Have I pruned too much? Should I take out

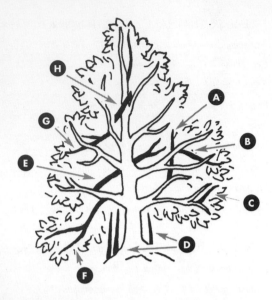

Figure 9.1 Prune tree-like shrubs for definition. You can moderately shorten some species but, in general, avoid size reduction. **A.** Too far up **B.** Too far down **C.** Parallel branches **D.** Suckers **E.** Wrong way **F.** On ground **G.** Crossing **H.** Moderate size reduction

this rubbing branch or the other one?" And be assured that the state of low-grade terror you feel when pruning never really goes away. You will just learn to push through it.

TYPES OF TREE-LIKE SHRUBS

I have further divided the tree-like shrubs according to their prune-ability. The *tree-likes that water-sprout readily* are very touchy and will explode into ugly, straight shoots (water sprouts) if you prune too much or attempt even moderate size restriction. They are therefore pruned only very lightly, using mostly small thinning cuts. The next group, *tree-likes that take thinning*, don't break bud easily and therefore can be thinned more extensively. Size restriction is still not advised, since these shrubs will lose

their nice branch structure or form. Some can be limbed up and made into nice-looking small trees (called *arborizing*). Exceptions to the rules always exist, and this is true for the tree-like category of shrubs. The third category is *tree-likes tough enough for shearing*. Some of the tree-like shrubs can be used for hedges, such as English laurel, English holly, and photinia, and complete information is included in this chapter. These plants can also be pruned selectively or let go *au naturel*.

CAMELLIA *(Camellia)*

When I spoke at the botanical garden in St. Louis, Missouri, one of the curators told me that her favorite task was tending the beautiful camellia collection in the greenhouse. She recounted her experience of patiently deadheading one day as she looked up past the green boughs laden in pink and red blossoms to see a wild, white snowstorm descending outside the glass windows. That image is as vivid in my memory now as if it had happened to me. There are some horticultural experiences that border on the sublime. I didn't have the heart to tell her that in Seattle camellias are generally treated as personas non grata, horticulturally speaking, that is.

I suppose, as always, it's because people plant camellias (usually *C. japonica*) too close to the house and then shear them into goofy big balls. Then, too, camellias have the unpleasant habit of hanging on to their blooms until they turn the color of aged apple cores. Finally, they drop the blossoms intact, all gawdawful orange and brown, onto the ground below. Magnolia blooms—which turn just about as yucky in color—at least have the decency to shatter and fall to the ground in pieces. Winter camellias (*C. sasanqua*) are much more appreciated since they have a looser habit, their blossoms shatter, and they bloom and smell sweet in winter months. People in gloomy climes need a lot of cheering up from November through February. The winter camellia is well placed where you park the car, so that you can see and smell the flowers as you dodge the raindrops on the way inside. They make nice espaliers too. But then I think *C. japonica* makes an even nicer wall plant. Which brings us to a major plus of both these camellias—their incredible pruning malleability.

Camellias are, in my opinion, almost as tough as English laurel. I know of an 8-foot-high, sheared camellia hedge that looks greener, tidier, and healthier than the laurel hedge next to it. And once a year it blooms! However, the average homeowner is well advised to refrain from shearing camellias (or any other plants for that matter) if they are not planted as a formal hedge or topiary.

Size Reduction

Camellias, unlike many other broadleaf evergreens, take kindly to the selective heading cut. The new growth tends to match the old growth, meaning it doesn't emerge as a fright of water sprouts. Nor do the branches tend to die when pruned hard. Always search for a nice big side branch facing out—and cut back to it, rather than to no place in particular (nonselective heading). Then look for the next branch which is too tall. Follow it inside the shrub to a side branch and cut it off there. The uncut, shorter branches then become the perimeter of the shrub. The key to selective pruning is to hide the cuts inside, like a shag haircut, rather than cutting back each and every branch at the perimeter, nip, nip, nip.

That said, I should warn people that the average adult size of a camellia is about 6 to 8 feet tall and 5 feet wide. And they eventually get twice that size (and sooner than you think). It's best for everybody if your plant has that much room to live. Otherwise you wind up fighting against nature, which is usually too much work, even when it works well. People just have the mistaken notion that shrubs are, or should be, about 4 feet tall and 3 feet wide.

Thinning

If a camellia seems oppressive, the best way to prune it (and other plants in the tree-like category) is to thin it out (see Figure 9.2). This is the art of selective pruning. As a good pruner, start by crawling into the bottom of the shrub. Using loppers, a hand saw, and good hand pruners, work up and out. Foremost is the removal of all the dead leaves, twigs, and stubs. Then look for crossing/rubbing branches, wrong-way branches, and ones that head too far up or too far down. Don't try to eliminate all wrong branches, just take out some of the worst. Every space should be filled, but with fewer branches. Don't strip out the branches, leaving only foliage on the ends. Selective pruning means

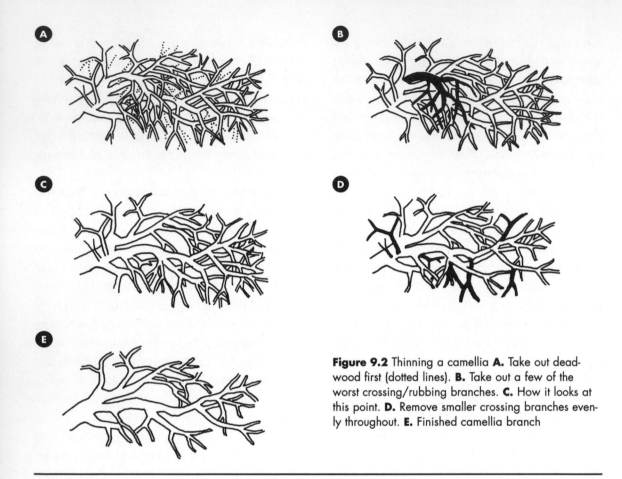

Figure 9.2 Thinning a camellia **A.** Take out dead-wood first (dotted lines). **B.** Take out a few of the worst crossing/rubbing branches. **C.** How it looks at this point. **D.** Remove smaller crossing branches evenly throughout. **E.** Finished camellia branch

that you take some, and leave some, fairly evenly throughout.

John Hushagen from Seattle Tree Preservation told me, "You know when you're done pruning a camellia when you can stand up inside it." That sounds about right. I like to finish up with a little judicious thinning from the outside, too. When you finally break up the solid wall of green, you get a lattice of foliage revealing the finely pruned internal branch structure of the camellia.

Camellias can take fairly heavy thinning and shortening because they don't tend to grow water sprouts. However, there is still a certain amount of good-sense aesthetics involved. Once I consulted at a house where I noticed, but tried not to comment on, an overthinned camellia. The husband said, "I went to a pruning class, and the guy said to prune a camellia so that a bird could fly through it. When my wife saw what I did she said, 'He meant a sparrow, not a goose!'"

Arborizing

Sometimes an ill-sited camellia that seems "oppressive" to the homeowner can be turned into a nice little tree by removing the lower limbs and thinning out what remains above. Before embarking on this path, take a moment to study the branch structure within. Imagine what it will look like without certain branches. The main trunk should be old and very thick. Otherwise you might get a "lollipop," not a "tree." But you often can't tell how it will really look until you're done. High excitement in the garden! Some people are so impressed with the effect that they proceed to strip up everything else in the yard. Good for some is not good for all.

Rehabilitation

Can a previously sheared camellia be returned to a natural, looser shape? I think so. In fact, I have succeeded in doing so. But it took all the bravery I could muster. The first spring or two I selectively thinned out the clumps of branches. Once light reached the inside, I radically (which is to say nonselectively) headed-back some branches inside the plant to try to force some new, interior green growth. It worked. As the homeowner requested, it is now several feet shorter and more natural looking. On similar plants in the future, I think I'll be more radical sooner, to get rid of the "ball" outline by staggering cuts throughout. I guess that's how you learn the limits of plants, by pushing them.

Radical Renovation

Whereas I worry about every cut, as do most of the pruners I know, the world is full of people who don't give it a second thought. Such is my neighbor who, soon after moving in, cut that too-big "green bush" in front of

his window down to a 3-foot clump of stubs. He felt bad when he found out it was a camellia. It looked like heck for a couple of years. Now, about five years later, it's about 4 feet, green, healthy, and blooming again.

Cutting a shrub back to stumps (or in the case of cane-growers, back to the ground) and starting them over is what I call radical renovation. Camellias in particular are excellent candidates for radical renovation; the survival rate is high. But camellias, unlike rhododendrons, are not particularly good transplant candidates. I have successfully transplanted some large ones (6 feet tall), but many others have died. So if a very old camellia is really, really too large for its location, it is wiser to radically renovate it than to try moving it. If you decide to risk it, do your cutting in the spring, keep your plant well watered for the next year, and visit it occasionally with kind words.

Summary

Don't shear your camellia into a ball. If your shrub seems oppressive, thin it out. You can thin it a lot. And you can take off lower limbs, making it look like a little tree. Camellias can withstand heavy heading, although it isn't a nice thing to do and doesn't look very good. Mal-pruned camellias can be renovated by cutting to a very low framework (a foot or two) in the early spring.

COTONEASTER (Cotoneaster)

New gardeners are apt to make their first and most embarrassing phonetic faux pas when they mispronounce cotoneasters as

Figure 9.3 Cotton-Easters

"cotton-easters." "Ka-TONE-ee-ass-ters" is correct.

Like most plant species, cotoneasters come in a variety of sizes, from the impressive *C. x watereri* 'Cornubia', almost a tree at 20 feet, to the tiny-leafed *C. microphyllus*, bred for people who like cute buns. I'm partial to the ubiquitous but highly underrated *C. horizontalis*, commonly called fish-bone, herringbone, or rock cotoneaster. I think it has great architectural qualities. Planted against a fence or chimney, it espaliers itself in a tower of fans (see Figure 9.4).

Figure 9.4 *Cotoneaster horizontalis* espalier **A.** Front view **B.** Side view

It reminds me of the ice feathers that form on your windshield in the winter, too.

It's been so long since I took plant ID that I get my midsized cotoneasters mixed up. I think it's the *C. parneyi* (now *C. lacteus*) that I prefer to *C. salicifolius*. Latin names— I lose more of them every year. I'm surprised I can't actually see them falling out of my ears. And curse that secret society of heartless taxonomical dictators who change plant names. Did you know that common garden mums (chrysanthemums) are now really *Dendranthema* (will they be called common garden ma's?). There ought to be a law.

What cotoneasters share in common is their nice display of red or orange berries and their arching branch pattern. They like dry soils and sun, but are generally tolerant of all kinds of abuse and neglect. They get around well on their own, spread by hungry birds who eat the berries in late winter when the finer fare is gone. You are apt to find a lone cotoneaster growing in the cracks of a sidewalk or sprouting out of the middle of a field of junipers.

Although I like cotoneasters, I admit that (on the great unspoken horticultural plant-status scale) they rate rather low. I know this because of what I found myself saying when I went on a consultation with another professional gardener. We went over her client's yard together, where many plants had been mal-pruned, mostly sheared into balls. The client asked what to do about the sheared cotoneaster and the sheared evergreen azalea. I told her that it wasn't worth the effort to rehab the cotoneaster (a lengthy process). "Just dig it out." I moved on to show her how to unshear the azalea (with relatively rapid, good results).

No Pruning

Like all shrubs and trees, cotoneasters do a pretty good job on their own. My favorite *C. horizontalis* isn't pruned at all. I saw one last year, smothered in berries like a giant red bow. Next to it sat Sugar, the snow-white cat. It was as pretty as a Christmas card.

The Most Common Mistake

The most common pruning mistake people make is to shear cotoneasters (and everything else, for that matter). Actually, cotoneasters fit the criteria for plants that are good as formal hedges (small-leafed, evergreen, and tough) and can be used as such, which is to say topiaried or sheared into continuous hedges. But most selective pruners express a more than average disgust when they see cotoneaster balls because such pruning subverts the best feature of these plants—their arching branch pattern. And

also because once cotoneasters are sheared, the future results are startlingly horrid. I know of no other plant that grows back from heading cuts with as many straight shoots.

Near my home, I have examples of three pruning techniques. One apartment complex sports a silly "row of soldiers"—all cotoneasters sheared into separated, tight globes. Nearer my house is a condo with a steep rockery that a hard-working, yet wholly ignorant, grounds crew swarms over once a month to shear cotoneasters into rather pleasant-looking smooth masses. It's reminiscent of some formal Japanese gardens I've seen. Between shearings, the shrubs resprout and don't look so tidy. In point of fact, the condo association is paying a lot of money to have these plants look ultra tidy half the time, and twice as unkempt the other half of the time (see Figure 9.5).

Next to the condo is a shorter rockery belonging to the church parking lot. It has unpruned cotoneasters spilling and arching

Figure 9.5 The most common mistake with cotoneasters: using nonselective heading cuts to make the plant smaller. **A.** Original plant **B.** Heading cuts make it look tidier for now, but... **C.** they cause ugly regrowth, making it twice as unkempt later.

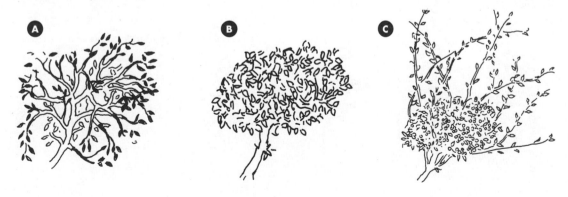

gracefully, like a waterfall, down the rocks. Nobody ever prunes them and they look great *all* the time. Unfortunately, grass and weeds are starting to invade, and when that happens, can the motorheads be far behind?

Shearing also invites disease problems in plants. Cotoneasters under stress get cotoneaster webworm, ick! Thinning reduces the occurrence of this ugly bug, shearing invites it.

Size Reduction

As with most tree-like shrubs, avoid trying to shorten or otherwise restrict the size of cotoneasters. If a branch actually interferes with people walking down a pathway, rubs on the house, or sticks out too far into a neighboring plant, see if it can be removed with a thinning cut, taking it off where it joins a larger stem, or altogether, by cutting it to the ground. If this is not possible, use a selective heading cut. This is not necessarily the *smallest* cut possible along the branch. Follow the branch back from the tip trying to locate a *largish* side branch to cut back to. (see Figures 9.6). It's a difficult thing to grasp, but this is the essential part of selective pruning that retains the natural grace of the branches and reduces the amount of water-sprout regrowth.

Avoid overall size restraint, though. Even if all the cuts are selective heading, you will get an upsurge of water sprouts, impossible to eliminate and ugly to behold.

If you research the mature size of your plant in a plant encyclopedia, and your plant doesn't have enough room, by all means *take it out*. (I rarely try transplanting cotoneasters. It's just not worth the effort, since they die easily, are easy to replace, and are not considered particularly choice.) Correcting mistakes as soon as they are spotted is good garden policy. (But then, so is waiting to see how it goes.)

Figure 9.6 Selective heading is the right way to shorten a branch, but **A.** this smaller cut may not be as good as **B.** a larger cut to a larger lateral branch.

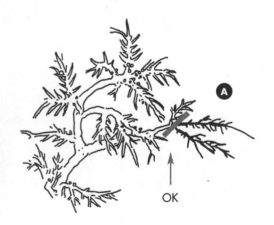

OK

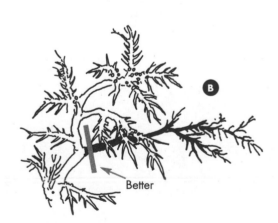

Better

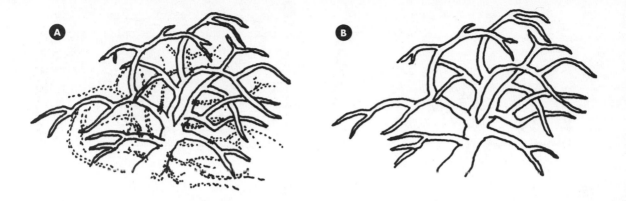

Figure 9.7 Deadwooding **A.** Deadwood makes plants look dirty. **B.** After deadwood removal

Deadwood

In pruning any plant, 80 percent of all the cuts made should be to remove deadwood—dead twigs, dead limbs, and stubs (see Figure 9.7). Cotoneasters, in particular, clean up well with deadwooding. The dead twigs are often so brittle that they can be simply brushed (crunched) out with a gloved hand. Take care to remove any stubs that might remain after the quick brush-through. What a difference! You will quickly discover that most deadwood occurs on the lower parts and inside of the shrub, where growth has been shaded out. Two other plants that particularly look better after deadwooding are pines and pieris.

Bottom Up and Inside Out

God bless garden writer George Schenk for his description in *The Complete Shade Gardener* of the pruning process. He writes, "Prune from the bottom up and the inside out" (see Figure 9.8).

I remember when I started my business many years ago, my partner would disappear inside shrubs, sometimes crawling into the base of them on hands and knees. I felt like asking her to stop fooling around and get to work. But as the minutes passed, and cut limbs and twigs were shoved outside the plant, the shrubs would start looking cleaner, better, and—well, more beautiful. This is the art of pruning.

Most books say to remove crossing/rubbing branches and to open up the center to improve plant health, which it does. But the real reason it's done is to make your yard look better—that's the point of gardening anyway, unless you are gardening to provide wildlife habitat. In that case some tangles, brambles, and deadwood are a good thing. So before you do any size reduction, thin a bit, doing more at the base of the plant than elsewhere, to see if that will solve the real or perceived problem.

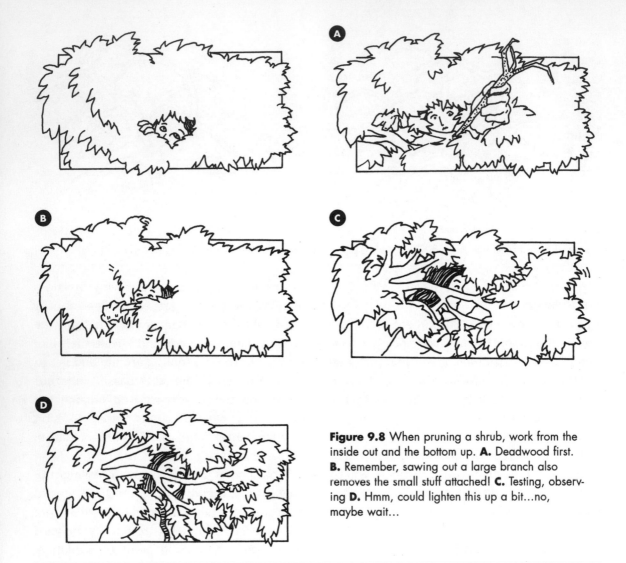

Figure 9.8 When pruning a shrub, work from the inside out and the bottom up. **A.** Deadwood first. **B.** Remember, sawing out a large branch also removes the small stuff attached! **C.** Testing, observing **D.** Hmm, could lighten this up a bit...no, maybe wait...

Rehabilitative Pruning

I can't actually recall spending the time and effort to restore a previously headed or sheared cotoneaster. It's too daunting. On the other hand, it makes perfect sense to try radical renovation on a mal-pruned cotoneaster. Cut it to the ground. After three or four years you may be surprised to find it has regrown into a graceful shrub. Or maybe not. Then return to plan B, removal. If and when it does recover and regrow into a nice, natural, arching shrub, sneak hubby's hedge shears out in a Goodwill donation bag for pickup the next day.

Summary

Stay away from shearing or overall size reduction on cotoneasters, as they will explode into a million wild water sprouts. Deadwooding and removal of some lower or inside branches often makes them look amazingly better. Selectively head or thin back the few branches interfering with walkways or nearby shrubs.

DECIDUOUS AZALEA

(Rhododendron)

Deciduous azaleas, like evergreen azaleas, are a subset of rhododendrons, but they look and prune quite differently. They are larger than evergreen azaleas, seeming less formal—tall, upright, open, and finely branched. Many have spicy, scented flowers in the spring, and nice fall color, too. For this reason I think they go particularly well in Pacific Northwest woodsy areas, and they add seasonal interest to overwhelmingly broadleaf evergreen yards. They are among a very small list of plants that are suitable for "skinny" places, like next to the walkway that goes along the side of the house.

Pruning for Definition

Deciduous azaleas are best pruned for definition, which makes them more beautiful, not smaller. By following the guidelines below, you will be able to clearly "read" the shrub's branch structure in the winter. The branch structure on deciduous azaleas is intrinsically pleasing to the eye, but it will be even more so with good pruning, looking cleaner and crisper. One of those maxims that opened my eyes as a novice gardener was "A shrub should look as beautiful in the winter as it does in the summer." Before I heard that, deciduous plants just disappeared for me when the leaves fell.

Deadwood

Deadwood is hard to spot on deciduous azaleas in the winter. I often set aside some time in the summer to deadwood them (as well as deciduous viburnums and lilacs) because it takes a lot less time to sort out what is alive.

Size Reduction

Overall size reduction on deciduous azaleas, unlike their evergreen counterparts, is not recommended. It doesn't hurt, but it does compromise the beauty of the branches as seen in the winter. One of the things that makes the branches of tree-like shrubs beautiful is the uninterrupted tapering of the stem and the even division of branches (called ramification) to ever smaller and finer branches. It is the *taper and even division that is the source of a branch's beauty.* When a large heading cut is made, the resulting regrowth is a cluster of skinny, straight shoots heading up from a large, blunt end. This is not the smooth transition of a normally grown branch. Therefore, I avoid heavy heading (selective or nonselective) on deciduous azaleas whenever possible. But the news is good if your deciduous azalea is too big for its location. Like rhodies and evergreen azaleas, they have compact, fibrous root systems, making them among the best candidates for transplanting.

Thinning

As with most plants in the tree-like category, thinning accentuates the nice branch pattern of deciduous azaleas. Using mostly thinning cuts and a few selective heading cuts, prune evenly throughout the plant. Look for branches that actually rub others or wander too far from their point of origin (i.e., that start on the outside and grow the wrong way, through the center and out the other side). Look for laterals that dip down into the layer of branches below. Look for duplicating branches, ugly previously headed branches, or kinked ones. Look for crowded spaces where branches meet the main stem (called crotches or branch attachments). Look for branches hanging on the ground. Prune off some of the worst of all those that are found, though never all.

Azaleas, unlike many of the shrubs in the tree-like category, can take a fair bit of pruning, both thinning and selective heading. I would say up to a quarter of the foliage can be removed. If you prune too much, the plant will not die back, but will easily break bud and send up new, straight shoots. An argument against heavy pruning, though, is that the branches will look less pleasing in the winter. The straight new shoots from *overthinning* are not as pretty as the older curved stems. The good news is that the straight new shoots of an azalea are stiffer than most water sprouts, and they rather quickly (in a year perhaps) develop a nicer, curved form.

Stimulating Replacement Stems

In several landscapes I know, old deciduous azaleas suffer from the sudden death of large old limbs. In such cases, I have had luck cutting the stems out almost to the ground (leaving, say, a 4-inch stubby cane). The new stems of the replacement shrub will grow from it. Check to make sure it is getting enough water in the summer before you make the cut, though. It's almost like pruning a forsythia.

Pruning for Health

Certain species of plants are reliably prone to certain diseases. Good pruning can't cure them, but it can help. And bad pruning (shearing, topping, overthinning) certainly makes disease problems worse. Deciduous azaleas tend to get *powdery mildew* that turns their leaves powdery gray and crinkly. It ruins their good looks in the summer. Although the mildews are often associated in people's minds with too much moisture and a lack of air circulation, I have found the primary cause is plant stress due to *insufficient summer watering*. So if you have an automatic irrigation system, increase the time on the clock. Improving air circulation may help, but only a little bit. Thinning out deadwood and crowded branches is okay, but more effective is transplanting too closely spaced shrubs or those that are in poor locations. Also note that many experienced gardeners have learned to simply overlook a certain amount of imperfection.

Old deciduous azaleas are also known to grow a lot of gray lichen on the bark, and sometimes green or gray balls of moss may also appear in the twigs and branches. This is not usually a serious threat to the health of the plants, but it is a sign of old age. I think of lichen as the gray hair of plants. It doesn't cause old age, it is just a sign of it. The look of lichen bothers some people. Others, including myself, think it adds interest. If you have a very, very bad case of lichen, meaning thick and covering *all* the bark, you probably should rub some of it off so the bark can "breathe." Increase irrigation if the soil is dry, and thin the shrub if that hasn't been done in a long time.

Summary

Deciduous azaleas are tough and can withstand a lot of pruning, but they look best gently and lightly thinned out for definition. Prune out deadwood in the summer when it is easier to spot. Many people underirrigate in the summer, inviting powdery mildew problems. If the shrub is too big, transplanting is easy and a better solution than pruning for size control.

ENGLISH LAUREL, ENGLISH HOLLY, AND PHOTINIA

(Prunus laurocerasus, Ilex aquifolium, and Photinia x fraseri)
What do English laurel, English holly, and photinia have in common? They all have large evergreen leaves; they break bud easily if pruned back to barren wood; and they eventually grow into either very large shrubs or relatively small trees (30 to 40 feet for laurel and holly and 10 to 15 feet for photinia).

No Pruning

If your photinia, laurel, or holly looks good and isn't in the way of anything, just leave it alone. If you want to help make it look better, taking out the deadwood almost always improves the appearance of any plant.

Pruning as an Informal Hedge
(Selective Heading)

Photinia, laurel, and holly make good mass plantings for background and informal hedges in the 8- to 12-foot range. If let go entirely, they can easily grow to twice that size. Don't try to keep them much smaller than 8 to 12 feet, because it won't work. Above that, they can be selectively pruned to shorten or tidy them up. Even though these shrubs can take frequent and hard pruning, it's usually the gardener who gives up because it really is too much work.

To prune selectively, locate the tallest or widest offending branch, follow it down *inside* the plant to where it meets up with a side branch or parent stem, and then cut it off there. Use a hand pruner or loppers of good quality. Then locate and shorten the next worst branch. It is very important to hide those cuts down inside the plant. It's the difference between selective pruning and shearing your shrub a twig at a time. After pruning for a while your shrub should look natural but shorter and tidier.

Pruning as a Formal Hedge (Shearing)

These big-leafed, evergreen bud-breakers are often planted as a formal hedge. However, they are really second-best as plants for sheared hedges. The truly best hedges are slower growing or have finer leaves (yew, privet, boxwood, Japanese holly). Finer leaves look more elegant. Slower growing means less work. The nicest hedge I know is a blue Atlas cedar hedge. It's 15 feet high. But only the very wealthy and devoted can afford such hedges. If you miss pruning one year and it gets away from you, you're sunk. Unlike photinia, laurel, and holly, conifer hedges can't be made small again. They can't break bud and green back up if cut back hard.

If you have (or want) a formal hedge consisting of any one of these big-leafed evergreens, go ahead and shear them. Use either hedge shears (they look like a giant scissors) or power shears (buy or rent them for the day). Rent a three-legged ladder if you don't have one. They are more stable on uneven ground than the four-legged house-painter variety. Also, the third leg can be threaded through or into the hedge, making it easier for you to get "up-close and personal" with your plants.

English laurel often looks tattered and stubby after a shearing. This can be improved by going back over it with loppers or a hand pruner to cut out the worst of the sliced leaves or barren branches. Some people have been known to selectively prune as much as 30 feet of laurel hedge, though this becomes quite tedious after a few years. Such pruning is too labor intensive for such a common and unremarkable plant. Reserve that kind of determined effort for your wisteria vine.

Photinia is just a dressed-up laurel, in my opinion. Its claim to fame is that its new growth is reddish or coppery colored. I guess I can still remember when I was mightily impressed and longed to possess some; actually, any plant is valuable when given a situation requiring its highest and best use. Every time photinia is sheared, it flushes out more interesting red leaves. Laurel and photinia are somewhat tender in regions like the Northwest, so be careful not to stimulate a late flush of growth by shearing it in the fall. It might not have time to harden off for the winter and will suffer freeze damage.

Using as Individual Shrubs

Both English laurel and photinia serve useful functions as fast-growing screens, either as formal or informal hedges. And they make nice small trees. But they are too large, in my opinion, to be used as individual shrubs in the garden. Even more difficult to accept is their use as *sheared* individual shrubs in general landscaping. You see them everywhere in commercial landscapes, repeatedly clipped into empty and meaningless boxes and balls. Each year they get a little bigger and more unwieldy (see Figure 9.9). A lot of maintenance money is being spent for limited value. They don't look good sheared and they won't stay small for long. Why not use something that grows to the right size and looks good with practically no pruning?

However, I must confess a slight fondness for the giant holly gumdrops seen here and there. Other gardeners find them objectionable. If such holly bushes are sheared every year from the time they are young, they develop a useful, incredibly thick and twiggy interior. Because of it, topiarians can then strap their 20-foot ladders directly onto the

Figure 9.9 The pruning cycle of a sheared laurel or photinia: **1.** First shear **2.** Regrowth **3.** 2nd-year shear **4.** 5th-year shear **5.** 12th-year shear **6.** Radical renovation **7.** It begins again.

bush and not fall through when they go up for the annual trimming. Even so, it's a painful and expensive proposition. Hug a holly? Not me!

Occasionally someone cuts the top off of one of these holly gumdrops, because, well, because it's gotten "too big." This won't hurt the holly, but it can be a visual disaster when the chainsaw reveals a trunk surrounded by a saggy donut of dead-looking branches

Radical Renovation

The good news is that these three plants can stand to be radically renovated. I once saw a full-sized holly chainsawed into the utterly leafless shape of a lava lamp. Next year it flushed out and looked great. Radical reno-

vations of laurel hedges are common. In the spring, saw the overgrown hedge into the desired shape, except perhaps a foot or two smaller than the final desired size. That's because it will need that room to resprout and be sheared into a thick green coat again. Be sure to cut your hedge narrow as well as short. It should be narrow enough for one gardener to reach across with a hedge shear. I have only seen one laurel hedge that didn't recover from this radical treatment. It has remained a perfectly square bundle of dead-looking sticks for years. I always want to stop the truck and ask the person inside the house what he or she did to kill it. But I guess that wouldn't be polite.

Please avoid heavy pruning on a hot July or August day, as you might burn up some internal leaves or scald the bark. If you renovate in the winter, you must stare at the ugly barren branches till spring. In the Northwest, spring provides the longest period of benign wet weather, which will help the plant to regrow.

Arborizing

I don't much care for laurels, hollies, and photinias as hedges or bushes, but I think they make great small trees. Arborizing, which means turning a shrub into a tree, is best done on very mature plants. Before doing anything rash, take a look inside and visualize how it will look stripped up. Are the trunks nice and thick, or will it look like an ostrich once it's limbed up? A little general thinning and cutting out of deadwood will make the crown look its best too. And don't try arborizing every plant in sight. Moderation in all things is the watchword.

When some friends moved into their new home, they inquired about what to do with the 20-foot laurel bush totally obscuring the living room window. "Limb it up and be done with it!" I replied. It turned out to have a lovely thick and sinuous trunk. Now it's a tree under which to store the firewood. There is just enough screening from the street, and just enough light is let in the window. And the birds love it for the berries. (I suspect that the delight of bird-watching is one of those pleasures that develops later in life. I don't recall being so impressed by them in my college days. But then it wasn't birds I was watching.)

The Perfect Plants for Views and Screens

Although I put laurels, photinia, and holly in the tree-like category, they are not among the Cadillacs of the plant world. They're more the utility vans of the plant world. They are quite useful for doing a specific job, though not particularly glamorous. This job is being the fast-growing screen that can be kept at a given height. For example, these plants would work for a person whose desire for water views is running smack dab into his downhill neighbor's need for privacy. He wants the tree cut down to see the water—but that would mean a sight line from his neighbor's window to the water is the same as the one from his bedroom window to his balcony. Another common problem occurs when the new neighbors suddenly add a second story to their house; the windows of their addition seem to stare out into your once private backyard.

If you are not willing to wait for a 'Pyramidalis' hedge (*Thuja occidentalis* 'Pyramidalis') to grow up (my first choice because it's

Figure 9.10 Resting under his laurels

no maintenance and guaranteed never to get too wide), then a planting of laurels, photinias, or hollies may be just the ticket. They will grow up quickly, providing privacy, but you can stop them from blotting out all sun and light by pruning at the exact height you want. People foolishly plant fast-growing trees for this screening purpose, and live to rue the day. Trees, real trees, can't be kept down successfully, and I would include in this the latest monster in the field, Leyland cypress (x *Cupressocyparis leylandii*).

Summary

Laurel, holly, and photinia are extremely tough and can take any amount or kind of pruning. They are often sheared as formal hedges. For least maintenance, use them as small trees.

LILAC *(Syringa)*

Next to roses, the most wonderfully evocative plant is the lilac (see Figures 9.11 and 9.12). In the spring the scent of its flowers is likely to transport you to a childhood time in granny's garden, even if you didn't have a granny. I think that just about everyone should have a lilac, even though they are not particularly gardenworthy the rest of the year. They get a host of pests and diseases that, though not life-threatening, will mar them. The leaves might get powdery mildew, or pucker, or get scorched tips, or they might get scored by miners. Rather than engage in a distasteful chemical battle, I

Figure 9.11 Lilac

suggest siting the shrub where it can be enjoyed in bloom and then ignored the rest of the year. That is to say close, but not too close, to the front entry.

Size

The adult size of a typical lilac is 8 to 10 feet tall and, left unpruned, they can get much taller. Don't bother pruning your shrub for the first five or ten years. Once they have reached their mature height (in seven to ten years), you may prune them if you so desire. But remember—like most all plants—they don't need to be pruned to look good, bloom, and do their job in the garden.

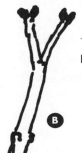

Figure 9.12 To ID a lilac in winter, look for double buds at the branch ends. **A.** Peace, man. **B.** Lilac, man.

Tall and Open or Short and Bushy?

In the Pacific Northwest, we tend to prune an old lilac like a little tree, taking out deadwood and a few minor crossing/rubbing branches (see Figure 9.13). I'm told that back in the Midwest they prune a lilac more like a forsythia, cutting a few large canes out to ground level every year or so. This creates a shorter but thicker shrub, as new canes (suckers, actually) arise from the base to grow into replacement canes in future years.

It's just one of those natural laws: You can prune to have a tall, open, delicately branched plant *or* a lower, broader, denser shrub. You will not succeed in pruning to create a low, delicate, open shrub. If it can't grow up, it *will* grow out—the growth energy must go somewhere. For people who desire a lower lilac without all the pruning, there are some dwarfish varieties that grow to about 5 feet tall and as wide. Examples are *S. pubescens patula* 'Miss Kim' and *S. meyeri* 'Palibin'.

Those Troublesome Suckers

Pruning books I read are always admonishing people to remove the suckers (straight, skinny, ugly shoots arising from ground level) "as soon as they are seen." I doubt that these people spend much time in the garden. After suckers are cut to the ground, they quickly regrow, except in greater numbers. This will happen year after year after year. There is a product on the market called Sucker Stopper (active ingredient NAA, Ethyl 1-napthaleneacetate) that you could spray on the cut ends, except that it really only stops suckers for about a year, and it's a

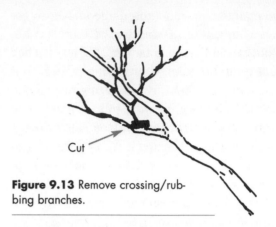

Figure 9.13 Remove crossing/rubbing branches.

chemical. Having fought the sucker battle on lilacs for many years myself, I have finally devised a new philosophy of sucker management. I let lilac suckers grow. Sometimes I reduce the number, cutting out the lesser ones, never expecting to eliminate them all. I call it the "country-thicket" look, which I make nicer by mulching and making sure that no weeds grow at the base of the shrub.

People often want their multitrunked young lilac to be a single-trunked, tree-like plant. I suspect that those shrubs are born, not pruned to be more tree-like. Also, older lilacs may have shaded out their own competing understory of thicket, resulting in fewer trunks. In any case, pruning the competing canes will probably just increase their number.

The lilacs of long ago were grafted onto the roots of the common lilac (*S. vulgaris*) or privet. Presumably, if you let suckers grow from below the graft union (the union will look like a bulge) the new growth will overtake and ruin your nice lilac bush. But how can you tell, unless you bought it yourself and know all about your lilac variety and whether or not it's grafted? So I tend to proceed under the assumption that the shrub is not grafted, or if it was, that it is already too late to do anything about it.

Deadheading

Books tell us to prune out spent lilac blooms (taking care not to damage side shoots just below the blooms) so that the plant's energy is not wasted by putting up seeds. Personally, I feel my own energy is wasted teetering about on tall ladders taking off spent blooms—not to mention that it puts me in danger of falling. I say, "Leave them alone." If, after many years, your blossoms get small and puny, then you may choose to deadhead to see whether it will improve them.

My Old Lilac Is Leaning

Very, very old lilacs get a hollow core and then start to fall over. As that leaning trunk dips down, dormant buds located down the trunk will break free (free from apical dominance) and begin to grow up as straight, skinny water sprouts. This is just the lilac's natural way of rejuvenating itself. If those shoots are left alone they will grow into replacement canes or trunks. That's their job. People tend to prefer the gnarly, twisted old trunk to the replacement canes, and therefore evasive action is sometimes taken. If there is something to cable the leaning trunk to, we sometimes do that. I do worry that the trunk will get half girdled by the wire-in-a-rubber-hose tie. Like the arborists, I prefer a small eyebolt actually screwed into the wood and then cabled back to the wall or other some object. An alternative is to use a "crutch" under the leaning trunk. You could use a piece of pipe or lumber for this job, but it looks more artistic to use a forked branch from some other plant. Throughout the year I keep an eye out for a few good forked sticks and gather them for just such purposes.

Radical Renovation

People are always telling me that their lilac is too tall and they can't get to the blooms. They never say that about their magnolia tree. There's nothing wrong with a tall lilac, and just about every shrub gets to be 8 to 10 feet tall. Usually the only thing trees and shrubs are too tall for is the person's idea of how big they should get. If you need some blooms for your vase, get out the loppers or the pole pruner.

That said, I must confess that I pruned my own lilac because it was too much the same size as everything around it (sounds a lot like "too tall"). Even though I know better, I first cut about half of the 10-foot canes down to about 6 feet. Sure enough, they resprouted at the cut ends and regrew to 10 feet in just one year. OOPS. So the next year I cut those same canes way, way down to about 1 to 2 feet from ground level. They sent out new shoots that rapidly grew to just the right height (5 to 6 feet), then they arched over and put on (bigger, better) blooms. This year I cut the other half down (see Figure 9.14).

I could have cut the entire shrub down at once, but like everybody else, I'm too scared. Such heavy-duty pruning is called radical renovation, and it is done in the winter or early spring. Do it only to well-established plants. Know that they will rapidly grow to two-thirds of their original height. Sometimes it takes a few years for the plant to bloom again. Don't do this more than once every fifteen years. It is a serious stress to cut a plant down, so be certain that it is reasonably healthy, is well watered, and has sufficient light for it to recover. There is always a chance that the shrub might die, but it's unlikely.

It Doesn't Bloom

I've heard that lilacs sometimes stop blooming. Be sure that your shrub is still in the sun (did a Doug fir grow up seemingly overnight?), and also remember that they prefer an alkaline soil. You might need to spread a little lime around. Garden lime or dolomite lime is calcium carbonate and is sold in bags at your local nursery or garden center. I've also read that root pruning them can force a bloom again. I've never experienced this, but a person who called me said that she had such an experience. She said that she had used a spade to root prune, but that it hadn't helped. So then she decided to dig up the lilac bush and throw it away. She got tired of digging before the job was done, and gave up trying for the year. Lo and behold, it bloomed in the spring.

Heart Transplant

I had a nice chat with a homeowner who told me that she had coveted her neighbor's lilac for more than thirty years. When that neighbor died and the house was sold to someone wanting to redevelop it, this homeowner talked a backhoe operator into digging up the

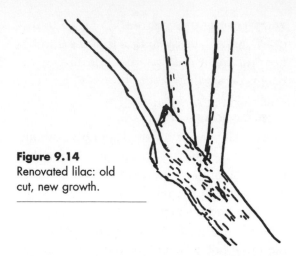

Figure 9.14
Renovated lilac: old cut, new growth.

lilac and putting it into her own yard. It lived, and bloomed and fulfilled a dream.

Summary

Lilacs can take a fair amount of pruning. Always deadwood first. You can prune a lilac like a cane-grower by removing a few of the oldest and tallest canes to the ground or a foot above and letting new suckers grow up into replacement canes. This gives you a lower but much broader and bushier shrub. Or you can prune it like a tree-like shrub, keeping it as a tall, open, finely branched plant. In that case, take out a few of the crossing/rubbing and wrong-way branches. If need be, selectively shortening (heading) a few branches by cutting back to an out-facing lateral (side) branch is okay. You don't have to deadhead unless the blooms are getting puny. I have never been able to stop suckers from coming up from the base of young shrubs. You can let them grow into canes, and/or perhaps they will be shaded out later.

RHODODENDRON *(Rhododendron)*

The problem with pruning rhododendrons is, well, they're unpredictable. Sometimes you head-back a branch to a node, and when you look next month you find that, instead of sending out new shoots, the branch simply gave up and died. On other occasions people reduce their rhodies to the height or width they want, only to discover that by the time the plants have developed decent, full, leafy crowns, they're back up to about the size they were before. Or the new growth is weird, all skinny and floppy. Or sometimes they do grow back shorter and look great. How are you to know? And another problem with rhodies is that all the leaves are at the outside edges of the plant. There's nothing green to cut back to.

My Rhody Is Too Big

A commonly seen situation is that of a large-growing, open-habit rhododendron (like the Loderi types) that someone is trying to keep shorter and more compact. An old gardener's saying is "Inside every rhody is a 15-foot tree trying to get out." The hapless pruner tries in vain. Even when following the "rules" by selectively heading-back branches to shorter laterals, the result is a "funny-looking" plant, which is to say it starts to grow in a roughly V-shaped pattern. With the above caveats in place, let's review seven solutions to the too-big rhododendron.

Prune It

A lot of people think their rhody is too big, but really it's just too oppressive and/or crowded. Real pruning for health and good looks often solves the problem (see Figure 9.15). The horticulturally correct pruner takes out all the deadwood. Do this first and always. Prune out a few of the worst crossing/rubbing branches. It often helps to take off some of the lowest branches, slowly working up and out from the inside. Also concentrate on thinning out the worst, most interfering branches that crowd into nearby shrubs, the house, the window, the gutter, or the walkway, and tidy up the top as needed. See if that just doesn't do the trick.

Increase Bed Size or Move the Rhody

Because of difficulties with pruning, it is often a better and longer lasting solution to increase the shrub's bed size to accommodate the plant. This is a creative but unpopular solution due to the removal of sod involved.

Rhodies have broad, flat, fibrous root systems and are a relative dream to move (see Figure 9.16).

Landscapers often move plants that are larger than people. Another old saying is "Your rhody will appreciate a trip around the house." It may require up to four strong backs and a tarp to slide the offending rhody out of its present home and to its new one. Don't be afraid to cut off 50 percent or more of the roots, both large and small, fishing around under the rootball with your loppers, trying to locate the roots that are keeping it tied down and foiling your shovel during the dig. After transplanting, immediate soaking is crucial. And give it lots of water throughout the first year. Moving is the only logical solution for situations where shrubs were

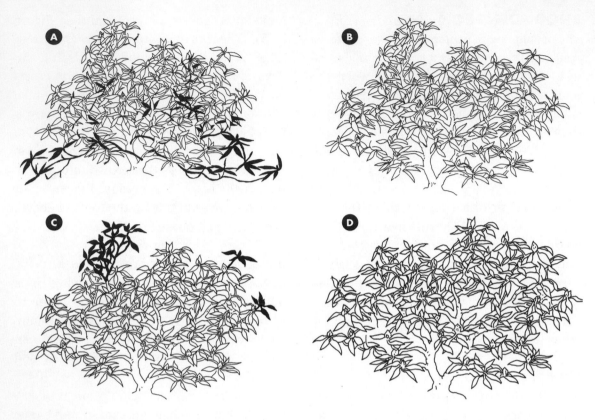

Figure 9.15 Maintenance pruning: Remove deadwood, a few crossing branches, and some lower limbs. **A.** Before **B.** After **C.** Tidy up the top as needed. **D.** Finished rhody

originally planted too close together or next to the walkway, as commonly seen in new landscapes everywhere.

Selective Reduction

Is it under the window? You can try to "work back" your rhody. You selectively head it a little every year. Locate the tallest branch and follow it down to a place inside the shrub where it meets a lower and shorter lateral. Cut it off there. Repeat with the next tallest branch. Continue until you sense you've gone too far. Quit; then come back

next year. Selective reduction works better on upward-facing branches (the top of the plant). The same pruning on the more horizontal branches (sides of the plant) tends to develop new shoots that look like spaghetti.

Stop It in Its Tracks

If the plant in question borders a high-traffic area such as stairs or a path, you might try snapping off the new growth. After the plant has finished blooming, you can either pinch out the new end-bud, or let the new supple shoot extend and snap it off with your fin-

Figure 9.16 Transplanting a rhody: Turn shovel upside down to chisel out the rootball.

gers or prune it off with your hand pruner soon thereafter, around May or June. Landscapers attest that on most rhodies this will not prevent blooming next year, though it is hard to understand why not. It is also exceedingly time consuming and must be done every year to restrict growth.

Arborize It

In special cases a "too-big" rhody can be thinned-up and turned into a nice small tree (see Figure 9.17). The plant in question should be very big and old. It should have a thick, curvaceous trunk. Be sure to meticulously deadwood it as well, and perhaps generally thin the upper canopy to prevent the "lollipop" look.

Radical Renovation

In especially desperate and hopeless situations, it is sometimes appropriate to cut the entire plant nearly to the ground and start it over. Like surgery, this is a serious move, and you should exhaust other possible solutions

first. Sometimes the plant dies. Most often it does not. I have been told that certain rhodies, the so-called smooth-barked rhododendrons (ones with *R. thomsonii* genes in them), cannot break bud and therefore will die under hard pruning. You will not likely spot a *thompsonii* hybrid by looking at it. I can't either. Their blooms are red, I know. But you can get a good idea by looking for the plumping buds on the lower portions of the trunks. No buds? Then the shrub is not a good candidate. Renovation works best on old and/or previously mal-pruned shrubs. Don't try to be nicer to a shrub by cutting less severely. Remember, after a plant is pruned the new growth starts just below the cut and grows *up* from there. It will be too big again very soon (see Figure 9.18).

And if your reduction cuts leave too much of the framework, you wind up with a mismatched plant. The new, smaller, leafy crown is stuck on top of thick old, thick "legs." It just doesn't look right. Plus you are more likely to produce the wild regrowth

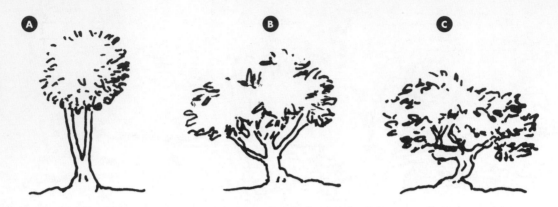

Figure 9.17: Arborizing a rhody: Turn a large shrub into a small tree. **A.** No lollipops. **B.** Limb up the lower trunk. **C.** Thin the crown to make it look less top heavy.

common on hard-pruned rhodies. But if it is cut lower to the ground, making a framework of 1 foot or less, the new shoots have no place to go but up (see Figure 9.19).

I also think it is wiser to cut the plant down (to a foot or so from the ground) all at once, instead of in stages as some recommend. If you cut one-third of the trunks to the ground, as you would prune a cane-grower, the remaining evergreen canopy is likely to shade out the returning new-shoot growth. Others advise cutting the entire plant back by a third, and then a third again the next year, and then again lower, to achieve a smaller shrub in stages. I have come to believe that this causes the plant more stress than a single, severe pruning to a low framework. The plant must deal with the injury three times instead of just once. But that's just my opinion.

When radically renovating a rhody, do it in the early spring, February or March. Don't fertilize. Water well throughout the next year. A radically renovated rhody will still need almost as much room to live and look

good in the long run. And remember that a the rhody will take several years to recover and look like anything.

Adjust Your Attitude

Most often the only thing a rhododendron is too big for is somebody's idea of how big it should get to be. In this case, the cheapest and best solution is to learn to appreciate mature plants. A mature rhododendron can grow to be 10 to 20 feet—that's two stories high. And some get up to 40 feet. Get used to it.

My Rhody Is Too Leggy

About fourteen years ago, I saw a rhody that a brave but unskilled gardener had over-thinned. Instead of looking like a nice little tree, the plant had internal branches that were so skinny and awkward they looked like a collection of broken arms and legs. And the plant continued to look that way for most of the following fourteen years. This year I noticed for the first time that the canopy had finally grown back together, hid-

Figure 9.18 Radical renovation: The most common mistake is not cutting low enough. When the rhody on the right grows back, it will obscure the window again.

ing the internal branch work. It looks okay. But no buds ever broke inside the shrub; all the new growth was at the ends.

Many people have skinny, leggy rhodies that are the result of bad culture, not bad pruning. By this I mean the rhody was planted in too much sun, too much shade (for example between two buildings), or that there has been insufficient water or too much competition from weeds. These are all cultural conditions that have caused a problem as opposed to pest or disease problems.

Like the rhody described above, there's not much help for these plants. It's a good idea to try to eliminate the cause of legginess, but it will still take a long time, and the plant may perhaps never look better. The best thing you can do is deadwood like crazy. Get inside and remove each and every bit. And take out the old yellow leaves, too. On many branches you will find a tiny ½-inch pointy peg of deadwood. It is the last bit of stem from an old bloom, still hanging on. Take those off. Remove any branches hang-

ing on the ground. Then the shrub will look cleaner and maybe sort of artistic, or at least not so annoyingly awful. And I recommend that you plant some lower-story plants to bring the eyes down. Use sword ferns, epimedium, or Lenten rose *(Helleborus orientalis)*. Or you could half-bury some interesting, low-maintenance rocks that will help shift the focus away from the rhody.

If the cause of the problem is eliminated (like cutting down the Doug fir nearby, or adding irrigation), you can try radical renovation. If the cause is not remedied, radical renovation will simply kill the plant or it will grow back leggy again. And take a moment to determine whether your rhody is one of the species that is naturally open (leggy). Most of these rhodies have large, long leaves. If so, think of yours as a tree (see Figure 9.20).

Nicking the Buds

An old landscaper's trick to renew a big or leggy rhody is to nick the buds. You can trick

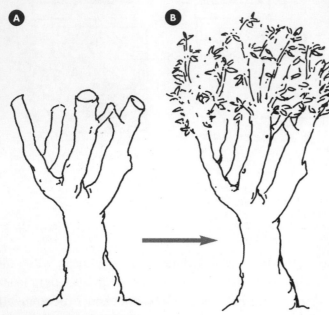

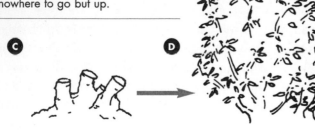

Figure 9.19 When renovating a rhody, cut very low—6 inches to 1½ feet above the ground. **A.** Rhody is cut too high. **B.** Regrowth is mismatched and "spaghetti" is likely. **C.** Cut low **D.** and growth has nowhere to go but up.

a rhododendron into thinking that its top is gone by doing so. In the very early spring, say February, locate the plumping buds down near the base of the plant. A bud will be about the size of a pencil-tip point. Use a razor blade to take a tiny wedge out just above the bud. You are removing the bark and the first layer of green (the cambium)

just below it. This will stop an auxin (a chemical like a hormone) from reaching the bud. This auxin comes from the apical bud (the one at the top end of the branch) and it tells the dormant buds below to stay asleep. Once the flow of auxin is interrupted, the dormant bud will think the top is gone and begin to grow out.

You can select five or ten buds to nick. Be careful not to girdle your shrub by nicking the branch all the way around like a ring. The vast majority of the cambium layer must be kept or the shrub will die. The cut should be about the size of a lady's fingernail clipping (not a gardener's, because we don't have nails long enough to clip). Just a little sliver of a moon, ¼ inch long, ⅛ inch or less deep (see Figure 9.21).

That year the bud will grow into a stupid looking whorl of leaves. But next year it will branch out into several leafy stems. The year after, you will have sort of a second shrub developing at the base of your old, leggy rhody. Then you can saw the top out. Again, this process won't work if the cultural problem has not been corrected or if it is a smooth-barked type of rhody.

People love this gardening tip, so much so that it worries me. In reality most of these people have perfectly good plants that aren't too big for anything. They just think their rhody is too big. I would much prefer that they transplant or simply accept their shrubs for what they are.

Layering

Another landscaper's trick is to layer mature rhodies, letting new ones grow up while selectively cutting out some of the large parent plants. If you stake or pin down a piece of green branch to the dirt, perhaps spreading a little soil over the point of contact, it will grow roots and become a new shrub. It's called layering, and it's how some people propagate rhodies.

My Rhody Is Ugly

The hardest plants to prune are old previously chainsawed rhododendrons. The new growth looks horrible. Although many can be brought back to a semblance of beauty with years of rehabilitative pruning, these casualties are often so indisputably ugly that removal is a more realistic solution.

Spaghetti

Some rhodies are not just leggy, their branches are ugly in the extreme. You look inside and all you find are long, skinny, roller-coaster branches that have only one pathetic whorl of leaves on the ends. The cause is usually mal-pruning. When a branch is headed back, the new shoot emerges, growing rapidly with soft wood. When the bud at the end blooms, the weight of the flower truss pulls the soft young shoot down. As the season progresses the shoot hardens off in that position. Next spring, off it goes again, headed up from the tip, then dipping down. I've heard these rhodies called spaghetti, and they are the most difficult plants I prune (see Figure 9.22).

Taking off deadwood as noted above may be the best you can do. If you go after the ugly branches, you are likely to open the canopy, giving an even better view of the remaining ugly branches. Remember that each of those pathetic whorls of leaves provides some valuable cover for the rest of the ungainly interior. In my experience, the internal branches never fatten up and look right. Your best bet is to encourage the canopy to cover and hide.

Figure 9.20 A. A leggy rhody caused by bad culture. **B.** A naturally open, tree-like rhody.

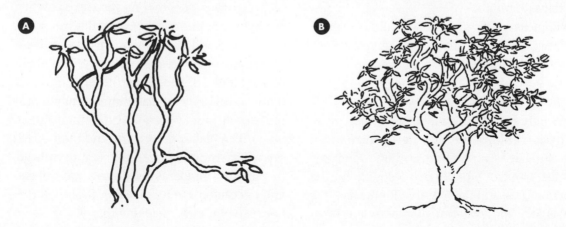

Figure 9.21 Nicking a bud.

That said, I sometimes do try to improve the spaghetti rhody just a bit, restoring it over many years to a better-looking plant. Here are the rules: Leave any branches that face upward and outward, no matter how horrible they seem. Cut off the lowest "hooks" of what I call "serial goosenecks" (see Figure 9.22h). As always, I remove any branches that actually touch the ground. Aside from detracting from the appearance of the shrub, these ground-touching branches act as root-weevil freeways, making it easy for the little guys to crawl up and munch on the leaves at night.

Needless to say, spaghetti rhodies are good candidates for renovation, assuming that they have their cultural requirements met.

Powdery Mildew

Some ugly growth is caused not by bad pruning or bad culture but by a newly introduced disease that is ravaging the rhododendrons of the Pacific Northwest, especially the hybrids 'Unique' and 'Virginia Richards'. It is a powdery mildew, but not the same powdery mildew that gets deciduous azaleas and Oregon grape. This is much worse. The symptoms don't resemble the gray powder of the other diseases either. Instead many of the leaves turn blotchy, yellow or sometimes brown, and fall off in the summer. (Some yellow, internal leaf drop is normal in the late summer.) Live buds will remain and the shrub will grow new green leaves in the spring. But then it happens again.

Rather than fight it with constant spraying of either chemical or organic compounds, I suggest removing the shrubs that continually look horrible. Some rhodies are more susceptible and others are more resistant. The disease also favors close quarters, shade, and high humidity. Some people hope that thinning will create enough air circulation to cure this and other fungal/bacterial diseases. It won't. Moving the shrub to a more open location might help. Just thought you should know.

Rootstock

And a final word about rhodies. The very first hybrids were grafted (spliced) onto the roots of a vigorous species, *R. ponticum*. When the hybrid is put under stress, the rootstock grows out and new shoots from the base eventually grow up and take over the plant. If you have a rhody with two colors of blooms, this is why. *R.* ponticum has a purple bloom (some people call it fuchsia-colored). The leaves are skinny and their edges are wavy. And the plants get very, very large. In parts of England they have naturalized and become quite a nuisance. I tell you this because you may have one that you want to

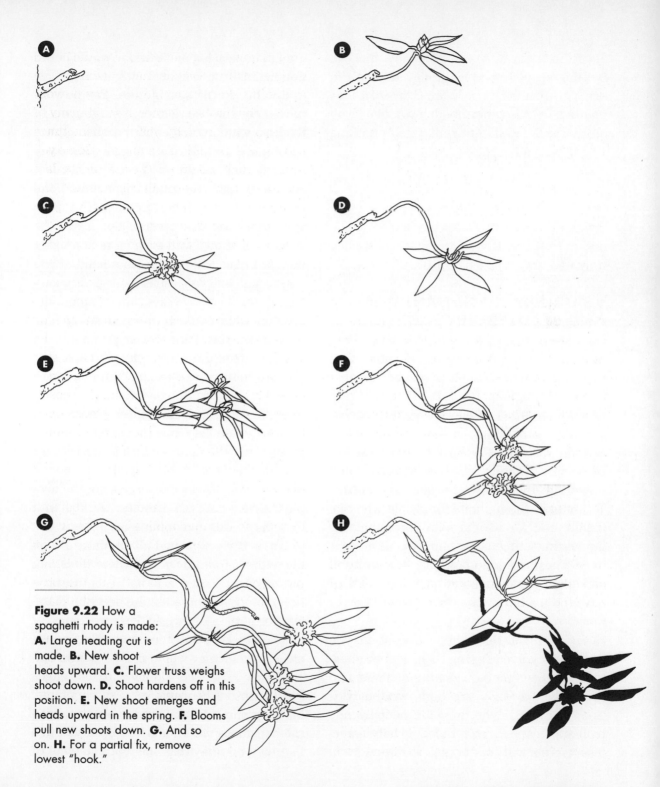

A

B

C

D

E

F

G

H

Figure 9.22 How a spaghetti rhody is made: **A.** Large heading cut is made. **B.** New shoot heads upward. **C.** Flower truss weighs shoot down. **D.** Shoot hardens off in this position. **E.** New shoot emerges and heads upward in the spring. **F.** Blooms pull new shoots down. **G.** And so on. **H.** For a partial fix, remove lowest "hook."

get rid of, and now you will know that it's nothing special. And it's not even what the original gardener had in mind when it was planted. On the other hand, if you like it, by all means keep it. After all, there's nothing wrong with a big rhody.

Summary

Rhododendrons are difficult to prune, especially for size control. But they are a relative dream to move. If your rhody is too big, dig it up and drag it to a better place.

VIBURNUM × BODNANTENSE AND BEAUTYBERRY (*Callicarpa*)

Both these plants do one thing well: They provide us with a winter treat. Beautyberries have clusters of brilliant purple berries that persist throughout the fall and into winter (see Figure 9.23). (Beautyberry, *Callicarpa*, is not the same thing as beauty bush, which is *Kolkwitzia amabilis*.) *V. bodnantense* has extremely fragrant clusters of small pink flowers in the late winter and early spring. This makes them plants for people who like plants, and for people who like something interesting going on in their gardens all year long. These deciduous shrubs are both tall and skinny. Beautyberry is 6 feet high or more. *V. bodnantense* grows to 10 feet or more. And you should pay attention. They really will get that big, sooner than you think; and you can't stop them with pruning.

The other common feature of these two plants is that they are both, well, gawky. They grow straight up with many skinny trunks or canes. From these, equally graceless laterals will shoot out in all directions in a most unpleasing and angular way. There's nothing to be done about it. It's just their natural habit, as the saying goes. People who have these shrubs are always wanting me to fix them with pruning either because (1) the shrubs are getting much bigger than they thought they would or (2) the plants just don't look right. Unfortunately, neither complaint can be fixed with pruning. The more you prune for size control, the faster the shrubs will grow (with even more and uglier upright branches). On the other hand, if you don't prune, and you just let them grow unmolested for twenty years, they eventually develop what could be termed an arching branch structure. Patience, not pruning, is the key to creating graceful, arching branches.

Horticulturists who are familiar with these shrubs don't find their habit disturbing. They know it's just how these plants look. Neophytes sort of expect all shrubs to look pretty much the same—which is to say fatter than they are tall, globe shaped, and about 4 or 5 feet tall. (That's the shrubs, not the neophytes.) It's how we drew the shrubs with crayons as kids and nobody corrected us.

It's as if we expected all animals to look like either horses or dogs. Where does that put elephants, ostriches, and eels? Beautyberry and *V. bodnantense* are sort of like the giraffes of the plant world. I'm sure they look quite natural to each other. And when you get used to them, they will look right to you too.

Replacement Pruning

Many pruning books recommend pruning the deciduous viburnums and beautyberries like they do forsythias—by cutting some of the canes to the ground every year. This will stimulate new shoots, called suckers, to grow up from the cut and become replacement canes over the course of the next few years. With *V. bodnantense*, if you don't cut out too many canes or too large canes, you might not even stimulate new shoot growth. That would be nice because then your shrub will stay thinned out, and, if the cane (or trunk) you removed happened to be the tallest one, you will have successfully made your shrub moderately shorter. I don't know if this system works for beautyberry, but I assume it would.

Thinning

For general-maintenance pruning I suggest using a light hand with these shrubs. If you prune too much (and it doesn't take much with the viburnums) you just stimulate a lot of ugly water sprouts to grow next season. Don't judge your pruning job just on how it looks right after you are through. If you prune out everything that is wrong, you will have a nightmare of regrowth the next year. Trying to restrain these really twiggy plants is especially hard on them. Just for starters, don't take out more than an eighth of these shrubs in a year. If you find that you get heavy regrowth the next season, then *do less*, not more. The plant is telling you that it must have a certain amount of leaves to stay healthy.

It is always okay to take out deadwood, dead stubs, and such. It doesn't count in the pruning budget, and it always makes things look better. It is the first thing good pruners do. Then go on to general thinning for good

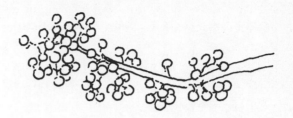

Figure 9.23 Beautyberry

looks. Concentrate on taking out a few of the worst lateral branches that hit the house or that threaten to poke passersby in the eye. Then look for Mr. Wrong Way. He's the branch that starts on one side of the shrub and crosses back through the center and out the other side. And look for ones that actually touch each other. Remove one of the crossers/rubbers, if to do so will not leave a big hole or exceed your pruning budget (see Figure 9.25). Keep moving. When in doubt, just leave the crossing branches in question and move on to another side of the plant. Get out before you do too much. Young plants probably should take only sixty seconds of pruning; old shrubs, maybe fifteen minutes to half an hour.

Radical Renovation and Rehabilitation

I don't like most renewal pruning systems. However, I occasionally do a rad-reno (radical renovation) on previously mal-pruned plants (e.g., if someone tried to prune their old viburnum or callicarpa into a big ball and now have a huge mess on their hands). I cut these unfortunate shrubs to the ground, or a foot or so above, and then let them regrow for three to five years.

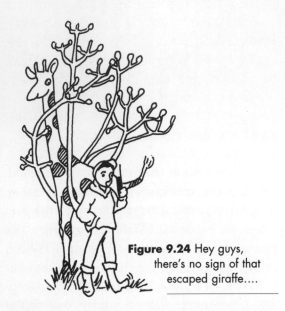

Figure 9.24 Hey guys, there's no sign of that escaped giraffe....

Radical renovation is the fast way to reestablish the natural habit of plants, although it will be a scary sight for a few years until they sort themselves out. The renovated shrubs will rapidly grow to almost their original size, and therefore the technique is not used for size control. It is also hard on plants' health. A little additional water in the summer is a good idea while the shrub is still in recovery.

There are other ways to rehabilitate these shrubs if they are mal-pruned plants. You can cut out one-third of the canes (to the ground) for three years in a row, letting new canes (suckers) replace the old. Or you can let the entire plant grow out for a few years after such cutting. The new growth will look horribly different from the old and will start to drive you nuts. It's a lot like growing your bangs out. After a year, go inside and thin out the worst clusters of overcrowded branches and simplify the hydra branch ends, as shown in the forsythia illustrations in the preceding chapter.

Timing

I don't care what the other pruning guides say, it doesn't matter when you prune these shrubs, if you are selectively pruning them. (Note that radical renovation and shearing are not selective pruning.) You will just lose the blooms on the branches you cut out. There will be plenty of blooms or berries left on the branches that are left unpruned. I don't know how timing got to be such a big deal. On these plants I prefer to prune them while they are in bloom or in berry so I can bring in the cut branches for table arrangements. It's not as though you will shock the rest of the plant into not blooming next year.

Figure 9.25 General pruning for *V.* x *bodnantense* and beautyberry **A.** Rubbing branch **B.** Mr. Wrong Way **C.** Branch on the ground

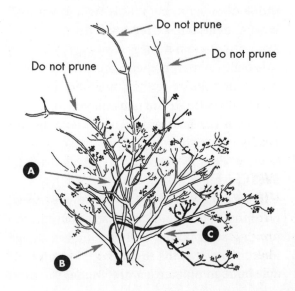

The Best Siting

The ideal pruning for these plants would be practically no pruning because they had been correctly sited. In other words, they should be placed where they have all the room they need to grow as high and as wide as they want. Put them in a bed that can be enlarged to accommodate their widening skirts, or put them in the back of a border. Place them where they can be easily seen in the fall or winter (or early spring for *V. bodnantense*), near an entryway or easily viewed from a window. But neither of these shrubs should stand alone as a focal point, nor be put too close to the main entry or window. They should be tucked in among more universally acceptable shrubs (or, alternatively, segregated in a mass planting in the winter garden). In other words, put these plants where they can be admired when they are doing their thing, but where their flaws can be easily overlooked the rest of the year.

Summary

Both these shrubs are naturally tall, skinny, and gawky looking. Pruning cannot turn them into tidier round shrubs. They also water-sprout like crazy if you head-back or thin too much, and it doesn't take much. The best you can do is a little light thinning and deadwooding.

WITCH HAZEL, DOUBLEFILE VIBURNUM, AND WINTER HAZEL

(Hamamelis, Viburnum plicatum tomentosum, and *Corylopsis)*
These three species all possess a very desirable horizontal branch structure. The "bones" of these plants when revealed in the winter are artistic, architectural, and elegant. Many cultivars also provide fall color for the garden. And the flowers are attractive and yet tastefully understated. None of these plants are prone to any particularly awful pest or disease problem. This means that horticulturists give these shrubs ten points out of a possible ten in gardenworthiness. Unfortunately, these shrubs also share another trait. They resent pruning and especially size control. If you prune too much or the wrong way, they will respond by growing back numerous straight, ugly shoots called water sprouts (see Figures 9.26, 9.27, and 9.28).

The key to success is to site these plants in a place where they can grow as tall and wide as they like, without ever needing to be pruned. That space is usually much larger than most people suppose. The mature size of these shrubs is 15 to 20 feet tall and often as wide, which is the size of a small tree in the mind of the average homeowner. Please don't kid yourself. They will get to be this size sooner than you imagine. You or some other poor soul will have to deal with them if you put them in the wrong place. And that means they will probably have to be cut down just when they are reaching maximum glory. Because these shrubs/trees are so good looking, many people are tempted to plant them close to the walkway, close to the street, or next to the front door. Don't do it! Plant them in the middle of a bed bordered by other shrubs of lesser importance, or by lawn that can be removed to accommodate their increasing size. They can, however, be planted flat against a fence.

General Pruning Guidelines

Limit yourself to pruning only a few of the small, most annoying crossing/rubbing branches; or the one branch that heads straight up, ruining the good looks of the horizontal pattern; or some limb that hangs on the ground (see Figures 9.29 and 9.30).

Of course, pruning off deadwood is always in order and is guaranteed to make things look better. Prune the shrub while it is in bloom to bring the cut branches indoors to put in a vase, or prune it anytime the spirit moves you. For beginners, limit yourself to removing less than one-tenth the foliage in a year. This goes for witch hazels, doublefile viburnums and winter hazels.

Witch Hazel

Witch hazels rule! They have the best of everything. Witch hazel blooms are always some variation of the color yellow, running to sulfur (I'm not allowed to use the color *orange* in print), with one type even having a raspberry hue. The bloom itself is sort of odd and spidery—looking quite fascinating, actually (on page 143).

The shrub blooms in the winter on barren, angular stems. And many varieties smell good, especially if a branch or two are pruned off and put in a vase, where they will automatically look as if they were arranged by a Zen master.

Suckers and Dead Leaves

Hamamelis mollis is one of the most commonly planted witch hazels. (I'm always tempted to say Hammammammalus mmm-molis.) It is also one of the parents of *H.* x

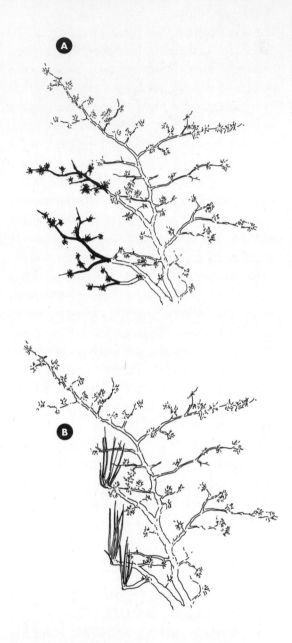

Figure 9.26 Don't: **A.** Making heading cuts to clear a path won't work because **B.** it causes ugly water sprouts to grow.

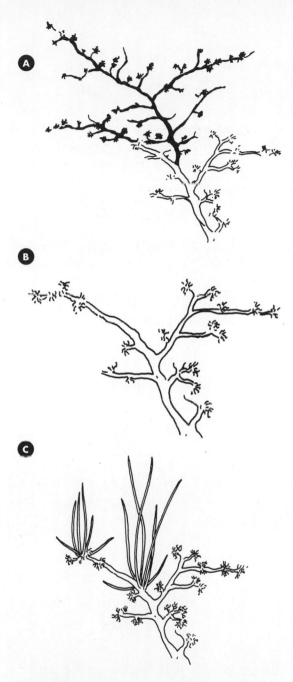

Figure 9.27 Don't: **A.** Trying to selectively reduce shrub size will look fine **B.** just after cuts, but **C.** water-sprout rebound won't be far behind.

intermedia, a witch hazel with great fall color. Either may be grafted to the roots of *H. virginiana*. The reason I mention this is that the graft union might fail if the shrub suffers from some serious stress. Then suckers from the rootstock will begin to grow out. If you see these suckers, you must remove them. And once suckers have begun to grow, you may need to remove them in increasing numbers every year. If you don't remove them, they will take over the shrub.

I had a client with a shrub that bloomed one color, then another, and half the plant refused to drop its ugly brown leaves. That was the rootstock that grew into half the shrub. I just killed the whole thing and started over. This unpleasant habit (of holding on to brown leaves just at the time when you should be enjoying the blooms) belongs to several of the species and cultivars, not just *H. virginiana*. If yours fails to drop, know that it's not your fault and there is no cure for it, except perhaps to carefully cut or pick the leaves off. It may vary from year to year.

As for general pruning, go easy. Use all thinning cuts, and relatively small and few ones at that. If you prune too much (and it doesn't take much) next year will bring you clusters of water sprouts at the site of each cut. Take those off and more return. Actually, more and more return. So you can see the importance of not stimulating rootstock suckers or water sprouts to begin with.

Doublefile Viburnum

Doublefile viburnums are called that because both the leaves and the flowers are arranged in two matched columns along the stems. The flowers are creamy white and quite nice. They bloom in the spring. The leaves turn a splendid fall color in the maroon segment of the color wheel. (Forgive my lack of colorful color descriptions. I flunked the "names of colors" class—just one several "girl" subjects I missed.) But take it from me, doublefiles are really pretty in the fall. A very old doublefile can be made into a sort of small tree by removing some lower branches. You may need to do this in order to continue using the path or something. Otherwise leaving the shrub dressed to the ground is fine.

Pruning Doublefiles: True Confessions

You prune doublefiles just like witch hazels (and winter hazels). Doublefiles are on their own roots, so if you see a ton of shoots springing up from the base, you can, and should, just ignore them long enough for them to turn into regular-looking parts of the plant. If someone has been overpruning or mal-pruning the plant (and I'm not accusing anyone), just leave it alone long enough and the evidence will disappear (in one to three years).

I have been the unwilling participant in an attempt to keep a doublefile to about 2 feet tall. It worked pretty well for several years. But remember, if it doesn't go up, it will go out. And this doublefile spread out a lot, which is to say it's easily 8 feet wide.

Doublefiles are utterly impossible to control in width, as are all of these species. It screws up their horizontal habit. Twenty years ago I planted two doublefiles next to my house in a narrow space. With all the

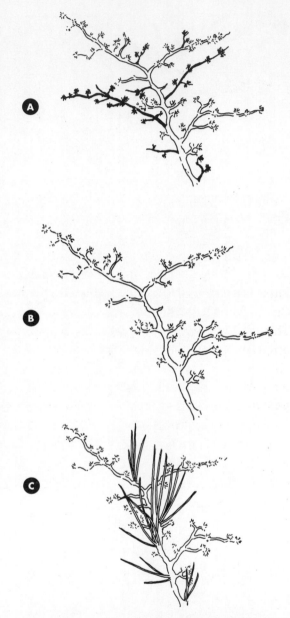

Figure 9.28 Don't: **A.** Making the right kind of cuts but too many is overthinning; **B.** it looks great just after cutting, but watch out—**C.** it stimulates water sprouts next year. Now you're stuck!

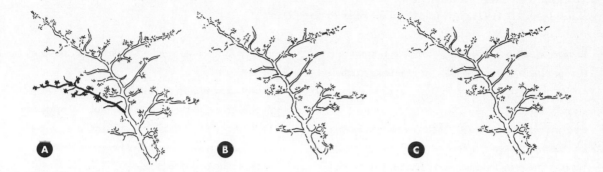

Figure 9.29 Do: **A.** Thin off one large, interfering limb, but nothing else, **B.** clearing a path for pedestrians **C.** without causing water sprouts next year.

hubris of a new selective pruner, I felt certain that I could control them. After all, I knew the secret of the selective heading cut. But it just made the branches look funny. This is how PlantAmnesty's adopt-a-plant program began—someone with more suitable space adopted my doublefiles. I feel better knowing that the plants have probably reached their full garden potential unmolested. The scars of my early training attempts are probably no longer visible. I

hope so anyway. Even though I still long to possess a doublefile, I know adoption was the best thing to do, for all those concerned.

But back to the 2-foot-tall doublefile in my customer's yard. Because of its ever-increasing width, I moved it to a new location, and I did so with an eye to the future. I looked up too. Even with diligent, knowledgeable, annual pruning, I knew that eventually the plant would be impossible to keep down. Finally, a year or two ago, I released it. Boy,

Figure 9.30 Do: **A.** Thin lightly if desired, using many small thinning cuts. **B.** This makes the shrub look better now and **C.** causes no water-sprout response.

Not One or the Other: In Between Mounding-Habit, Cane-Growing, and Tree-Like Shrubs

Beauty bush (_Kolkwitzia_). A big shrub that needs room to be 10 to 12 feet tall and as wide as a small outbuilding. Prune as a tree-like shrub, or renovate as a cane-grower.

Ceanothus (_Ceanothus_). There are many species and varieties of this plant; some are a low-trailing ground cover, some are mounding-habit shrubs, others will grow into open trees. All have small leaves, but many become large plants. They are drought tolerant and short lived. Pruning literature is contradictory on subjects of shearing, heading, and renovation. I suggest light thinning only.

European cranberry (_Viburnum opulus_). Preferably pruned as a tree-like or mounding-habit shrub, but can be renewed by cutting trunks/canes to the base. Wants to be 10 to 20 feet tall, the size of the garage. Cute dwarf buns (2 by 2 feet) are available in the nursery trade.

Mock orange (_Philadelphus_). Prune as a tree-like shrub; renovate like a cane-grower by cutting all trunks/canes back to a 1-foot framework. Must have at least 8 feet to look good—remember that this is taller than you, reaching almost to the bottom of the eaves.

Pearl bush (_Exochorda racemosa_). Prune as a tree-like shrub; renovate like a cane-grower. Grows 10 to 15 feet tall. Hybrid _E. macrantha_ 'The Bride' is smaller at 4 by 4 feet.

Quince (_Chaenomeles_). Can be pruned as a mounding-habit, cane-grower, or tree-like shrub. Withstands radical renovation. Difficult to keep from spreading by runners. Large shrub with mature height of 10 feet. Dwarf varieties now available.

Smoke bush/Smoke tree (_Cotinus coggygria_). Difficult to prune because of contrast between the newer, upright, unbranched growth and the older, loosely curving branches. Several systems are advanced in pruning literature: annual stooling, annual cutting to a 2–4 foot framework, or light pruning as a tree-like (which I prefer). Take note, the mature size is 25 feet; ultimate size is twice that.

Snowball bush (_Viburnum_ spp.). Several species are called "snowball." Prune as a tree-like or mounding-habit shrub. Can renovate like a cane-grower, cutting canes to the ground. All grow about 10 feet tall and wide, which is taller than you.

Spindle tree (_Euonymus europaeus_). Prune as a tree-like shrub, but canes can be removed to ground level. New canes (suckers) can be allowed to grow into replacement trunks. Mature height is 10 to 15 feet.

---

it shot up! It grew to 6 feet in a year! Then I skirted-up some of the very lowest of the old growth and it looks just fine now. (Promise me, you won't turn me in to the tree police.)

Winter Hazel

Winter hazel is sort of a witch hazel, but with skinnier branches and even less spectacular flowers. I mean, we're talking so understated you might not even notice them. Actually they're really quite nice, pale candle-yellow danglees (another Cass Turnbull technical term) that hang on barren branches in the early, early spring. I guess that makes the winter hazel the aristocrat's forsythia. And it smells nice too.

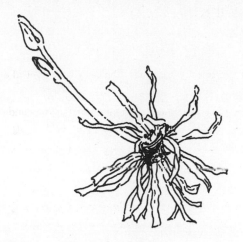

Figure 9.31 Witch hazel bloom

I've seen it used to wonderful effect in an early spring garden, with a yellow theme. The garden had winter hazel, daffodils of various types, and golden variegated grasses. Foliar contrast was provided by several of the always impressive *Euphorbia characias wulfenii* and groupings of the Corsican hellebore *(Helleborus argutifolius)*. Their chartreuse-colored blooms added just the right pizzazz to all that understated elegance. I know that chartreuse is a horrid color for a dress or a refrigerator, but trust me, it is fabulous in a garden.

Pruning for the winter hazel is the same as the other plants in this section, which is to say, prune as little as possible and let them do all the work, making your garden a four-season delight.

Summary

These plants water-sprout like crazy, so prune them very lightly if at all. Forget size control. You may thin them out a bit to accentuate their great horizontal branch structure. Take off less than one-tenth of the foliage when you do prune, using true thinning cuts, and smallish ones at that.

CHAPTER TEN

Vines

Vines are those plants that can't stand up on their own. No backbones, as it were. They need outside support to get up to the sunlight, where they will flower and/or fruit. In nature, the support system is usually a nearby tree or some other plant. Another word for "tree" is "arbor," as in Arbor Day. Was the first grape arbor a tree? Nowadays, vines have trained people to provide support for them—you know, like trellises, walls, arbors, and pergolas as well as ornamental trees and shrubs.

KINDS OF VINES

There are all kinds of ornamental and fruiting vines, and all kinds of ways to categorize them. I like to divide them into three groups, according to their support needs. Some, like clematis and grapes, *twine or lash* themselves onto an *open support system* (wire or lattice). Think of Indiana Jones using his bullwhip to lash onto a tree limb so he can swing across the open pit. Then there are those such as ivy, trumpet vine, and Virginia creeper that *cling or grab* onto *flat surfaces*. These vines have hairy, aerial roots or suction cups. Think of the suction cups on an octopus arm. Finally there are those that use the *grappling hook* method of getting up in the world, like bougainvillea and climbing roses. The pirate throws a rope with a grappling hook onto your ship and swings over with a knife between his teeth.

Why should you know these differences? So that you will use the proper support system. A *twiner* can't get up a concrete wall, but a *clinger* prefers one. Your hooker, er, I mean *hooking vine*, would like to get to the top of a pergola (or your shed roof) and spread out. Note that most climbing roses need some canes to travel horizontally in order to bloom. If you want to train the rose on a vertical trellis, you will need to tie it on, bend new lateral canes to the horizontal, and tie them in. And be sure to periodically remove the old ties before they girdle canes.

WHY VINES?

I like vines. I study gardens trying to figure out what makes them look good, and I have concluded that the easiest way to turn an ordinary landscape into a glamorous garden is to add a vine or two. They figure prominently in garden magazine photos and coffee table books. They can double your blooms or add a second season of color to a shrub or tree. My *Clematis montana* climbed into the lilac bush one year, blooming pink at the same time the lilac bloomed lavender. Suddenly catching sight of it, framed by the lace curtains of my living-room window, almost made me swoon. Another year it ran up a rhody that appeared to bloom soft pink (the clematis) and later, dark pink (the rhody).

A clever gardener of my acquaintance planted a clematis with dainty white flowers to grow through, and contrast with, the leaves of her purple-leaf plum tree. Fabulous! She plans her garden triumphs. For most of us, they are just lucky happenstance. Vines maximize garden space by growing up, and not out. This is great for people with small urban yards. Vines are also useful for hiding unwanted views—for example, filling an empty, blank wall or covering the top of a chain link fence or the face of an ugly brown board fence.

MINDING VINES

Unfortunately, vines are not, generally speaking, a low-maintenance proposition. Along with hybrid roses and fruit trees, vines are for the industrious and forgiving gardener. I think of vines as the problem children of the plant world. If you don't constantly mind them they get into trouble. They are known to run away from home, fall off walls, and go where they have been forbidden, and some can damage your house. Periodically, they get really scruffy looking. Many don't play nice with others. Some are rightly considered juvenile delinquents— English ivy (*Hedera helix*) and silver lace vine (*F. aubertii*). Still others have been tried and convicted as adults: kudzu in the South, morning glory here, and of late, the escaped clematis that is naturalizing and taking over greenbelts. But, don't get me wrong. I like vines; really I do. I own several. And my friends tell me there are even some well-behaved ones. Give me a minute and I'll try to think of some.

PRUNING VINES

Now that you know that your vine's mission in life is to climb up your tree and smother it, you can start to think of pruning as a way of keeping it controlled. A common scenario is that of the new gardener bringing home a vine from the nursery, say a clematis, and planting it next to the house. They tie it to that cute little fan-shaped trellis on the wall. The first two years it grows to the right size, blooms, and looks great. But a few years later, all the flowers are at the ends of the vine that has grown over the roof, into the neighbor's yard, and up his tree. The bottom of the vine (the part still on the cute fan-shaped trellis) has turned into fat, barren, ugly stems. And in the winter, the vine looks pretty bad. In fact, it looks like what the plumber pulled out of the P-trap under the clogged sink.

Pruning is done to keep a vine, especially the flowering or fruiting part of a vine, where it is wanted, which is to say, nearby. And pruning a foliage vine—say Boston ivy that has reached the top of the house—is done to keep it from heading into the gutters and onto the roof. And from covering up the windows. Pruning can also minimize the ugly periods in the life cycle of many vines, and that includes the evergreen *Clematis armandii* and the semievergreen *Akebia quinata*.

Such pruning can be quite radical looking. Some clematis vines are cut to a foot off the ground annually. Sometimes you take the power hedge shears to the tangled clematis or honeysuckle mess gathered on top of the fence. Sometimes you chisel, rip, and cut the clinging vine halfway back down the wall, or maybe even back down to the bottom. Don't worry. It will grow back as much as 10 feet or more in two years. Other vines have 90 percent of all *new* growth cut off annually, like the climbing roses, grapes, and wisterias. The practice of this large-scale pruning seems so radical that it is often incomprehensible to the new gardener.

WHAT CAN GO WRONG?

I suspect that not much can go wrong with pruning on vines, at least not the common ones listed here. If you prune your clematis at the "wrong" time it will just delay, not prevent, blooming. This is only a big deal if, say, you chose the variety of clematis to bloom simultaneously with the climbing rose it is threaded through. If you are pruning just to get it off of the woodpile, timing is not very important. And, I suppose if you pruned a vine too often, say every other week, it wouldn't have enough time to set up flower buds and bloom.

You must *allow time and space* for the plant to grow and set up flower buds. This is why it doesn't work to cut the vine back to the *top* of the fan-shaped trellis. After pruning, it resumes growth from the cut ends. It grows new shoots for a while, then it sets up flower buds and blooms on top of the roof. Instead, you need to cut a stem down to an inch or so from the ground. There it breaks bud and grows up with several new stems to 3 feet tall—where it blooms *on*, not over, the trellis.

RENOVATION FOR OLD VINES

Gardeners commonly renovate old, abandoned vines of all kinds by cutting them down to the ground, or more accurately, to a foot above. Or you may cut a vine way back to a manageable framework and then retrain the rampant new growth in coming years. The vines rarely, if ever, die. Instead, they grow back amazingly fast and look better than ever. Okay, *occasionally* making a big cut on a really old clematis stem/trunk will kill it. So if it has three big, old stems (by big, I mean ¾- to 1-inch diameter), only cut one or two this year. Save one for backup. If you have only one really big, old stem, grit your teeth and do it. Or you could decide you like the way your vine blooms on top of the basketball hoop.

MY BEST ADVICE

Having witnessed many people's successes and failures with vines, I proffer the following advice: New gardeners get to plant one and *only one* vine per arbor, trellis, or wall. Give your vine a lot of room. Really, *a lot more room* than you are planning. And use an arbor or arch that is much bigger than the ones you commonly see in garden centers. By the time a vine gets going and blooming on one of those, you won't be able to walk through it. The arbor needs to be 2 to 5 feet taller and wider than you so that the vine can gracefully spill off. A clinging vine needs a lot of room too, like one entire side of your house. It won't work to put it on the mailbox post. That's not enough space. And, given that many vines have an ugly phase, put that arbor or trellis *away from the front porch*,

Some Common Vines

TWINERS

Akebia (*Akebia quinata*). Semievergreen, small purplish blooms. Because of small blooms, vine is best located outside the back door or a window. Its ugly phase is fall/winter (black spots on leaves). Can produce unwanted seedlings and can rip off siding.

Clematis (*Clematis*). Beautiful flowers, interesting seed heads. *C. montana* and *C. armandii* are most vigorous. Many others are more well behaved. Ugly phase is winter (tangled mess) for all, including the evergreen *C. armandii* (yucky leaves). Difficult to get out of shrubs and trees.

Grape (*Vitis*). Ornamental and fruiting. Nice leaves, plus grapes. Most kinds could cover up a tree, easy. Annual pruning and tying needed. Grapes bleed (run sap) if pruned too late in the winter; scary, but doesn't hurt the plant. A really nice new purple-leaf ornamental grape is now available, *V. vinifera* 'Purpurea.'

Honeysuckle (*Lonicera*). Sweet-smelling flowers. Ugly phase is summer (chronically aphid-ridden) and winter (tangled mess, the "honeysuckle mattress").

Kiwi (*Actinidia*). Makes kiwi fruit, has nifty fuzzy stems. The fruiting kiwi vine needs to be tied to a stout and sturdy trellis. It wants 30 feet, which is the length of a house. Male and female plants are needed for fruit (most kinds) and, remember, one mature vine can produce fully one ton, that's 2,000 pounds, of fruit. There is a wonderful variegated ornamental species (*A. kolomikta*). Its leaves are green, pink, white, and rose on the same plant; many leaves are green splashed with white. It can burn in direct sun. It needs only 15 feet.

Passion flower/Passion vine (*Passiflora*). Exotic-looking flowers. Ugly phase is winter (tangled mess, dead stuff on bottom).

Wisteria (*Wisteria*). Beautiful blooms and, when pruned regularly, can have an interesting winter

structure. Reckless, fast growing, and strong. It gets under shingles, rips up fences, tears apart balconies, sneaks with runners on the ground over to distant plants, and jumps onto nearby trees. Prune off 90 percent of new growth every year. These are the runners/whips, soft, and about as thick as an electrical cord. Leave unpruned the stiff parts: the trunk, scaffolds, and flowering spur systems spaced roughly 1 foot apart.

CLINGERS

Boston ivy (*Parthenocissus tricuspidata*)/Virginia creeper (*P. inserta*). Great red fall color. These deciduous vines have nice winter pattern, especially on concrete walls with seams. Difficult to get off wood siding for painting, gets under shingles. Both need a lot of wall space, like 30 by 30 feet.

Climbing hydrangea (*Hydrangea anomala petiolaris*). A lovely, well-behaved vine. Pretty white flowers. Looks good in the winter. The only clinging vine recommended for growing up an established tree's trunk. Good for low walls.

Ivy (*Hedera*). *H. helix* (English) and *H. canariensis* (Algerian) are considered too vigorous. But others are better behaved. One, *H. helix* 'Congesta', a cathedral ivy, is a truly small vine with interesting overlapping spires when grown on a wall. Needs only 2 by 2 feet. Good for foundation walls, fences, the water meter (with a cutout for the dial face), lamp posts, and so on.

Trumpet vine (*Campsis*). Cool, orange, trumpet-shaped flowers. Needs a lot of wall space, like 20 by 20 feet. Not well behaved. Spreads by suckering roots. When dug, tiny bits left in soil grow into plants.

HOOKING VINES

Climbing rose (*Rosa*). Beautiful, sweet-smelling flowers. Needs tying. Bend young canes horizontally to promote flowering. Ugly phase is summer/fall (black spots on leaves). Like others of its kind, stems of these plants can cause pain (thorns).

maybe down below in the garden. With some distance, the vine still looks elegant even when the leaves are mildewed, black spotted, aphid-ridden, or gone for the winter.

SUMMARY

Many vines are pruned heavily, either once in a while or annually. This is done to keep them blooming and/or fruiting nearby, or to prevent them from overcoming the house, the tree, or the garden. Hard pruning can minimize the ugly stage in the life of many vines.

CLEMATIS *(Clematis)*
by James "Ciscoe" Morris

One of the plants that sometimes give pruners a problem is clematis. This is because there are three different kinds of clematis, and each kind needs a different style of pruning.

The key to pruning clematis is bloom time. One type of clematis blooms in summer or fall. Another blooms only in spring. A third type blooms in spring, followed by another bloom in summer or fall. Often it's difficult to tell which type you are dealing with. If you don't know, it's probably wiser to wait a year to find out and then prune accordingly.

Summer Bloomers

The easiest clematis to prune are those that bloom in summer or fall (bloom after the end of May). The classic summer bloomers are the *lawsoniana* hybrids. The huge blossoms flower on wood produced in the spring. These late bloomers are best pruned to

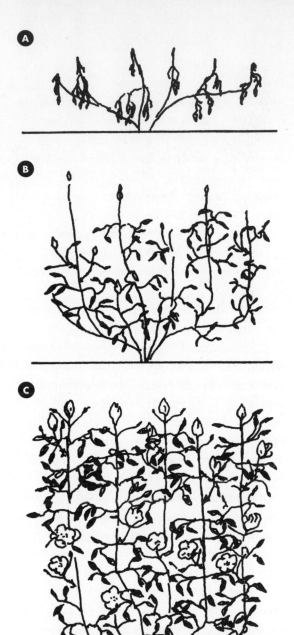

Figure 10.1 Summer-blooming clematis **A.** Summer bloomer pruned in spring **B.** Summer bloomer in mid-spring **C.** Summer blooming!

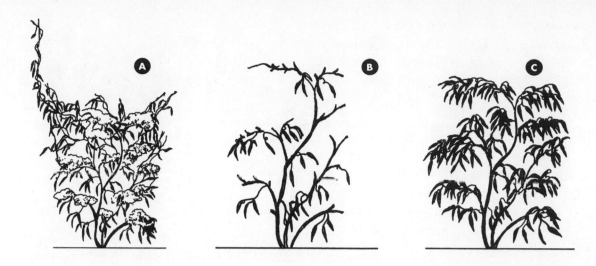

Figure 10.2 Spring-blooming clematis **A.** Spring bloomer blooming **B.** Spring bloomer pruned in late spring **C.** Summer regrowth

within about 2 feet of the ground every year. The summer and fall bloomers can be pruned in fall, once the vine takes on that dead look, or in early spring before growth begins (see Figure 10.1). I prefer pruning them in fall so I don't have to see that ugly, dead-looking foliage all winter long. When planting summer-blooming clematis, I usually prune it to within 6 to 12 inches of the ground for the first two to three years. That promotes low branching for a fuller plant with more flowers.

There is at least one exception to this rule. That is the relatively rare *C. maximo wicziana.* This plant blooms with small, fragrant, white flowers late in summer and is generally evergreen here in the Pacific Northwest. To preserve its evergreen nature, it should be pruned before growth begins in spring in the style described for *C. armandii* below.

Spring Bloomers

The spring-blooming clematis include the fragrant *C. montana* and *C. armandii.* These bloom only on the previous year's growth. Prune them a month after the bloom fades in spring (see Figure 10.2). These plants quickly resemble rat's nests if they are not kept under control. I prefer to keep them thinned out in a style that I refer to as the tracery effect. To achieve this, prune out all but two or three basal stems. Allow only as many lateral stems as the trellis can support without looking crowded. Prune all other growth back to the main branches. To prevent *C. armandii* from becoming bare at the base, pinch low-growing branches and train laterals to cover the base.

Repeat Bloomers

Clematis that bloom in the spring *and* again in the summer (or fall) are the most confusing.

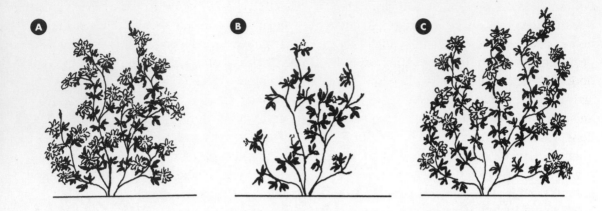

Figure 10.3 Repeat bloomer **A.** Spring repeat bloomer **B.** Pruned in spring after bloom **C.** Fall bloom

The China native *C. lanuginosa* with its attractive 6-inch flowers is a good example. These bloom on old wood in spring and new wood in summer or fall. To preserve the old wood that will produce the spring bloom, prune lightly in fall or late winter. Remove only deadwood and weak, spindly growth. In spring, immediately after the bloom, cut back branches that flowered to the main framework branches (see Figure 10.3). This will promote the new growth that will bloom in fall, and again in spring. The only problem with the spring and fall bloomers is that the need to preserve the old wood for the spring bloom makes it necessary to leave the ugly dead-looking foliage on the trellis all winter long. I guess a little ugly foliage during the winter is a small price to pay for two displays of spectacular clematis flowers each season.

The Young Clematis Vine: A Note from Cass

I caution gardeners not to heavily prune a clematis before it gets established, which can take up to five years. Sometimes hard-pruning a young clematis can kill it. (Although many books recommend cutting new clematis vines to three buds, i.e., 2 inches, I assume, to create multiple stems.) In fact, it seems to me that new clematis vines are prone to dying at the drop of a hat in any case. Don't bump it, or step on it, or let your dog near it for a few years. Maybe protect it with a little chicken-wire fence. But if you do that, don't let the vine grow *through* the fence; later, the clematis will be tough as nails.

WISTERIA*(Wisteria)*

"Wisteria is Latin for work." I wish I knew who said that. How true it is! Under those beautiful color photos of arbors splendidly vine-laced and hung with glorious lavender blooms, there ought to be a warning label: "This Vine Can Be Dangerous." It wants to cover . . . everything!

Ciscoe Morris, renowned Northwest media horticulturist and author of the preceding section on clematis pruning, tells a story about the time he was house hunting. He saw a home advertised for sale in the paper—three bedroom, two bath, in a desirable neighborhood. The price was unbelievably low. Upon arriving at the site he realized why. Two ancient wisteria vines had overcome the home, actually lifting it off its foundation. Their stems were as big as tree trunks. I doubt it was an exaggeration. I have seen wisteria tear off balcony banisters and smother entire trees, and everyone knows what they'll do to your roof and gutters.

I guess I didn't know when I planted mine against the railing of the covered porch eleven years ago. But I'm not sorry, either. Despite the work, there is nothing quite as wonderful as a wisteria. I love the high excitement of watching the spring buds plump up and then expand. It's so . . . erotic. Later, when it's in full bloom, I watch people point and sigh as they pass my house. It makes my entryway look so horticultural. And wisteria smells sweet. In the winter the long fuzzy pods dangle down just above my head, as if asking to be petted. And I must oblige.

Early Training

I read a lot of pruning books. They amuse me. I especially like the one that insists that you make your wisteria vine single trunked. To do that, I think you'd have to guard it twenty-four hours a day with a flashlight. Although I have seen single-trunked wisterias, the more common sight is a main trunk composed of twisted and coiled stems. They look like an unruly rope. Wisterias just grow

like that. I don't know why they don't girdle themselves, but they seem to do just fine.

If you want to force side branching at a particular point, you head-back (lop) the main stem at that point (see Figure 10.4). In my case I planted a vine at the front porch post. I wanted some framework scaffolds to run along the handrail. *Scaffold* is a word meaning one of the main branches of a tree, or in this case a vine, as opposed to the main trunk or the many smaller side (lateral) branches. Then I wanted the main trunk to continue up to the little porch roof and grow along the trellis over the entryway stairs. At the place where the little vine was headed back—the level of the handrail—four or five new shoots developed. Two of the new shoots were tied into position to become the handrail scaffolds. Another one was tied to the post to continue up as the main trunk. Another shoot was shortened (to about 3 inches) in hopes of forcing it to bloom. And the last shoot was cut completely off to prevent overcrowding.

People are often reluctant to head-back a wisteria, wanting it to get as big as fast as it can, and not wanting to hurt the poor little dear. But trust me, heading will in no way slow it down, and a small cut on a young plant does little harm. It simply makes it branch out. Major scaffolds on a wall or lattice should be spaced at least 1½ feet apart to allow room for the blooms to dangle down without running into each other.

All along the major scaffold branches (about every foot or two) you will want to create persistent frameworks of lateral branches reminiscent of the spur systems

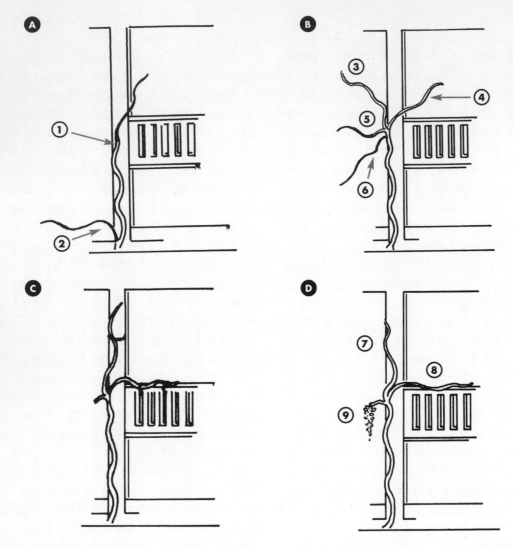

Figure 10.4 Training a wisteria vine **A.** Use a heading cut where scaffolds are wanted. **1.** Cut tip. **2.** Cut off low runner. **B.** Train new shoots that came from heading cut. **3.** Tie up. **4.** Tie down. **5.** Shorten. **6.** Remove. **C.** After cuts **D.** It blooms in the spring! **7.** Trunk **8.** Scaffold **9.** Bloom

found on an apple tree. These spur systems hold the fat flower buds that expand into blossoms. Each little spur system will be a woody framework of branches ranging from about the size and shape of a hand to (after many, many years) roughly the size and form of a forearm.

Instead of growing a series of these tidy, well-behaved spur systems, the young wisteria branches will send out a lot of skinny, rapidly-growing, soft, vegetative shoots (which

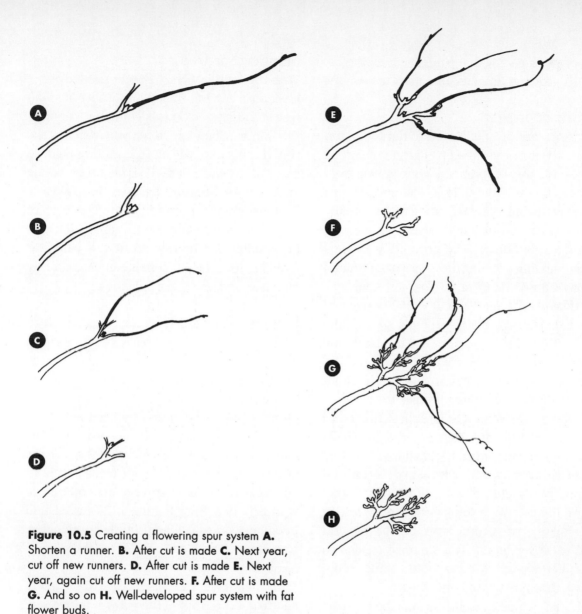

Figure 10.5 Creating a flowering spur system **A.** Shorten a runner. **B.** After cut is made **C.** Next year, cut off new runners. **D.** After cut is made **E.** Next year, again cut off new runners. **F.** After cut is made **G.** And so on **H.** Well-developed spur system with fat flower buds.

make leaves, not flowers) in the spring and summer. These shoots are called *runners*, or sometimes *whips*. You will need to force some of these runners into becoming a spur system by heading them back to 3 to 6 inches from where they join their parent scaffold branch (see Figure 10.5). The majority of the runners should be completely cut off at the scaffold. Most of the shortened runners will fatten up and become spur systems, but some may die and become stubs. And still others seem determined to be vegetative, taking off with a vengeance next year and refusing to produce flowers. Don't ask me why.

Arbor or Trellis

Wisterias are often allowed to run to the top of an arbor or overhead trellis and to spread out, with the blooms dangling down from above. Quite lovely. This too necessitates frequent pruning or the wisteria eventually piles up on top of itself, creating a mess of dead canes below and preventing blooms from hanging down. After it has been trained to a framework of scaffolds and spur systems, you will need to cut off 90 percent of the *new* runners every year and shorten the rest. Whenever necessary, whack back any lateral runners that try to escape off the sides of the trellis or that threaten to climb into neighboring plants or structures.

I think that wisterias look best trained to an overhead trellis. Such an arbor or trellis needs to be very strong and sturdy. Use 4 by 4s, at the very least, as the main posts and the top piece should be made of 2 by 4s. Forget those flimsy lattice things you see for sale in catalogs or at garden stores. Your wisteria will eat it for lunch. The smartest trellis I've seen is a system of metal pipes, sunk in concrete, disguised with some lattice.

If the wisteria trellis is attached to the house, I strongly recommend that you plant the vine on the *farthest* post and let it fill in by growing toward your house. You will be glad that you gave yourself that slight edge in later years as you find yourself tugging and tearing runners out of your gutters and shingles. And trust me, you need only one wisteria.

Standard or Tree

With the help of a very sturdy stake or two, a wisteria can be trained into a sort of small free-standing tree. This is commonly done in the South. When the young vine reaches the top of the stake, whack the wisteria back to force it to bush out. The resulting young shoots later become the main scaffolds or framework of the tree canopy. The idea of the wisteria tree appeals to me since it can be situated in the middle of the yard, far from anything else. There it can be vigilantly watched and pruned on all sides.

Summer Runners

With all wisterias, scores of runners will reach out into empty air every summer, hoping to grab onto a nearby helpless victim. These runners are roughly the thickness of a phone cord. Cut them off before they strangle a sleeping dog or trip the gardener. This can mean pruning every month if the runners are in your way, say on your front porch. In any case, be certain to prune them off before winter, when they harden off (stiffen and become woody, holding tightly to shingles, tree limbs, etc.) and are more difficult to remove.

In the summer I whack back the runners just to get them out of the way (making them about 5 or 6 inches long). I do more detailed thinning and pruning in the winter, when all the leaves have dropped off and I can see what's going on. After the summer pruning, my wisteria vine looks sort of like a feather boa, just to give you an idea. By the way, those runners can be used to make a tasteful

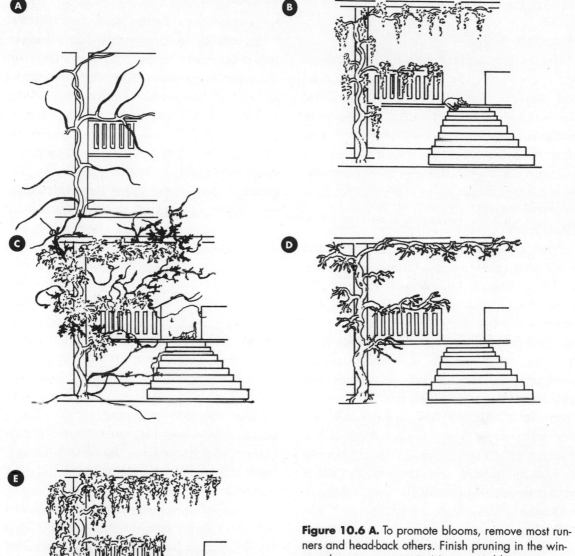

Figure 10.6 A. To promote blooms, remove most runners and head-back others. Finish pruning in the winter, when you can see. **B.** Next year's blooms **C.** Summer runners: Watch out, here they come! Cut them back every two weeks to get them out of the way. **D.** Finish pruning in winter, removing runners but leaving woodier parts. **E.** Each year there are more and longer blooms, and trunks and scaffolds thicken.

simple wreath. Just wind them into a circle. Same with grape vines.

Underpruning

The most common mistake is to not prune a wisteria enough. More than 90 percent of the *new* growth (the zillions of long runners) needs to be cut off annually. A single runner can grow 12 feet in one year. After the framework is established, shorten many of the runners to six buds. Remove the vast majority completely, every year! (see Figure 10.6.)

Overpruning

I didn't think it could be done, but I have witnessed three novice pruners overprune wisteria. Given a mature flowering vine, the pruner is tempted to remove not only the runners but the desirable, woodier, persistent spur systems as well. Very old vines have flowering spur systems that are as long as your arm. If they are pruned off or even shortened too much, the vine will appear sparse and have too few blooms. And the next year, such overpruning will result in a wild (wilder than normal) resurgence of flowerless runners. The general idea, then, is to shorten or remove all the long, wild runners, and leave all the spur systems to flower like crazy.

Radical Renovation

If it gets away from you or you have moved into a home that already has an enormous wisteria tangle, grabbing and strangling everything in sight, show no mercy. Lop, saw, and chainsaw whatever is necessary to get it back down. I suggest you cut several feet below where you want the regrown vine to be, since you will experience an upsurge of new shoots the following spring.

As with all heading cuts, the new growth will occur directly beneath the cut and will head up from there. You will need some room to let the wisteria regrow over the next few years. New growth will be vegetative (not flowering) and rampant for a few years. I wouldn't be surprised if some major stems die back partially or totally, if you make cuts 1 inch in diameter or more. But I doubt that you will kill the plant. As some stems die back, cut off the dead bits. Other stems will supply the replacement shoots to be tamed in upcoming years.

Tools

My relationship to grapes and wisterias changed dramatically when I finally bought a specialized tool called an ARS long-reach pruner. No, it's not a traditional-type pole pruner. It's a lightweight, expanding, aluminum pole, with a trigger and a standard scissors-type pruning head. Some (interchangeable) heads have a sort of "grabber," perfect, I imagine, for pulling tough runners out from under shingles and fascia boards. Such a tool saves hours of ladder work, but can cost about eighty dollars. I got mine from the A.M. Leonard tool catalog (1-800-543-8955; *www.amleo.com*); ask for the wholesale catalogue.

The long-reach pruner is only good for water sprouts and vines. It lacks cutting power for thicker or woodier branches. The only other tools required for wisteria are loppers and hand pruners. Occasionally you may need a pruning saw. Don't forget the twine and nails or whatever you use to tie up the vine. And retie as needed to prevent girdling.

My Wisteria Won't Bloom

The most common comment I get at classes is "My wisteria won't bloom." It's natural for these vines to take between three and seven years to start blooming. I have read that frequent, proper pruning may help them to begin blooming sooner, or at least more. On the other hand, some people have old vines that have never bloomed. I'm told that these are seed-grown plants or "mules."

I have often heard root pruning recommended to force an older vine to bloom. Basically, this means that you use your shovel to cut the roots in a circle (or dotted circle) a foot or two from the vine. I have also heard people recommend fertilizer formulated to encourage blooms (relatively low in nitrogen). However, I have been faced with such a vine and had no luck with either technique. In that case, as with all nonperformers, removal is the best option, and no one will blame you for it.

How to Kill Your Wisteria (and Other Woody Plants)

If you just cut the offending plant to the ground, it will not die. Instead it will regrow rapidly. If it, or any other woody plant that you want to kill, is impossible to dig out, I recommend using Roundup (glyphosate). Roundup is a liquid herbicide often used to kill dandelions and other weeds. Farmers use it to kill weeds before planting, since it does not poison the soil. The herbicide binds tightly to soil particles, making it unavailable to kill other things. It is quite deadly to the plants it touches, though, and is translocated throughout the plant system including the roots. Although I would never declare this or any chemical (organic or nonorganic) safe, it seems to pose the least threat to the environment, given what we know.

As an herbaceous weed killer, Roundup is mixed with water and sprayed on weeds. This is best done on a dry, hopefully warm, spring day. In two weeks the weeds will be yellow and dead, and the soil will be ready for replanting and mulch (to prevent weed seeds from germinating).

In the case of woody plants, like the non-blooming wisteria, volunteer holly, blackberry, ivy, cotoneaster, or what have you, you use Roundup as a "cut-stump treatment." Purchase the jug of concentrated Roundup, usually about 18 percent active ingredient (the glyphosate). You'll use only a small quantity of liquid, to which you'll add the same amount of water. The directions should say "Apply a 50 to 100 percent solution of this product to freshly cut surface immediately after cutting." They don't say how. I use a glass rubber-cement bottle that I have gone through great pains (involving emptying glue and then peeling residue out with my finger) to prepare for use as an herbicide container. It has a brush built into the cap, and the bottle fits nicely into my tool-belt pocket. But it is an imperfect system, as the cap corrodes and leaks, and it is illegal to store the herbicide in that container. I regret that there is no appropriate commercial applicator available. Be sure to wear rubber gloves and safety glasses, and take care not to get any in a stream or on yourself.

The cut-and-paint system is best done in late summer, not spring or winter. The only serious problem I have heard of arising from the use of Roundup as a cut-stump treatment is the situation where a desirable plant, usually a tree, is "attached" to the sucker, sapling, or tree being cut and painted. Trees of the same species in close proximity can have roots that graft to each other underground. One man e-mailed me to say that after he poisoned the stump of a bigleaf maple he cut down, the poison "flashed-back" into a nearby bigleaf maple and killed it. Think the situation through, please.

Roundup used as a cut-stump treatment could be a powerful tool in the war against invasive exotics such as ivy, Scotch broom, and wild clematis. Unfortunately, those good people who are most willing to do the work (the volunteers) are often the least willing to use chemicals of any sort. I can tell you,

though, that Roundup is the last chemical that even organically minded professional gardeners give up. And I would be sorry to see it banned.

Summary

Prune wisteria a lot, removing up to *90 percent of the new foliage* every summer. Cut off all those skinny runners and/or shorten some to about 4 to 6 inches from the scaffold branches or trunk. This will encourage them to turn into persistent, blooming branch systems (spur systems). Leave all the older, previously shortened branch/spur systems that are attached to the main trunk(s) and scaffold framework. You can tell the branch/spur systems from the runners because they are thicker and stiffer (woodier), and have relatively fat flower buds on them. Summer pruning is done just to keep the wisteria from taking over the world. More precise pruning is done in the winter, when all the leaves are off and you can see all the trunk, scaffolds, spur systems, and runners.

CHAPTER ELEVEN

Trees

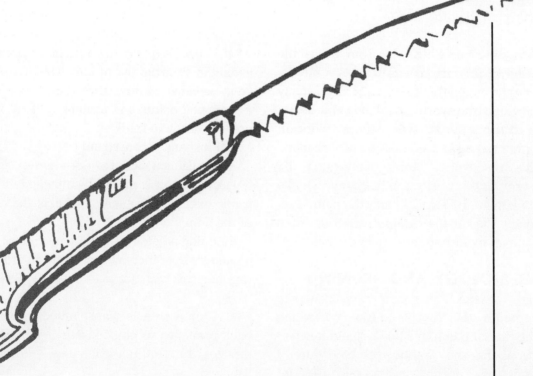

Thank God for Dr. Alex Shigo. I feel lucky to be living at the same time as Dr. Shigo, and to have been privileged to hear him speak in person on numerous occasions. Dr. Shigo is a Ph.D.–type doctor, as opposed to a medical doctor (M.D.). He has been described as the "Sir Isaac Newton of Arboriculture" (the study of trees). As the chief scientist for the USDA Forest Service, he did pioneering research on how and why trees decay (rot). And he has finally described exactly how a tree limb is attached to a tree. Previous to Shigo's work, engineers could not explain how a limb could withstand wind stresses and snow loads. These are only two of his contributions to the field of arboriculture.

Not only has Shigo done an incredible amount of primary research, he is a powerful public educator. He travels extensively throughout the world speaking (and listening) to the arborists who actually work on people's trees. And he tells them that many of his "discoveries" are actually not really new, but that his main job has been to make them known. He says, "I carry the club." Presumably, he means the club used to wake people up by hitting them over the head.

TREE BIOLOGY AND PRUNING

Shigo's research has now been generally accepted as the "New Tree Biology" (which is the title of one of his books), and it is revolutionizing the practice of tree care. I include this information here because a lot of new research (in the past ten or twenty years, both by Shigo and by others) counters what many people hold to be true. The following is a partial list of conclusions based on these new scientific findings:

• Wound paints and pruning seals do not prevent decay in trees.

• "Flush cuts" cause rot.

• Fertilizing a sick tree does harm.

• A tree limb is not really attached to the trunk, except for a small portion at the base of the limb.

• Adding amendments (like peat moss) to a planting hole increases neither the growth rate nor survival rate among newly planted trees.

• After a tree is transplanted, pruning-back branches to compensate for root loss reduces, rather than encourages, reestablishment.

• Weaker trunks develop on those trees that are tightly staked at the time of planting.

I could go on, but you get the idea.

For those wishing to find out more, or for those who still have serious doubts about any of the above, I recommend getting a copy of the third edition of *Arboriculture Integrated Management of Landscape Trees, Shrubs and Vines* by Richard W. Harris, James R. Clark, and Nelda P. Matheny (published by Prentice Hall, Upper Saddle River, New Jersey, 1999). Arborists just call it "Harris." It's a very large and expensive textbook, but it comes as close as anything I've found to being the Compendium-of-All-Horticultural-Knowledge. It references and summarizes the major scientific findings in the field. Unfortunately, like most textbooks, it makes for some very dry reading. Those wanting to go right to the source will want to locate either *A New Tree Biology* (1986) or *Modern Arboriculture: A Systems Approach to Trees and Their Associates* (1991), both by A. L. Shigo (published by Shigo and Trees, Associates, Durham, New Hampshire). These are also large textbooks, and like Harris they may be hard to find in the local library. If you don't care about the subject that deeply, you may just continue through the tree section of this book, which you already know is lightweight, cheap, and easy to read.

Compartmentalization

The world can be roughly divided into inanimate objects, plants, and animals. Animals often avoid injury and death by moving away from the wound source. Pain, caused by fire for example, is the signal to move away. Trees cannot move away from the source of an injury. (An old saying is "Trees will stand for anything, because they can't run.") When an animal is injured, it must stop the bleeding and mend the damaged part (the broken bone). When a tree is injured, it must stop the *decay* (same as rot) that wants to eat it up, and grow a new replacement part, say a new limb. If you back the car into a tree, thus breaching the protective bark, the rotting organisms can then charge in and start to eat (decay, rot) wood. The decay begins with the injury. A good analogy in humans is gangrene that follows a war wound. Unfortunately, there are no antibiotics for trees. And pruning paint or wound seal does *not*, as we all once believed, keep decay from entering the tree. The tree does the defense work internally.

Trees are the largest, longest-lived organisms on the planet. The reason is an incredible defense mechanism called *compartmentalization*. When it is injured, a tree *walls off* or *compartmentalizes* the injured area internally by chemically altering the wood in predictable patterns. Trees don't heal; they set up barriers to rot and then try to outgrow it. Sometimes a tree compartmentalizes well, and only a small pocket of rot remains sealed off inside the trunk as the tree grows larger. Or perhaps decay spreads up and down in a long column. It varies. The only wood that is guaranteed not to decay after an injury is the new wood—the rings of wood laid down after the tree was damaged. If you see a hollow tree, you will know that the size of the hollow is exactly the size the tree was when it was topped or injured.

Compartmentalization is why that pocket in your tree where a limb rotted out doesn't get bigger; it just makes a cute home for a squirrel. It's easiest for a tree to wall off a dead or dying limb (see Figure 11.1). It's somewhat harder for the tree to wall off a gash on the trunk (see Figure 11.2). It's hardest for it to wall off the rot that comes charging down the trunk when a tree has been topped (see Figure 11.3). It's sort of the difference between bruising your knee, cutting off your hand, and cutting off your head.

This new understanding of tree biology means that arborists no longer bother to dig out a rotten "cavity" in a tree and fill it like a dentist. And we especially don't dig back into "sound wood" or drill a hole to drain water out of a cavity, since both these activities make a brand-new wound, allowing decay to enter previously protected areas of the tree. The tree must then set up new barriers, taking up valuable space and energy.

Whether your particular tree dies back totally or partially when wounded depends a lot on how well it walls off wounds generally.

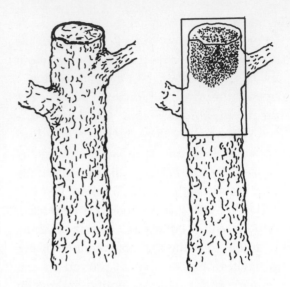

Figure 11.2 Look inside: pattern of decay after a topping cut.

This varies according to a tree's species or genetic makeup—even among members of the same species there is genetic variation. There are several species of trees that don't compartmentalize well. In the trade they're called "rotters." They include bigleaf maple (*Acer macrophyllum*), alder (*Alnus* spp.), willow (*Salix* spp.), and poplar (*Populus* spp.).

You want to help these plants by prompt removal of injured limbs and by avoiding wounding or cutting (pruning) healthy green wood. Cut out the deadwood and little else. Leaving deadwood rotting on a tree acts, as Shigo says, like "a big stick of sugar" drawing in the rotting organisms. Besides, it's UGLY.

The Branch Collar

Shigo tells us that branch wood is different from trunk wood. This is a hard one to get your mind around, but it explains how limbs

Figure 11.1 Look inside: pattern of decay from a stub cut limb.

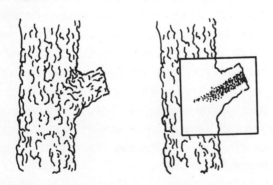

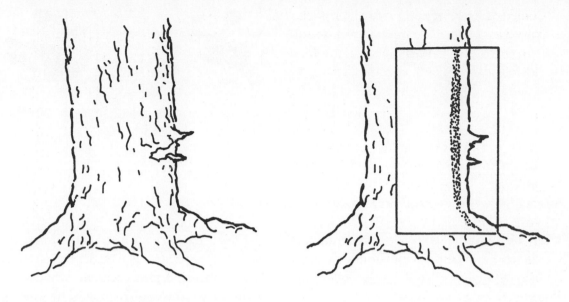

Figure 11.3 Look inside: pattern of decay after a trunk injury.

are held onto, and into, trees. In the spring, a tree will wake up and add a layer of wood (the new ring) to a branch. Then the trunk wakes up and puts on its own new layer of wood. Where the trunk wood meets the base of the limb, it laminates over the limb, creating sort of a bulge called the trunk/branch collar. For short, this area is now referred to as just the *branch collar*. The branch is, for the most part, separate tissue from the trunk and is just held in place, buried inside the trunk by each year's new ring of wood. When a knothole drops out of a piece of lumber, you are seeing the branch wood drop out of the trunk wood.

This lamination process is repeated every year. When you prune off a limb for whatever reason, you should be careful to cut off only the branch wood and avoid cutting or wounding the trunk wood. This means you cut *to* the collar but *not into* it, since that would open up the trunk to decay.

If you cut *too far out*, though, the branch will die back to the collar, leaving a stub (see Figures 11.4, 11.5, and 11.6). The dead stub changes color and, in response to the cut, the collar plumps up. Next year the collar starts to creep out the stub, trying to enclose it (this process is called *wound closure*).

In general, the right place to cut is almost like a dotted line where the branch starts to get fatter near the trunk. People always want me to tell them the right "angle" to make the cut, but that angle varies, as do the collars themselves. Some species have big and fat collars, some species have their co-lars inside the trunk (another hard one to visualize). But by studying illustrations and looking at the collars on real trees, you'll soon get the idea. Looking at recently dead branches,

Figure 11.4 Where to cut **A.** Stub cut (too far) **B.** Collar cut (just right) **C.** Flush cut (too close)

with the plumper collar and different colored wood, can help you determine the characteristic angle of your tree's collar (see Figures 11.7 and 11.8).

Flush Cuts

Older arboricultural literature recommends cutting a limb off "flush" with the trunk. Shigo recognized and explained how damaging flush cuts are to trees. The practice of flush cutting began as a misinterpretation of a true observed phenomenon. When a limb is removed, the tree responds by covering over the wound in the process called wound closure. With a flush cut, closure can happen faster than when a proper collar cut is made. Wound closure is important because it seals off the *entryway* for decay and allows the tree to continue adding rings of healthy new wood. Even if the entryway is closed, some decays can continue internally, but the real problem with flush cuts is that, unlike collar cuts, they open a second door through which decay reaches trunk wood (remember that trunk wood is different from branch wood). Any possible benefit of rapid closure is far outweighed by the unnecessary damage a flush cut does by opening up the trunk to decay. Arborists of the past mistakenly equated closure with the tree being "healed."

Also note that while it is true that rapid closure can be the sign of a healthy tree, artificially inducing closure with flush cuts is still bad. It is sort of like making a hospital patient get out of bed and run. While it is

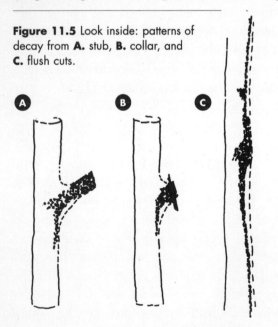

Figure 11.5 Look inside: patterns of decay from **A.** stub, **B.** collar, and **C.** flush cuts.

true that a person seen running is probably a healthy person, causing a sick person to run will not make him well.

How Trees Die

People mistakenly assume that since a tree didn't die right after having nails or a car driven into it, it's all right. Wrong! Trees usually die from a series of blows over a long time, and when one dies it's usually because of the proverbial straw that broke the camel's back. You may have a giant column of dead rotten wood walled off inside your tree from some old wound and when the drought hits, well, whammo! You have a dead tree. Your trees can wall off a lot of abuse, but that doesn't mean you should abuse them.

How to Prune a Tree Limb

When pruning heavier branches and ones that have narrow crotches (branch attachments), it is wise to use a multi-cut system of removal. Remove the weight of the branch first by cutting it off farther out from the trunk. Start by making an undercut, then saw from the top down. The undercut will prevent your saw from getting stuck. Once the weight is gone, more accurate pruning to the collar is easy. Then, at the bottom of the collar, also make a correctly angled undercut. This will prevent tearing the bark when you make the final cut from the top down (see Figure 11.9). If it is a very narrowly angled branch crotch, you may be forced to saw completely from the bottom upward; otherwise, you will inadvertently cut into the collar (see Figures 11.10 and 11.11). This is awkward, but necessary, since the nicest thing you can do for your tree is to make *a good collar cut*. In fact, most pruners spend a fair amount of time correctly positioning themselves, checking from different sides, before they begin to saw.

Summary

The nicest thing you can do for your tree is to figure out where the branch collar is and

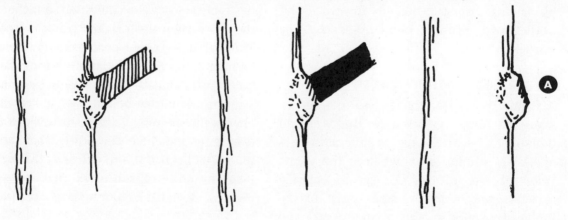

Figure 11.6 Branches die back naturally to the collar. **A.** The collar is usually obvious as a bulge.

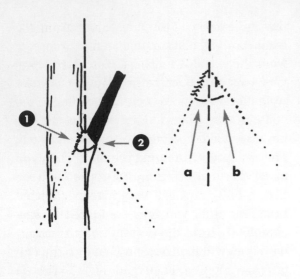

Figure 11.7 If no collar is visible, locate the branch bark ridge and use geometry. **1.** Branch bark ridge **2.** Collar **3.** Angle *a* = Angle *b*

cut the limb off to, but not into, it. The branch collar usually looks like a bulge at the base of the limb. If it is a big limb, take the weight off it first by cutting the limb off farther out. For the final cut, make an undercut first, before sawing down. This will prevent ripping the bark. If the crotch angle is narrow, you may have to make the entire cut by sawing from the bottom upward. Don't bother with pruning paint or seals. They don't work.

PRUNING YOUNG TREES

A young tree is one that is less than fifteen years old. Shigo says it's a tree that is still all dynamic mass. Such a tree is difficult to damage with pruning. But, whereas the young tree *can* take a lot of pruning, it generally doesn't *require* much, since most of the limbs of a young sapling are temporary and will be removed as the tree grows up. But by knowing what to cut and why, the pruner can solve many problems before they become serious and much harder to correct later in the tree's life.

The main goals of young tree pruning are (1) removing suckers, (2) removing temporary limbs, and (3) minimizing included bark.

True Suckers

Suckers are the straight, thin, rapidly growing shoots that arise from the trunk, the *base of the trunk* (which is called the *trunk collar* or *butt flare*), the roots, or below a graft union. Trunk suckers are often caused by wounding, such as flush-cutting limbs or mower/string-trimmer damage. Suckers can also occur when a graft union no longer suppresses the growth below. Remember, suckers are *not* the same as water sprouts, which occur on tree *limb*s when they have suffered injury or mal-pruning.

Graft Union Suckers

The *graft union* is the place where two parts of a plant are spliced together, usually a desirable top portion (the *scion*) attached to the more vigorous, original trunk or roots. The graft union on a weeping cherry tree will be high up on the trunk and will look like a bulge just beneath the weeping branches. The trunk below belongs to a standard cherry, the weeping limbs just above are the desirable branches. On other trees, graft unions on the trunk, either near the crown or near ground level, can be spotted as a sudden change in bark color or trunk diameter.

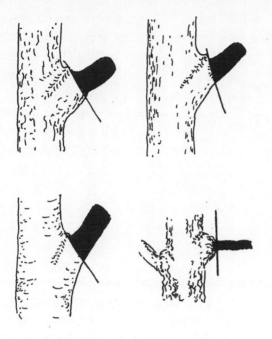

Figure 11.8 All are correct collar cuts: There is no set angle for a cut.

Graft unions sometimes fail, especially if the tree has suffered from drought, malpruning, late freeze, or other cultural stress. When this happens, dormant buds below the union begin to grow out into suckers. These suckers must be removed on a young tree (even if they have gotten rather large) or they will overtake the tree (see Figure 11.12).

Getting Rid of Suckers

You have the greatest chance of success by correcting sucker growth on young trees. Cut the suckers off just as they meet the trunk. If a sucker is a few years old, it may even have developed a collar. Cut to it, but not into it. Cutting suckers too far out (leaving stubs) or too close (flush cuts) stimulates even more suckers to grow. But note that even if suckers are pruned "just right" they may keep returning to plague the tree owner for a lifetime.

Moderately better luck can be had by pruning in the summer, though even this is not a magic bullet. Sucker Stopper claims to prevent regrowth for up to a year. Beware that it is a powerful growth regulator that can damage live wood. It should therefore be used only on one-year-old sucker growth, not as a treatment for regular pruning cuts. The best "cure" for suckers remains prevention, and that is done by keeping the tree healthy.

Ground-Level Suckers

Suckers sometimes arise from below ground level, from a young tree's roots located near the trunk. This is often the result of the tree being planted too deep. This is a common problem both in the landscape industry and in volunteer and homeowner tree-planting projects. A survey conducted by the Bartlett Tree Research Laboratories found that 93 percent of the test group (363 trees) were planted too deep by professionals (see "National Epidemic Reported: Improper Planting Is Killing Trees," by E. Thomas Smiley, pages 36–39 in the December 1991 *Arbor Age Magazine*). This is indeed an astounding percentage. Not only do these trees send up troublesome suckers, they fail to thrive and many can die before reaching maturity. (Shigo once said that if he was granted one wish, it would be that trees not be planted too deep.)

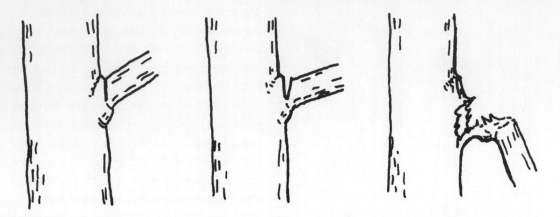

Figure 11.9 A common mistake in limb removal: No undercut causes bark to tear.

If you find such a tree, and it is young, dig it up and replant at the correct level. If it is too large to dig, just pulling the soil away several inches from the trunk collar (hopefully with positive drainage) can help immensely. You will know where the correct level is by carefully digging down the trunk with a trowel until the trunk flares out, turning into the major roots of the tree. This is the *trunk collar* or *butt flare*, and in a correctly planted tree it would be above ground, with roots disappearing just under the soil. If the tree has been planted too deep for a few years, know that some new roots may have developed in the higher soil level. They are an emergency system, like their aboveground counterparts, water sprouts. Such roots are thin and pale and they don't enlarge where they meet the trunk. Ignore them and continue to dig down looking for the characteristic flare of trunk collar, which will be the tree's original and correct soil level.

Temporary Limbs

As the urban tree grows up, it is usually necessary to remove the lower limbs to create clearances for people, cars, houses, and such. Almost all the limbs the new owner sees on a young tree are these *temporary limbs*.

A limb on a trunk "feeds" the portion closest to it, making that part of the trunk stronger, and giving it good taper. A poor nursery practice is to tightly stake a sapling tree and quickly limb it up. This creates a

Figure 11.10 Another common mistake in limb removal: Cutting from the top down, the narrow angle forces a flush cut.

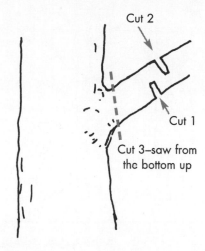

Figure 11.11 The three-cut system. On narrow, angled branch crotches, you may have to saw entirely from the bottom upward.

(diagram labels: Cut 2, Cut 1, Cut 3–saw from the bottom up)

taller tree, faster. But they are weak trees that may even flop over when untied. When limbing up a young tree, you need to do it neither too soon or too late. Delaying pruning until the limbs have become large is equally bad for the tree. Older trees are less able to deal with the larger pruning wounds. Also, if cuts are made one directly above the other, pockets of rot may coalesce between them. It is therefore best to vary cuts at different heights and sides of the tree over the course of years.

A good rule of thumb is that at any given time two-thirds of the length of the tree trunk should be covered in a leafy crown. Another good rule is to *prune off temporary limbs before they become half the diameter of the trunk.*

If the young sapling tree is planted on a narrow median strip, the only limbs in existence may interfere with people walking down the sidewalk. In this rare situation, it is recommended that the temporary limbs be headed-back, out of traffic's way, but allowed to continue feeding the lower portion of the trunk (see Figure 11.13). This is one of the few exceptions to the rule, "Don't head-back tree branches." When enough of the crown is above head height, begin to slowly remove the temporary limbs, perhaps two a year from opposite sides and different heights on the trunk.

And, of course, all cuts should be made to the branch collar.

Included Bark and Double Leaders

The other target of early pruning is included bark and the correction of double leaders. When a tree has two equal leaders (a *leader* is the uppermost or leading part of the trunk), separated at a narrow angle, bark can get trapped between them (called *included bark*). There is no connecting wood holding the two leaders together. As the two leaders expand they may push each other apart, and the tree can break. Another common

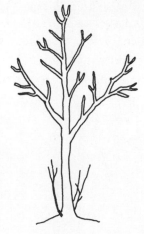

Figure 11.12 Remove suckers from the base of trees.

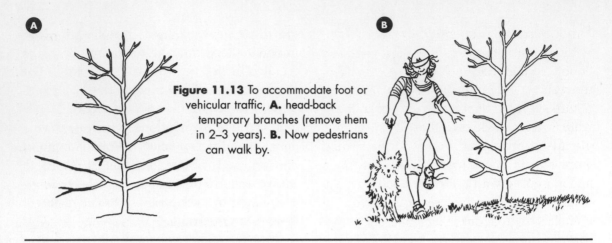

Figure 11.13 To accommodate foot or vehicular traffic, **A.** head-back temporary branches (remove them in 2–3 years). **B.** Now pedestrians can walk by.

included-bark situation arises between the trunk and a large side branch when the crotch angle is narrow. As the tree grows larger, the area of disconnect increases, as does the weight of the limb. These limbs are the ones prone to breakage, damaging the tree and ruining its good looks. Worse yet, if the tree is on a right-of-way or near a structure, people or property could get hurt. A little enlightened intervention early in the life of a tree can prevent a major disaster twenty years later.

Not all narrow crotches have included bark. If the attachment is a good one, you will see a little rumple of bark at the point of juncture. If there is included bark, the bark will disappear in a fold. V-shaped crotches often have included bark. U-shaped crotches are okay (see Figure 11.14).

If you find an included-bark branch on a young tree (a young tree that is going to grow up to be a big tree), go ahead and prune it off to the collar. In the case of a double leader (in which the two main leaders are the same size, with a narrow crotch), one of the leaders should be removed. The result can look quite severe, and the tree may even become lopsided. But fear not. The tree will grow new scaffold limbs higher up on the trunk and right itself naturally. Because there is no collar on a double-leadered tree, the cut will seem too steep or flush; but it is a proper cut nonetheless (see Figure 11.15).

Figure 11.14 Spotting included bark on a narrow-angled crotch **A.** In a V-shaped crotch the bark disappears into the trunk. This is a weak attachment. **B.** In a U-shaped crotch the bark is pushed up. This is a strong attachment.

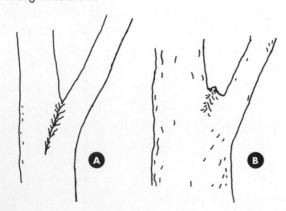

The Causes of Included Bark

A fair amount of branch crowding, including double leaders and included bark, is again the result of poor nursery industry practices. A three-year-old sapling looks like a buggy whip (it has no side branches). Nursery people discovered that homeowners would more readily buy a tree if it looked like a miniature tree with a crown. Such a tree is created by heading back the sapling, forcing branches to grow out in a cluster at the top. Unfortunately, the person who bought the tree must then spend the next several years training it back to a central leader and then slowly removing the lower, temporary branches as it gains height. And so it goes.

Other trees just seem prone to growing with included bark and double leaders, especially trees with an opposite branching pattern. Responsible nurseries maintain a strong central leader on shade trees and

do follow-up pruning to alleviate over-crowded branches.

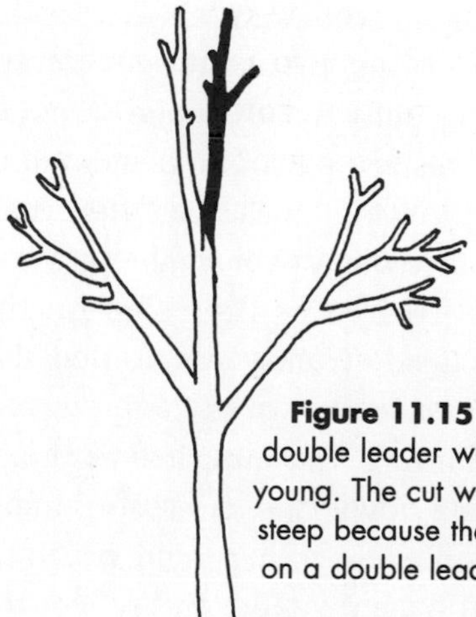

Exceptions to the Rules

Small maturing ornamental trees (as opposed to large, shade trees like oaks and elms) may already have their major limbs chosen, and they should not be trained back to a central leader. And they may be crowded at the point where the major limbs meet up. Certain cherry trees are an example. To "correct" it would mean ruining the tree.

Learn the natural habit and the estimated mature size of your tree. A nursery person can readily supply this information. Take, for example, the Florida or Eastern dogwood (*Cornus florida*). It often grows with an open, U-shaped, or even V-shaped double trunk. These forms have even more aesthetic interest than the single-leadered ones. And since dogwoods are sensitive to pruning cuts, don't try to make one into a single-leadered tree. The crown of a purple-leaf plum tree (*Prunus cerasifera* 'Atropurpurea') is likely to have mostly included-bark scaffolds. To try to eliminate them would be to eliminate the entire crown, creating a nightmare of water-sprout regrowth and perhaps even killing the tree. And, since this tree rarely gets large enough to do major damage when the limbs fail, the situation is best ignored. Another small tree, the Japanese maple (*Acer palmatum*), often has a crown consisting of included-bark scaffolds. Many of the new *fastigiate* (narrow growth form) trees developed to fit street right-of-ways consist mainly of included-bark limbs. But since these limbs are of relatively small size,

Figure 11.15 Correct a double leader when the tree is young. The cut will be very steep because there is no collar on a double leader.

and their angle to the trunk remains acute to the end, they are not considered dangerous.

On a medium- or large-growing young tree, you will sometimes come across a side branch or double leader that is too large to remove (i.e., a cut more than 2 or 3 inches). In this instance, attempt to suppress *one* of the leaders or the competing branch by selectively heading it back to a large lateral.

Large Trees with Included Bark

At some point the cut will be too large, and the tree too old, to remove included bark. At that point a professional arborist should be called in to do a *hazard tree evaluation*. Find an arborist who is certified by the International Society of Arboriculture (ISA). Only these people should be used for large tree work of any sort. Look for that information in the yellow pages under "Tree Service," or call the ISA's toll-free phone number (1-800-335-4391), or visit the Pacific Northwest chapter's website *(www.pnwisa.org)* to request a listing of local arborists. Of the arborists listed, only some will have the necessary training and sufficient field experience (years of removing fallen trees after storms) to be qualified to do hazard tree evaluations and not just tree work.

Find out if the tree poses a significant risk (ask for the hazard rating in numbers). Possible hazard mitigation procedures include cabling, bracing, thinning to reduce wind resistance, or some combination. Removal of the tree must also be considered if there is high risk of damage or injury to people or property. It can be a hard decision. You might want to ask your arborist, "What would you do if it were your tree?"

Summary

Young trees can take a lot of pruning, but they don't usually need much. Remove any suckers growing from the base of the tree. As the tree grows up, you may remove the lower limbs, a few at a time, from opposite sides of the tree, to allow for foot traffic. A few thoughtful cuts minimizing included bark (which causes weakly attached limbs) can prevent serious damage from occurring many years later. The old headmaster's adage goes "As the twig is bent, so grows the tree." It's true for the student, and it's true for the tree.

PRUNING TREES FOR POWERLINES

There is no good way to make (or feasibly keep) a big tree small. It just can't be done. They just grow faster and look uglier. And we can't let trees grow through the powerlines or the lights would go out every other day (and a lot of people would get electrocuted). This is unfortunate, since trees are pretty and wires are ugly. The best solution is to remove the big trees (that's the hard part) and replace them with smaller-growing ones. Or we could site the large-growing trees farther inside front yards so that they can crown out *over* the wires.

Undergrounding the utilities of major arterial streets, over the course of many years, is feasible and to my mind worth the cost and traffic aggravation. But reflect that it would *also* require the removal of long rows of large, existing trees. And the initiative for undergrounding would need to come from the public (not the utility companies). The combination of negatives—traffic trouble, increased utility rates, and removal of trees—could prove very unpopular.

Without permission to remove trees, the very best that line clearance crews can do is to prune trees to grow around the wires (usually in a V shape). This still looks funny, and it isn't good for trees. But it is better than topping, and there just are no other options (see Figure 11.16).

POLLARDING

Pollarding is a form of pruning "art." A special ornamental effect is achieved in keeping a big tree small: The thick trunk is in strong contrast to a relatively small, compact crown. Some trees are pollarded to accentuate secondary features, such as increasing leaf size (*Catalpa, Paulownia*) or stimulating bright-barked water sprouts (*Salix*). Correct pollarding is achieved through species selection, early training, and extensive, dedicated annual maintenance. Like other examples of pruning art, pollarded trees are rarely planted as individuals, but are best suited to mass plantings and/or as part of an overall formal design.

Pollarding vs. Topping

Pollarding bears a superficial resemblance to tree topping. But then again, to a man from Mars a surgery looks a lot like a mugging. In both cases somebody puts a knife in the subject's stomach and relieves him of all his money. The big difference is that one of

Figure 11.16 Three examples of proper line-clearance pruning: not a good thing, but doing a bad thing well. **A.** After under trimming **B.** After through trimming **C.** After side trimming

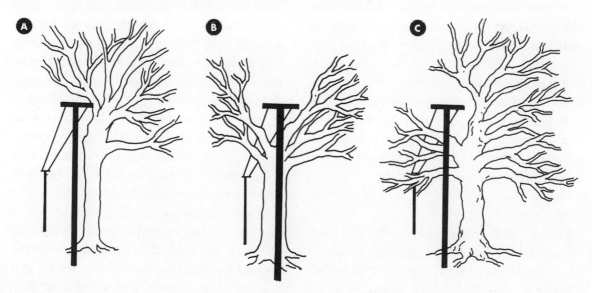

the procedures maintains the long-range health of the subject. Pollarding, like topping, eliminates the natural beauty of a tree's branch structure. It is extremely high maintenance, just like tree topping. Unlike topping, it maintains the long-term health of the tree. In Europe, pollarded trees have survived for five hundred years, actually living longer than their natural counterparts.

How Did Pollarding Start?

Pollarding began in Europe as a practical way to harvest a tree without killing it. A young deciduous tree would be headed back at a point above the reach of foraging deer and livestock, and then regrown. The resulting water sprouts (also called suckers by some) would be cut off every year or two to be used as animal fodder, made into baskets or brooms, or bundled together for firewood. Soon the tree would form a callused knob from which the water sprouts would regrow. The water sprouts regrow annually from dormant buds on the pollard head and are cut off again and again at their points of origin.

How Is Pollarding Done?

The right species must be used. Species that are traditionally pollarded include plane trees, sycamores, *Paulownia*, *Catalpa*, linden (Tilia), tree-of-heaven (Ailanthus), and horsechestnuts (Aesculus).

The Essential First Cut

The tree trunk or branches are headed back to the point where the pollard heads are to be located. The first training cuts on the tree should be less than 1 inch in diameter and should be made when the tree is young (Shigo defines a young tree as one that is under fifteen years old). Starting with large cuts on an older tree is unacceptable. The pollard head protects the trunk from rot. If the pollard head is removed, the trunk rots out and the pollard is ruined.

Pollard Styles

Usually trees are trained to a single head or to a series of pollarded branches originating from one point. As a simple guideline, one-third of the total height of the tree should comprise the crown and two-thirds the trunk. If the pollard heads are located too far out on the branches, the branches may break. Other styles exist, including vertical and "free form."

Sprout Removal

Sprouts that regrow from the pollard head are removed every year. Annual upkeep is essential not only for aesthetic appearance but also for tree health. Removing the sprouts every year from the time the tree is young ensures that the tree never becomes dependent on more canopy than it can grow in one year. Furthermore, if sprouts are left to become older they develop heartwood and become less able to react to the cutting, once again allowing rot to enter the tree.

To determine whether a certain tree is a true pollard or simple mal-pruned, ask the following questions.

1) Is a suitable species used?

2) Are all cuts made during the life of the tree under 1 inch in diameter?

3) Does it have a pollard head (or heads)?

4) Are sprouts removed every year?

5) Was it chosen and planted in this spot to be used as a formal pollard? (i.e., is it part of a larger overall formal design, such as castle grounds, a rose garden, or a boulevard?)

6) Is it likely that the tree will have the sprouts removed every year through several "owners" for perhaps a hundred years? (i.e., are people being charged admission to the garden where the trees are located, or are they city trees on the public dole?)

Summary

Pollarding looks like tree topping, but it isn't. Unlike tree topping, pollarding protects the long-term health of the tree. To be real pollarding, the process starts early in the life of the tree. No cut should ever be greater than 2 inches in diameter. Pollarding can and does keep a large tree small, but maintenance is costly and can never be deferred. Numerous shoots must be removed annually for the life of the tree. Pollarding is a very formal style and should match formal surroundings.

DOGWOOD *(Cornus)*

I like the entire genus of dogwoods. There is a reason the old favorites are old favorites—they're nice. The dogwood trees (as opposed to the dogwood shrubs such as *Cornus stolonifera* and the ever-so-cute but hard-to-grow dogwood ground cover, *C. canadensis*) have nice flowers and fall color. Many have attractive fruits, and some have an elegant winter branch pattern.

Water Sprouts

With regard to pruning, the most important thing to know is that dogwood trees throw water sprouts at the drop of a hat. (See Chapter 3, Suckers and Water Sprouts.) Prune too much (and it doesn't take much), and the next growing season will bring a bushel basket of water sprouts growing from the site of each cut.

With most trees, professionals advise that you can remove up to one-fifth of the foliage once every five years or so. But when pruning a dogwood tree, I say you should prune even less, maybe something like one-eighth of the foliage, or perhaps even one-sixteenth. If your dogwood doesn't grow a bunch of water sprouts from the pruning cuts in a year's time, then you have not overpruned, and you may try some more. Or not, if you don't want to tempt fate.

Bleeding and Timing

I am told that dogwoods bleed if pruned too early in the year. I have never seen this myself. When a tree "bleeds," it oozes sap from a pruning wound at a scary rate. I have read that bleeding does not hurt the plant, but it does bother the tree owner. The bleeding will stop once the tree's leaves emerge. For these reasons, and others, you usually prune in the early dormant season or in summer.

Sunscald

A dogwood's bark, especially that of the eastern dogwood *(C. florida)*, is thin and prone to sunscald—another reason not to overthin. I have heard a garden columnist advise people to shade the trunk by planting shrubs to cover it. But I think this just makes everything look crowded and messy. I would rather people just retain enough lower limbs on the tree trunk itself, or if not, try to see that that the tree is protected by high shade of other trees nearby. Dr. Shigo has stated that there is no such thing as sunscald caused solely by exposure to sun, not even on a dogwood. His work indicates that the splitting bark (sunscald) is a result of two cuts being made one directly above the other or that it comes from improperly placed cuts, specifically flush cuts (which remove the collar). In either case, the "take-home" message is avoid limbing up dogwoods whenever possible.

Common Sense Pruning

That doesn't mean that you shouldn't prune. If a limb is growing out into the pathway, prune it off to the branch collar. And certainly take off any deadwood, which is easy to spot in the summer because the dead branch has no live leaves on it. Old, previously mal-pruned or anthracnose-ridden trees will have plenty of deadwood. The greatest pruning secret is to remove deadwood. Good pruners do it first, and do it always. We also look for any obviously broken or damaged branches.

Size Reduction

Do not attempt height control or reduction! It won't work. Even using proper selective heading cuts, a dogwood tree will explode into a wild regrowth of ugly water sprouts. Prune those off and three times as many grow back!

Only on rare occasions is the selective heading cut used on a tree, especially a dogwood tree. I can remember such a cut I made on a previously mal-pruned eastern dogwood (C. florida). The branch in question had been headed before, and the end of it sported a nasty snarl of water sprouts. It was not an option to take the limb off entirely because it was too large and, in addition, the cut would have left an unbalanced-looking tree. So I followed the branch back from the tip to a place where there was a large, well-placed lateral branch and cut back to there. The remaining cuts on the tree were all true thinning cuts, removing lateral branches at their point of origin.

Thinning

Many of the remaining branches to be removed will be located near the crotches. Pruning out small branchlets from the space nearest where the branches attach to the trunk seems to make the tree look better defined and cleaner. On many dogwoods, especially the eastern dogwood, you can also accentuate the elegant branch structure by taking out some (never all) of the duplicating or parallel branches. In this species a branch of tends to have a smaller branch attached to it that exactly parallels its parent. Pruning off the "baby" branch may make your plant look better (see Figure 11.17). This sort of general thinning is the artistic part of pruning and is quite enjoyable. But be careful not to over-prune. This is hard once you start seeing how much better your tree looks thinned out. The overriding law is to stay within the pruning

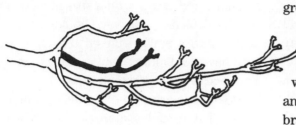

Figure 11.17 Remove the parallel "baby" branch.

budget—and remember, the budget is extremely small for dogwoods.

In general, you should work from the bottom up and the inside out, going in a generally upward spiral fashion. When confronted with a difficult pruning decision, I have found it best to skip it and move on. Just remove those branches that you are quite certain need to be removed and that will not leave a large "hole." Whenever I find myself paralyzed with indecision, I just move over to another part of the tree. I know I can come back later, after the rest is done or when I have viewed the tree from many angles.

Rehabilitative Pruning

Because dogwoods have such a lovely branch structure and because they water-sprout back so horribly, gardeners consider the mal-pruning of them as particularly bad. The three common forms of mal-pruning are topping, shearing into a ball or other shape, and overthinning. The good news is that, given enough time, dogwoods can be pruned back into good shape. But it's hard, and it takes nerves of steel. The overwhelming impulse is to remove all the ugly water sprouts, but that won't work—more just grow in their place.

The four steps to rehabilitative pruning are (1) wait, (2) thin, (3) wait, and (4) thin. The water sprouts will shoot way, way up, but they will eventually arch over and turn into youthful, pretty decent looking branches. The problem is that they will look different from all the original old branches, which are more curved and generally better looking. It is the contrast between the two types of branches that drives people crazy. As a professional I have developed specialty pruning that is done to mitigate the intolerable contrast. This keeps the tree owner calm long enough for the tree to outgrow the mal-pruning. It also does help the tree regain its natural shape sooner. Such pruning is counterintuitive, and it is very hard not to overprune while working on the tree. It will take five years or so before the tree is fully restored.

This is what you do: Take out all of the deadwood and stubs. Then wait a year. Go back in and take out just *a few* of the water sprouts from some of the clusters along the branches. Take out more of those closest to the branch crotches. Wait another year. Now, begin to make the two branch types (the old curved and the new straighter) look more uniform. Do this by removing some of the pretty curved branches, leaving straighter old growth (that's the part that doesn't make sense). Then cut off some of the most impossibly ugly, long, or wrong-way shoots of the new growth, leaving the shorter, more curvaceous new shoots. Now the top and the bottom (or the interior and the exterior) more closely resemble each other. Only do *some* of the pruning now. Come back next year or the year after and do more. One year you will come back and everything will look pretty good. Ah, success.

If you are having difficulty identifying a tree as a dogwood, refer to the old horticulture joke: How can you tell a dogwood? Answer: By its bark.

Cornelian Cherry

Cornus mas is a plant lover's tree because it blooms very early (February) with small, cheerful yellow flowers, and, like forsythia, it blooms before the leaves come on. In the fall, the cornelian cherries have big black fruits reminiscent of cherries (hence the name). Plant lovers tend to be blind to the faults of this tree: It lacks, shall we say, structural grace. Its branches tend to be skinny and straight, crossed like Ts, and parallel all over the place in a most unfortunate way. Only in great age do they develop more arching grace. Go easy on these trees. Pruning more won't make the branches any prettier, and water-sprout regrowth could make it a lot worse.

Eastern Dogwood

The eastern dogwood (*C. florida*) is a favorite small garden tree. It comes with either pink flowers or white, and there are even some with tricolor leaves. They bloom in May. They have the classic "turban's cap" buds—good for winter identification. They have good fall color. And they have the elegant branch structure I love to look at in the winter. They are more densely branched and shorter than the western dogwood (*C. nuttallii*). Many eastern dogwoods grow with a spreading double leader—which, by the way, should *not* be corrected into a single-trunked tree by people who have read more about pruning than they have actual pruning experience.

Dogwoods are also extremely prone to a nasty disease called anthracnose, in which all the leaves turn crispy brown in the summer and then fall off. Not all the eastern dogwoods have the disease. The healthy ones I see tend to be living in tall, open shade or mild sun as opposed to being tightly jammed in a courtyard. Good circulation is important. However, don't try to create good circulation by overthinning. You will just cause a billion water sprouts to regrow, and they really make the tree thick and prone to disease. On the other hand, cutting down the Douglas fir next to your dogwood can help. If you are not averse to a chemical program, there are products that can be sprayed on the tree that will effectively control the disease. Or you can just learn to live with the sight of crispy leaves in the summer.

By the way, all the dogwood trees look a little more drought stricken than they actually are. In the summer, the leaves directly exposed to sun start to fold, looking roughly like taco shells. This is normal and is even an identifying characteristic of the tree. This is not to say it's okay not to water. It's just something to know.

Kousa Dogwood

The kousa dogwood (*C. kousa*) seems to be somewhat disease resistant (meaning it doesn't get anthracnose as badly) and it is quickly becoming a new favorite small, street tree (especially for under powerlines). It can be a multitrunked, twiggy tree that in older age develops a nicer fan-shaped branching habit. Sometimes it blooms so heavily it pulls the limbs over. Very impressive. It is one of the trees that, when I was first becoming interested in gardening, I actually stopped the car and tracked down, going through several yards to find out what it was. (The others were ginkgo and paulownia.) The reason I was interested was that it bloomed solid white in the summer (when most everything else was through blooming) and then *faded to pink*! Ooooo! All the girls will want one. The same pruning rules apply as with other dogwoods.

Western Dogwood

My favorite dogwood tree is our native one, *C. nuttallii*, but I never recommend planting it because it is extremely susceptible to, and defenseless against, anthracnose. I have seen many trees die from this disease and it makes me so sad. Western dogwood is a much taller and more openly branched tree than the eastern dogwood. Its flower bracts are a creamy yellow-white, tinged slightly green. The flowers load up the trees in early spring, and one can see why it is British Columbia's provincial tree if you drive the country during the bloom time. They're everywhere and they're beautiful. And sometimes there is a second bloom in the fall. They have, in my opinion, the nicest branches, like delicate ripples of water, and nifty seed heads.

My opinion is not shared by all. When I was first learning gardening, I found two city gardeners in a Parks Department truck and picked their brains. I asked, "What's the difference between the eastern and western dogwoods?" They agreed that one was much denser that the other and they both said one was better than the other, though it turned out to be a different tree for each.

In an effort to simulate the feeling of a western dogwood in my yard (but without the anthracnose problem), I purchased an 'Eddie's White Wonder', a cross between the eastern and the western dogwood. I like it, though the flower bracts are not quite the same. It does have lovely fall color and only gets a little anthracnose at the bottom (where there is less air circulation). For several years I would go outside to find the top foot of the tree broken. I never figured out why, though I suspect a crow or squirrel had something to do with it. Following each break it would send up several new shoots, and I always felt I should be a good pruner and go up on a ladder and train it back to a single leader. But I found that if I just put it off long enough, the tree would choose its own new leader and the other competitors would subside into side branches. Now when people ask me if they should train a new leader on a broken top, I'm not sure what to say. Sometimes you should work on it (to prevent a double leader from developing), and sometimes you can ignore it and it will go away on its own. I have found this to be true of many problems in life. The hard part of problem solving is knowing which kind is which.

Summary

Because dogwood trees water-sprout easily, prune them lightly. No size reduction is allowed! Use thinning cuts, preferably small ones, and always cut to the collar. Remove no more than one-eighth, and more like one-sixteenth, of the live crown. Taking out deadwood is always okay and doesn't count against the pruning budget.

FRUIT TREES

Ask five knowledgeable gardeners how to prune fruit trees and you may well get five very different answers. This is because fruit trees have been grown for centuries as food sources rather than as ornamental trees. Therefore, everybody and his brother have developed a system to maximize fruit production and to make it simple to pick all the fruit, fast, and to make it easy to spray and to do more intensive pruning to produce more and more fruit.

If you want to maximize your fruit production, most county extension services have inexpensive bulletins. They will explain early training of young trees, pruning for production, and what to do with that ugly old apple tree to bring it back into good shape. You will learn the single leader method, the open center method, and the modified central leader method. You will learn about Type IV tip bearers with "blind wood." You will learn how to spread open young limbs (some people use clothespins) or to shore up old limbs with 2x4s to keep them from breaking. All the information in these bulletins will help you produce lots of fruit, but if it seems like too much work and you don't want to learn that much, try the Turnbull method of pruning fruit trees. It is less work, and you don't have to concentrate as hard. It makes your tree look good and will produce enough fruit to feed all your friends and family before the fruit rots.

Pruning Errors

First, let's go over what not to do. The two most common errors in pruning fruit trees are: (1) topping and (2) creating umbrella trees whose crowns are laden with ugly water sprouts. Topping is unequivocally bad for any tree, including fruit trees. The water sprouts that shoot back up from a topped fruit tree will not only be ugly, they are too busy trying to get enough leaves back in order to feed the tree to make much fruit.

However, many orchardists will reduce the height of apple and pear trees using the dropcrotch method of lowering trees. Dropcrotching means you selectively head back to a side branch of a decent size, say one-half the diameter of the parent stem. This is hard on the health of old trees and opens them up to rot. Younger trees (fifteen years old or less) withstand this height reduction better. Dropcrotching reduces the amount of water-sprout regrowth, as compared to topping, but does not eliminate it. On an old apple or pear, do not make a dropcrotch or thinning cut that exceeds 2 or 3 inches in diameter at most. Do not use it as a way to keep your ornamental tree small. Don't prune too much (no more than one-fourth of the total leaf surface) in any one year. And don't try to fix it all in one year. If

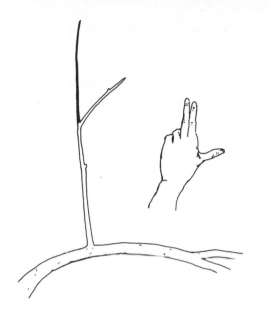

Figure 11.18 An upright 1-inch branch (width of two fingers) can be cut back to a half-inch side branch (width of one finger).

you have a tree that needs a lot of work, do it over several years.

The second error is the creation of "umbrella trees." This is the result when the pruner cuts to an outside branch year after year (called *bench-cutting*)—something you might be tempted to do if you already know something about pruning.

Apical Dominance

We now need to understand apical dominance. This is the only hard, technical part. Here is some basic tree and plant biology, which, when you get it, will make everything else clear to you, and you can also impress your friends with some fancy words. First, we will talk about the last bud on the end of a branch (the terminal bud). This bud releases a chemical that, moving via gravity, keeps the buds on down the line rather subdued. Think of it as the boss bud. When you cut off the end boss bud, or even bend it over, the chemical flow is disturbed and the other buds begin to grow.

Umbrella trees have terminal (boss) buds that are too low. Gravity prevents the chemical from reaching buds down the line, so a crown of water sprouts develops at the top. To help keep your old apple tree from producing excessive crown water sprouts, thin back low branches (they look like hooks) to a branch facing more up and out.

Pick out a major (scaffold) branch and follow it with your eyes. Does it dip down quite far, crossing other, lower scaffold branches and cluttering things up? Then you may selectively head back (prune) to one of its side branches that faces more upward and outward (a 40-degree to 60-degree angle is ideal). The scaffold branch now ends in a boss bud with greater *apical dominance*. This will reduce the number of returning crown water sprouts farther back as well as improve the looks of your tree. Keep in mind apical dominance if you attempt to reduce the height of your apple or pear tree. It is a good idea to cut back a tall vertical branch to a shorter branch that also faces upward (see Figure 11.18). Basically you are not trying to eliminate all vertical branches; you are simply replacing them with shorter, younger, and fewer vertical branches. This retains some apical dominance and allows the tree to grow a little every year. It's like a volleyball game—you rotate out a few of the tallest old watersprouts every year. You may have a forest of water sprouts that are the result of previous bad pruning. If you remove all of them, they all come back. Leave some to apically dominate the rest, shorten some to create a second story up, and thin out the rest. Note that the natural state of many old fruit trees is an umbrella, which is all right if the umbrella is low down on the tree where you can get the fruit, and if you don't care how it looks. But often the umbrella occurs high up on the tree, shading out the fruit below, and spoiling the overall good looks of the tree.

Pruning Fruit Trees

So, how do you prune an apple or a pear tree? The easiest way is just to prune it like other trees: for health and good looks. First, and always, take out the deadwood. Be thorough. Then take out some of the worst crossing or rubbing branches and the worst branches going the wrong way. These are the ones that start on one side of the tree, head the wrong way through the center, and come out on the other side. Also, thin or selectively head back some of the branches, especially toward the top (even a few big branches, up to 1½ in diameter) to increase light penetration and to lower your tree. This helps ripen the fruit lower down. It increases air circulation, too, which is important in order to discourage the numerous bacterial and fungal diseases that spoil the fruit. Look for narrow, weak big-branch crotches. Heavy, fruit-laden branches need to be strong. Narrow crotches are the ones that break. Now, you could stop here and you would have a pretty good-looking apple or pear tree without too much trouble. It will have fruit. But if you want to do more, read on.

Pruning for Fruit Production

Certain kinds of branches make more fruit buds or spurs than others. These are the ones that are situated in a not-too-horizontal position. You can pull or push new branches into such a position, or you can just start cutting out the ones that aren't in the right place and leave the ones that are. Nature makes fruit by sending up a young, straight-up soft branch. It flowers on the tip, and the flower turns into a fruit. The weight of the fruit pulls this supple branch over. As a branch gets older, it stiffens in a more horizontal position (see Figure 11.19). As the branch tips over, the apical dominance of the terminal bud weakens, and buds farther down the branch are released to form nice little side branches (laterals) and on them, teeny, tiny ¼-inch branches called spurs. These tiny spurs have fat flower buds (fruiting buds) rather than skinny leaf buds. We want the laterals and spurs.

In the winter, it is the fat-budded spurs that you see on trees that make you think what you're looking at might be a fruit tree. You can encourage some, but not all, of your side branches (laterals) to make spurs by heading (also called tipping back) to two or three buds. This works on pears and apples, but it doesn't work on cherries. And plums, apricots, and peaches are totally different. Now, if your main branch gets pulled too far over—past 90 degrees—apical dominance is diminished, too many buds are released, and

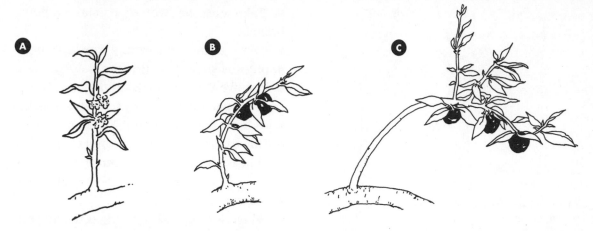

Figure 11.19 A. Vertical shoot flowers. **B.** Flowers become fruit weighing branch down to 45 degree angle. **C.** More horizontal branch develops laterals and sends up new vertical shoot.

those miserable water sprouts start charging back up.

In some senses, pruning fruit trees breaks all the rules for ornamental tree pruning. You try to keep your tree small, something that should never be done to other trees. Pruners often reduce fruit trees dramatically, which would be extremely bad pruning on a maple or oak. We also head a lot. We head side

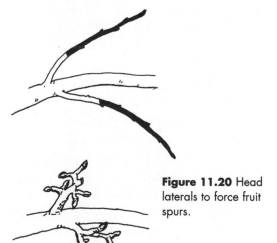

Figure 11.20 Head laterals to force fruit spurs.

branches (laterals) to force them to make spurs (see Figure 11.20). We shorten major scaffold branches with heading, especially young ones, so that they won't swing in the wind and lose fruit (see Figure 11.22). Heading causes these branches to get fatter or stouter. We need stout branches to hold up heavy fruit. On apples and pears, especially, we do a lot of heading.

Other Fruit Trees

Peaches, nectarines, and Japanese prunes are pruned quite heavily, with scary-looking large heading cuts. Instead of setting up persistent spur systems, as apples and pears do, these trees make fruit on new wood. The heavy pruning is done to force renewal shoots to grow, and also to keep the branches short enough that they don't break under the fruit load.

And then there are the cherries and European plums, which you shouldn't prune

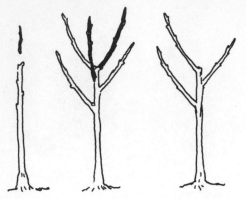

Figure 11.21 Heading a "whip" is done to create a low crown. In year 3, remove crowded branches and those with included bark (weak crotches).

much at all. Deadwood removal is always okay.

Let's recap what we've gone over thus far. Prune your fruit tree like any other tree:

1. First, and always, take out all of the deadwood.

2. Take out the worst crossing, rubbing branches.

3. Take out the worst wrong-way branches.

4. Take out some, not all, of the water sprouts.

5. Remove weak crotches if they are or will become part of the main framework (scaffold) branches (see Figure 11.21.).

6. Thin (don't strip) all those branches rather than heading them, and do more thinning on the top to encourage light penetration and air circulation.

When dealing with water sprouts on your apple or pear tree, remember to cut some out altogether; leave some alone (don't cut off the tips), since they will flower and fruit and be pulled over and produce more spurs later; head back some water sprouts to thicken them up into second-story branches. Try to head back to another upright side branch and not to a horizontal branch that would water sprout back madly (see Figure 11.23).

Figure 11.22 Training a young fruit tree. **A.** Before **B.** Growth after

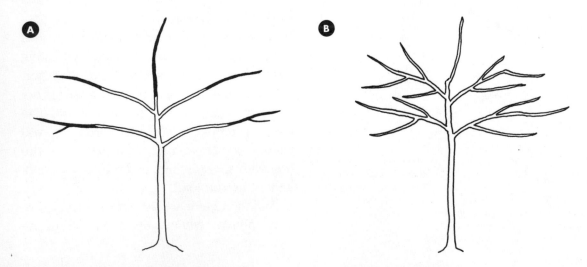

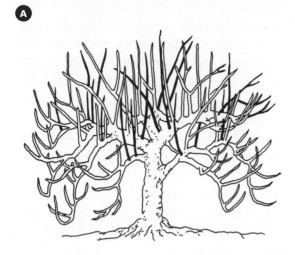

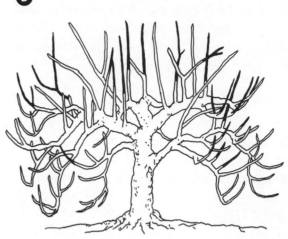

Figure 11.23 A. Leave some water sprouts, cut some out altogether, and shorten some. Remove water sprouts up to 2 inches in diameter.

B. Shorten some water sprouts to a side branch or bud.

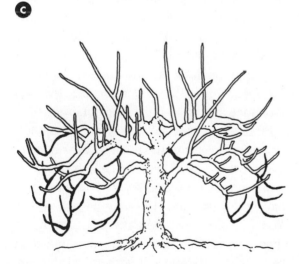

C. Remove lowest "hooks" to reduce the recurrence of water sprouts and make the tree look better.

D. Finished apple tree.

If you want to encourage more fruiting on your apples and pears, you can prune for more horizontal branches. You can bend back laterals to force more spurs to form. See, you're an expert already!

More About Fruit Trees

• Pruning of young trees (under six years) is done to develop strong, low framework branches and not much else. In fact, it may take a while longer for your tree to fruit. Go easy in the early years. There are some newer varieties that fruit earlier.

• Old trees can be invigorated by heavy pruning to produce new wood and spur systems, although you may experience a temporary drop in production when you cut off older and lower limbs or "hooks."

• Summer pruning of fruit trees is all right if the tree is vigorous and healthy and well watered. Spotting deadwood is easy in the summer. Summer pruning can be useful in reducing the spread of fungus-bacterial diseases that like damp weather, and it will help reduce water sprout regrowth. It generally slows the growth rate and will help restrict the size of your tree. It is harder on the plant, however, so go easy, and never prune during a drought.

• Many fruit trees need a cross-pollinator tree in the neighborhood. The cooperative extension service in your area has lists of what type of tree pollinates what for you and which fruit trees do well. Cross-pollinators are something to consider when you are planning your orchard.

• New dwarf varieties called "spur type" apples don't need to be pruned to make them set up spurs. They do it themselves. In fact, be careful that you don't prune the spurs off.

• Bee activity is needed for pollination. If it has been a very wet spring, you may not get enough bee activity. Bees, like some Parks Department workers I know, won't work in the rain. On the other hand, if you don't see any bees and it has been sunny, it may be that someone in your neighborhood has inadvertently killed them with pesticides. Misapplication of some commonly used pesticides can wipe out entire hives. If your neighbor doesn't read the label and applies something like Sevin on plants in bloom during the middle of the day, a bee might bumble into a flower and then carry the poison back to the hive and kill the entire hive. This is a tragedy for the orchardist as well as the bees.

• Fruit trees need sun in order to flower and fruit. If your tree never sets fruit, stand next to it and look up. If you see big trees or condominiums, this may be your problem. You're in too much shade. Try removing your fruit tree and planting a vine maple, Japanese maple, or some other understory tree that will look nice and do well in these conditions.

• Fruit trees, especially Gravenstein apples, sometimes get into the habit of bearing fruit every other year. This routine can be somewhat modified by pruning. If you wish, you can ignore it. Your tree may be too young. You'll have to wait, be patient! Or your tree may be too old. You'll have to prune it or remove it and replace it with something you like better.

• You can improve the size and quality of your fruit by thinning branches so that more light gets to the interior of the tree. Also, you can thin spurs and baby fruit so that more energy gets put into the remaining branches or buds for bigger, tastier fruit. (Mother Nature will do some fruit thinning for you. In the "June drop," the tree will shed away any small apples that have not developed seeds.)

• There is a difference in the severity of pruning of European and Japanese plums. Japanese plums should be pruned heavily, like peaches; the strong upper wood should be cut back to weaker branches. European plums should be pruned very lightly. Japanese plums and European plums will not cross- pollinate each other.

• These days you don't have to suffer with big fruit trees; nurseries now have new dwarfing rootstocks. So if you want fruit and less work, chop down that old tree and plant a new dwarf one. Dwarfing rootstocks come in small, smaller, and very small. Check them out with your extension service. A really smart-sized fruit tree is about 4 feet tall. Unless, of course, you love that old tree—then keep it.

• Do not try to make your cherry tree small again by topping it. It won't work. They have yet to develop a really good dwarfing root-stock for cherry trees, although there are a few available. That's why that big bucket truck with the 70-foot extension is called a "cherry picker."

• People often want to lower cherry trees because they cannot stand the waste of the fruit on the top where they cannot reach. Removing the top will not actually increase cherry production down low. Other people welcome the day when the tree gets tall enough that the birds leave the lower cherries alone.

If much of the information in this section seems very confusing and self-contradictory—well, it is. Even people who specialize in fruit tree pruning are often unsure and easily swayed to other methods and ways. Take heart—teachers send students out to practice on apples and pears because these trees are so forgiving. In Eastern Washington, machines mow them to force fruit production. Stay away from topping—especially your cherry tree—and you'll do okay.

Summary

• Traditionally, fruit trees, like roses, are for people who like to prune and spray a lot. Try buying very, very disease-resistant, and very dwarf trees to reduce these maintenance chores.

• You can, if you like, prune fruit trees as you would ornamentals, for health and good looks, and leave it at that.

• Horizontal branches bear more fruit than vertical branches.

• All fruit trees are not created equal.

Group A. Head a lot. Prune hardest.
Peach, apricot, nectarine, Japanese plum

Group B: Keep young trees short. Head laterals to encourage fruit spurs. Prune less than Group A.
Apples, pears

Group C: Hard to keep trees short with pruning. No topping. No heading laterals. Train early by bending branches. Prune least.
Cherries, European plums

JAPANESE LACELEAF MAPLE

(Acer palmatum 'Dissectum'*)*

The laceleaf maple is king. Who would deny it? The magnificence of its winter branch pattern is such that even most hedge-shear maniacs will halt before its awesome delicacy and grace (see Figure 11.24). If you're looking for the perfect focal point for a small and frequently viewed area, you'd be hard pressed to do better.

But just how to properly prune a Japanese laceleaf maple is a source of great concern for the average homeowner, and a source of great joy (and income) for the knowledgeable professional.

What Doesn't Work

Don't try to keep a laceleaf maple small. I have seen gardens where people have diligently tried to contain them, using selective thinning cuts to keep the top down and selective heading to restrain the width. But the heavily thinned branches seem to rapidly age, peel, and crack—a sign that dieback is next. Overthinning and overpruning can also

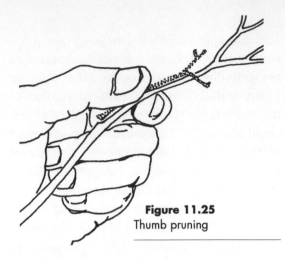

Figure 11.25
Thumb pruning

stimulate a resurgence of shoots, which are always a warning bell that something is wrong.

The most common cause of mal-pruning is mis-siting. Usually the dainty baby maple is perched at the front stairway's edge, ensuring inevitable obstruction of foot traffic. The best solution to the severely mis-sited tree is to transplant it. Go ahead. We (that's the royal "we," meaning John Turnbull) recently salvaged a forty-year-old laceleaf maple (8 feet by 8 feet by 5 feet tall) and transplanted it to the Turnbull Home for Orphan Plants. When moving a Japanese maple, take special care not to break the branches—they are quite brittle. Immediate water is the key to success, as is diligent watering the first full year.

I have only seen one full-grown Japanese laceleaf maple that has been successfully reduced in size. It was in a Japanese garden within a larger botanic garden in Missouri. Farther on in the same landscape was its twin. But that one looked sadly nipped and nibbled on, no doubt from a similar attempt to "control" it.

Figure 11.24 The Japanese laceleaf maple has beautiful winter branching.

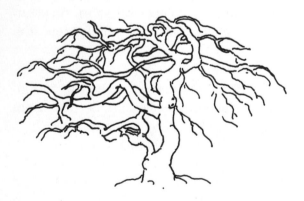

The Miracle of Deadwooding

Gardeners love to get their hands on an old, neglected laceleaf because they are assured of transforming a scraggly brown mop into a piece of artwork. I remember one impressed client who said, "I thought I just didn't have the right kind." And it's so easy! Eighty percent of the work is simply the removal of collected dead leaves and accumulated deadwood. Just gently run your fingers through the branches, combing out the leaves. I always feel like the hairdresser of the Goddess Flora. Then the gardener "thumb prunes" out the tiny dead twigs that have occurred since last year. They are easy to spot, since they are light gray in color, not matching the rest of the living branch. Using thumb and forefinger, the pruner gently squeezes, until the dead twig snaps out (see Figure 11.25).

Larger dead and dying branches should also be removed. They are usually located at the bottom and inside of the tree, where they have been shaded out. Which brings me to correct positioning. Work from the bottom up and the inside out. Like an auto mechanic, the pruner is often found lying under the tree, legs sticking out, working on his or her back. It's a fine place to spend a warmish summer day

Prune not only the dead branches but also the limbs that have been so severely shortened that they are of no further use (and would probably die sooner or later anyway).

Timing

I like summer pruning because you can gauge when the tree has been sufficiently opened up to see inside to "the bones." Laceleafs tend to get a bit heavy and thick looking in full sun, and they can be successfully thinned out to give them a lacy feel. Take care not to thin or overthin in very hot weather, since the bark is easily sunburned (despite how it sounds, sunburning the bark on any tree is a serious problem). Or you can prune laceleafs in the early winter. For novices it is easier to follow the branch patterns when the leaves are off, but it can be harder to spot dead wood. To make sure a limb is dead, use your hand pruners to peel back a tiny bit of bark. If the thin sheath of cambium just beneath the bark is green, the branch is still viable. If it is brownish or worse, cut away!

Not long after the winter solstice, the sap begins to rise in maples, and if you prune before the leaves are out, you are likely to see the cuts "bleed." I am told that this doesn't permanently damage the tree, but it looks scary, and most good gardeners wait to do

Figure 11.26 Summer pruning: Assume the position.

major work until the leaves are out. Once in late January I cut a large limb on a sunny day. It wept heavily, and I worried that as the temperature dropped to below 30 degrees that night the wet area might freeze and crack.

Tools

More so than on any other plant, it is important to use high-quality, sharp pruning tools when pruning laceleaf maples. The cuts must be exact, neither leaving the hint of a stub, nor cutting too close (see Figure 11.27). In the first instance the stub dies back and ruins the good looks of your elegant plant; in the other case, the flush cut can open the branch to disease and decay. I vividly recall my Japanese pruning instructor showing us "shell pruning." He ran his hands along the branch and extolled the virtues of "smoothness" and "agedness" in our pruning endeavors. The branches on laceleafs are so brittle, and the bark so thin, that it's easy to make pruning cut mistakes, tears, or stubs. Invest in a professional pair of bypass pruners and an ARS-type folding pruning saw. ARS, Felco and Corona are the three brands recommended most. Julie Hale, a PlantAmnesty gardener, has located a special tool called a Japanese keyhole saw, which works especially well to make the fine and exacting cuts required on Japanese maples.

Some little maples are so engineered that their skirts drag in the mud. That is to say, the lower limbs flow down to the ground and beyond. Remedy this situation by taking off some of the lower limbs entirely to the trunk (even some fairly big ones) and selectively heading some of the others. Always cut back

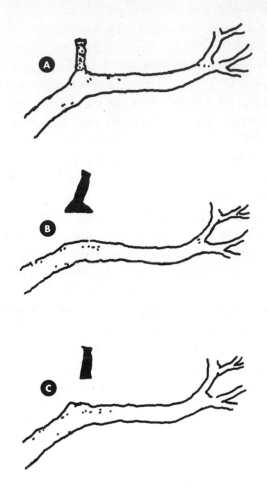

Figure 11.27 Where to cut **A.** Don't cut too far out; it leaves a stub. **B.** Don't flush-cut; it's bad for the plant. **C.** Cut just right.

to a side branch that is big enough to take over as the branch end. Usually the side branch is at least one-half the diameter of the parent stem, and faces out.

The rest of your pruning is done either to solve a problem (e.g., removing the one most interfering limb that sticks out into the sidewalk) or to lend definition to the plant (see

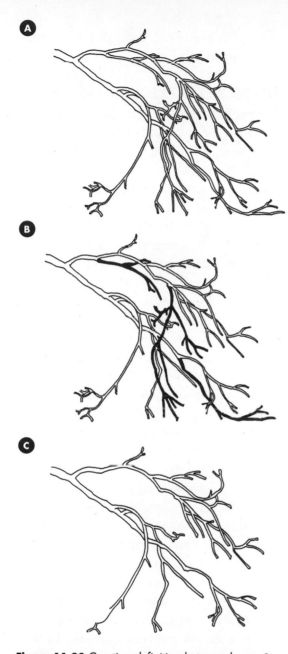

Figure 11.28 Creating definition between layers **A.** Original side branches **B.** Remove lower branches with selective heading and thinning; always cut to upper, out-facing branches. **C.** Layers are separated on the finished branch.

Figure 11.28). Thinning out branches uniformly throughout the plant will give it that airy look. Be careful not to "strip" them all out to the ends. Better to take some large and some small branches, frequently standing back and walking around to judge your progress. It helps me to think that I am separating various layers of limbs rather than thinning each branch separately. When selective pruning, always take off the lower portion of a branch, cutting it back to a side branch that "leaps" upward and outward. It reminds me of opening an umbrella.

Remember, it's easy to take it off, hard to put it back. New pruners tend to overthin. It is true that you take out crossing/rubbing branches, but remember you are not trying to eliminate them all, especially if they represent a fair portion of the plant. To remove all the crossers/rubbers would mean total destruction of a laceleaf, whose branches tend to wander and double back in curious ways. It is more important to spot the branches that wander too far from one side of the tree to the other, that are too straight (not as pretty as curving ones), and that have little taper to the stem (see Figure 11.29).

Finish by thinning the top of the plant, which I find the most difficult part of the job. I often do this portion from outside. In the end the plant should have a uniform "beaded curtain" or "lace" effect.

The entire process of pruning a large, neglected laceleaf maple can take between one and three hours, so remember to be patient and move slowly. In the end you will be amply rewarded. The laceleaf does all the

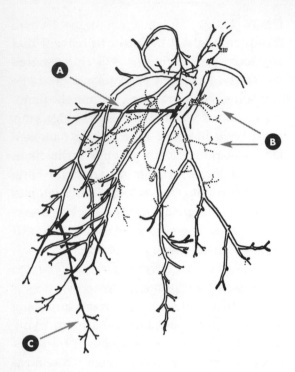

Figure 11.29 Remove deadwood (dotted lines), some branches that rub, and ones with little taper or curve. **A.** Too far, too straight, no taper **B.** Deadwood **C.** Touches the ground.

work, but you'll get all the credit. Long live the king!

Summary

The art of fine pruning is seen at its best on the Japanese laceleaf maple. Working from underneath the plant, flat on your back, deadwood and remove dead leaves first. Then use a combination of selective thinning and selective heading cuts to lace-out the plant. Favor branches that curve pleasingly and those that face upward or outward. Create layers. Save the topmost part for the end, with final touch-up pruning being done from

outside. Do not try to keep this plant from getting larger.

JAPANESE MAPLE *(Acer palmatum)*

Pruning Japanese maples is easy, and it reveals the inner beauty of the tree so that it can be seen even in the summer when it is cloaked in leaves.

When I landscaped my yard almost twenty years ago, I put a Japanese maple (the kind that makes a small tree, not the weeping Japanese laceleaf maple, which I'll discuss a few pages further on) in front of the living-room window. Through the years I have watched it grow. I love how the raindrops hang on the limbs like a string of pearls. I love how a winter snowfall traces a white line atop each of its dark and delicate limbs. Because it's a deciduous tree, it was a good choice for the south side. My south side isn't blazing hot and totally exposed, as it's a bit set back from the street and it's in temperate Seattle. I suspect that in a more severe climate a southern exposure might scorch the leaves. The Japanese maple is an understory tree, preferring a slightly shaded and sheltered spot. The shade, in turn, results in the classic open canopy that shows off the Japanese maple's fine trunk and branch structure.

Thank heavens my maple lets the precious winter sunlight in, but keeps the hot summer sunlight out. But because it's in a sunny spot, it grew up thick and full. After only a few years, my window was totally obscured. I signed up for a Japanese pruning class to learn how to prune it so that I could continue to see through it. Now I sit on the sofa with my morning coffee and newspaper and peek through the branches. I can observe my little corner of the world without totally exposing myself to it. I make note of neighbors walking to the bus stop and the kids going to school. And I can take appropriate action when I see stray dogs enter the forbidden territory of my yard or a squirrel start to dumpster-dive for bulbs.

My tree has grown quite large, standing 20 or more feet, crowning out over my front porch roof. Ever since we adopted a full-sized Japanese laceleaf maple for the backyard (Little Red), we refer to the one in front as Big Red. Sometimes in the afternoon the sun casts a shadow of delicate leaves inside the house. It looks like someone painted a Japanese mural, except that the gray shadow leaves will occasionally shift and sway on the wall. And looking directly out at the tree is impressive too. The window frames the trunks, which curve and recurve artfully.

To add to my viewing pleasure, a flock of the tiniest little round birds come to visit my tree every fall. Out of nowhere they start appearing, zipping in one by one, and soon the tree is chock full of tiny, chirping budgies. They busily groom the branches, defying gravity as they do, sometimes hanging upside-down or walking up vertical limbs to eat unseen insect tidbits. And then, after a while, the birds leave. It ends as it began, with just one or two birds flying off at a time. And then suddenly they're all gone. The tree is empty and quiet again.

My Mistake

The Japanese maple I brought home was a perfectly globe-shaped, multiple-trunked tree. I thought myself pretty smart to situate it far enough, about 4 feet, from the window. As it turned out, it was still poorly placed, growing easily thrice as big as I had imagined (and still going). Years ago rain-laden limbs were hanging down, intruding onto the pathway, onto the porch, onto the roof, and into the wires (the telephone line). Not so smart after all. Had I chosen a fan-shaped tree I would have had a much easier job training it to stay out of harm's way. I feel guilty every time I have to prune another limb.

Japanese maples—like snowdrop trees, dogwoods, and many other small trees—are mis-sited by landscape designers all the time. They place them as a garden's focal point, too close to the walkway or road, as if "small tree" meant "doesn't grow." Small trees or shrubs will still shock the owner with their increase in size over the years. Yet these plants are correctly labeled because when they grow up, they will still be relatively much smaller than the vast majority of trees (which are 40 to 80 feet or more). As you may have surmised, I know most of the common garden mistakes because I've made them myself.

Heading-Back Temporary Branches

At the suggestion of a friend I tried containing my tree's size by selectively heading-back its limbs, all over, every year. Selective heading means making a branch shorter by pruning it back to a smaller side branch. (Selective heading is the right way to make a branch shorter.) Each cut I made was less than ¼ inch in diameter. I kept pruning Big Red in this way for several years. I did the tree no harm, but I still failed to stop it from increasing in size. The tree just seemed to redouble its efforts to grow to its predetermined size.

I watch landscapes over years, and I've seen many people try to keep Japanese maples and most other trees small, both the right and the wrong way; I've never seen it work. Actually I saw it once. A two-story Japanese maple had been arduously pruned for a water view from the upstairs windows. The owner wanted to know if her arborist had "butchered it." I said no, it looked amazingly good for an attempt at the near impossible. The result of years of dropcrotching was that the branches splayed out like a giant candelabrum. I told her that it would be better for her to choose: tree or view. (Later I heard that I had told her to "take the tree out!")

Over the long haul, I suspect that the best you can achieve with dedicated, annual pruning for size control is about a 10 to 15 percent reduction in size as compared to an unpruned tree. The constant time, money, and effort it causes rarely justify the difference. I now think of tree pruning as a way to channel or direct growth, not as a way to stop or even to slow down growth. One good adage I've heard is "You exert your control over trees when you choose which one to plant."

Selective heading works only as a temporary holding measure to keep lower branches out of the way until such time as they can be completely removed. You might well ask the question "Why not remove them as soon as they are spotted as being in the way?"

It is recommended that the lower limbs of all young trees be kept for a few years. The reason is that the photosynthate made by those limbs (or, more accurately, by the leaves of those limbs) is used to strengthen and fatten the lower portion of the trunk where they are attached. And we want strong, well-tapered tree trunks because they are less likely to break in windstorms. For street trees, owners are admonished to shorten and keep the lower limbs until two-thirds of the tree is above head height. Then the limbs should be removed slowly, one or two a year on different sides of the tree trunk and at different heights. Avoid pruning two branches located one directly above the other during the same season.

On the other hand, you shouldn't wait too long to remove the lower limbs on a Japanese maple or any other tree. In nature, the young, lower limbs are naturally shaded out as the forest grows up. In the city and in the open, the limbs are surrounded by sun and will stay on indefinitely. Your job is to prune them so that they don't interfere with foot or vehicular traffic, before they get too big. How big is too big is, of course, a relative situation. For example, a 2-inch-diameter branch on a massive 100-foot tree is nothing, but on a 15-foot Japanese maple, it's a major limb. Taking off large limbs does harm to trees, even when done properly, so minimize the damage by timing your pruning cuts just right. Not too soon, or too late in its life—but just right.

Branch-Collar Cuts

Hopefully, all readers know how to make a proper collar cut by now. If not, be sure to read the section "Tree Biology and Pruning" at the beginning of this chapter. Remember, the very nicest thing you can do for your tree is to learn where to make the cut. (Skip the pruning paint—it doesn't work. Skip the fertilizer spikes. Skip the trunk wrap.) New pruners are apt to cut off the bottom part of the collar. A few years ago I instructed my apprentice on collar cuts and assigned her to cut off a lower limb of my maple—just to help her get her courage up. I came out later to find an oval face, instead of a round face, on the trunk. (*Face* is a term referring to the light-colored area that shows where the cut was made.) It hurt like a poke in my eye; a flush cut on my tree! As soon as she left, I rubbed a bit of dirt on the face, hoping to hide it from my arborist friends.

Thinning

Generally speaking, pruning a Japanese maple consists of thinning out the tree using a combination of larger and smaller thinning cuts spread evenly throughout the crown (meaning you don't just strip out all the internal branches). You start from the bottom and work up and out. First, remove all of the deadwood: dead twigs, dead stubs, and dead limbs. They are easy to spot in the summer because they have no leaves. But even in the winter deadwood is a different color from live wood. On Japanese maples it's gray and snaps out easily when pressure is applied.

Also look to remove interfering branches, say the one that sticks out at eye level into foot traffic. Before you do, though, consider how your tree will look without that particular branch. And what, then, will your next move be? Plan a few steps ahead. Sometimes it helps to have a friend standing outside the tree. You jiggle the branch you want to remove and they tell you if it will look right. Then switch places. Perhaps you should head it back for now. Perhaps not. If the in-the-way branch is a major portion of the tree, it is often a better solution (though certainly more difficult for people to accept) to move the pathway to accommodate the tree.

Other candidates for removal are branches that rub other branches—if they're not too large, that is. More than once I've seen people destroy their tree by blindly following the pruning rules.

After this, the rest of your pruning is to create definition between the layers of branches. As you work up the tree, follow the individual scaffold branches with your eyes. Look to remove branches that head too far up or dip too far down (see Figure 11.30). In my mind, I think of the floating lady in the magic trick. The magician appears to pass a hoop over her body to prove that she is not suspended from wires. My branch is the lady, and as I move the imaginary hoop over her I run into the wrong branches (too far up or too far down). I cut them off, leaving a relatively level plane. The Japanese pruning term for this sort of thinning is *fan pruning*.

Keep moving as you prune, lest you overthin the tree. When considering any particular area of branches, I prune only the easiest choices. When I find myself at a loss as to which branch to cut, debating in my mind the pros and cons of removing this or that branch, worrying if I will create too big a hole, I take it as a signal to move on. You needn't, and probably shouldn't, finish cutting off all the "wrong" branches. Remember, you can come back to it later—later in the day, or even next year or the year after.

The Pruning Budget

The overriding factor in pruning is the pruning budget. This is rarely referred to in pruning literature, but it is critical. In fact, if you prune out *all* the "wrong" branches in a Japanese maple or any other plant, you have overpruned it. Each plant has a set point, and if you prune more than it likes, you stimulate water-sprout regrowth and/or dieback of branches. The set point varies by species, but in general the pruning budget for trees is much less than for shrubs. The commonly quoted "one-third" rule is for forsythias, not maples. Try to limit yourself to removing no more than one-eighth or less of the leaf canopy in a year. (Deadwood doesn't count in the budget—it's dead.) You can come back next year for more, assuming that you don't do too much now.

Go especially easy on young trees (less than five years old) in your landscape. In an effort to get that open, fan-tree look, people are apt to prune too much too soon. How will you know? Next year the tree grows out with fast, skinny, floppy new shoots. They look a lot like suckers or water sprouts except that they originate from perfectly good, uncut tips of branches. My friend Tina calls them "maple squirts."

The pruning budget also varies among different members of the same species. There is a variegated (two-tone) Japanese maple that has become quite popular recently that is naturally much more stiff and twiggy. I've been asked to prune it to make it look more like its airy and graceful cousins, but I resist. It is much better to let it grow for a few years and then begin the thinning process, slowly, and wait to see how it responds next year. If the tree responds with a lot of weak and

Figure 11.30 A. Thinning a branch includes the removal of a dead lateral (dotted line) and laterals that reach too far up or down. **B.** Finished branch

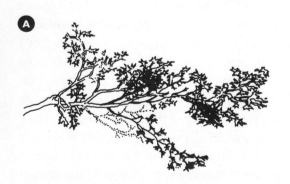
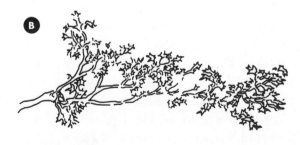

spindly shoots, it has been pruned too much. Do less, not more, in the future.

Correcting Mistakes

One common mistake in pruning a Japanese maple is overthinning. Another mistake is to top or tip it. Although I think of the Japanese maple as sort of a delicate tree (perhaps because of the thin bark or because it gets sunburned and windburned), it recovers pretty well from the various forms of mal-pruning. New branches will form out of the regrowth of water sprouts.

I remember gardening for a charming Scandinavian lady in Bellevue. She loved her garden. The hepaticas in it reminded her of home. She fed me cookies and very strong coffee at lunch. Among my chores was seeing what could be done with the three full-grown Japanese maples that had been topped a few years earlier. They were a mess. The mal-pruning had simply been a mistake on her part. People see topping done and they assume it must be okay. Well, two of the three trees looked quite a bit better after some rehabilitative pruning. The worst one, however (cuts 2 inches in diameter!), never made it back and finally had to be cut down.

The first step to rehab pruning is WAIT, and it's the hardest. It's impossible to believe that all those horridly floppy water sprouts will ever turn into anything substantial, but they do. Over time (a year or two) they actually stiffen and lift back up. It's true. I swear. I've seen it with my own eyes. Then you can begin to take off the lesser of the new branches: the ones that still flop, head the

wrong way back into the center of the tree, or are too crowded with the others in a cluster. Deadwood and especially dead stubs from mal-pruning are always fair game, and the biggest aesthetic improvement will be in removing them. Do your rehab pruning (except the deadwood) over a few years. If you take off too much, too soon, guess what happens? A bunch more water sprouts are stimulated into growing out.

Summary

Japanese maples are good candidates for thinning. They take an average amount of pruning, for a tree. Remove no more than one-eighth of the live crown, plus all the deadwood. You may want to prune to create layers, called fan pruning. No heading, no size control. If removing a lower limb or two solves a problem (like interference with foot traffic), then do so if the limbs aren't too large (no thicker than half the diameter of the parent trunk).

MAGNOLIA *(Magnolia)*

Every year I regret more and more every cut I've ever made on a magnolia tree. That's because no matter how few or how small the cuts, they always seem to turn into a mess of water sprouts, ugly as sin and impossible to get rid of.

That's a real shame, given that the branch patterns of the deciduous magnolias are some of the best Mother Nature has to offer. I have to stop myself from bringing pruned branches home from work. (My house would be full up in a week with the interesting flora I come across.) Not only do the magnolia's branches divide often, but the tips are fattened like fruit-tree spurs, and they end in eminently touchable fuzzy buds, an identifying characteristic of the species.

The three most common magnolias in the Pacific Northwest are the saucer magnolia, the evergreen or southern magnolia, and the star magnolia. Take care not to ask too much of a magnolia tree, or she will punish you for a lifetime. But given just the right spot and the freedom to grow unaltered, a magnolia will reward you with much of the best that trees have to offer: bloom, scent, and a lovely winter silhouette.

Pruning Magnolias

My best advice about pruning magnolias is—don't. Having said that, I confess that sometimes I do. If the lowest limb stretches into the driveway or runs through an unmovable shrub, I may prune it off to the trunk or to a likely upper lateral. If an upper scaffold dips down too far, crowding another major limb, I may lighten it up with many small thinning cuts or I may remove a large lateral or two. Then it springs up and out of the lower network of limbs. That looks better. And I have been known to thin an old crowded branch. This is good fun, and the results are a crisper, cleaner-looking branch pattern.

But earlier this year I noticed an unflattering, straight water sprout on a star magnolia that I had headed back the previous year, ever so lightly and selectively, to get it out of the concrete pathway. Now when I prune, I do so with even greater guilt and apprehension. I suggest you do too. And avoid it altogether if you can.

Rehabilitative Pruning

The good news is that magnolias are good compartmentalizers. This means that if some misinformed, well-meaning neophyte tops the heck out of a magnolia tree, the tree won't die. The tree will instead wall off the incoming rot organisms, explode into a bazillion water sprouts, and grow back to its original size in a year or two. Of course, it looks horrid, as does any magnolia that has been mal-pruned—topped, tipped, or overthinned. Overthinning is, by definition, pruning to the extent that water sprouts are formed in response to the cuts. (Over-thinning is harder to determine in many conifers, since as a general rule they can form few waterspouts in response to cuts.) In the case of magnolias, whether or not any particular thinning cut responds with water sprouts will depend on several factors: the size of the cut, how well it is made, the total amount of foliage being removed, and whether or not the remaining branch is exposed to sun. You may get away with making a few small, internal, well-made collar cuts. Otherwise, expect to see water sprouts next growing season (see Figures 11.31 and 11.32).

If you leave the water sprouts growing long enough (and they do get long!) they will turn back into branches. It's true! With a little judicious reduction in the numbers of sprouts (cutting out a very few of the smallest, wrongway, or crowded sprouts in each cluster), you can eventually, over the span of four or five years, get a crown of sorts back on the tree. I have personally trained a group of water sprouts from a skinned-up saucer magnolia back into a blooming branch system. Not as lovely as the original, but passable, and I no longer have to remove water sprouts that make the tree look such a fright for half of the year.

When rehabilitating the crown of a previously mal-pruned tree, I am more tempted with magnolias than other plants to head-back some of the skyrocketing water sprouts in hopes of building a crown with some lower internal branching. I'm not thoroughly convinced this works, but a knowledgeable arborist of my acquaintance assures me that it does.

Saucer Magnolia

The saucer magnolia (*M.* x *soulangeana)* is a really nice tree. It gets listed as a small tree in garden books because it tops out at about 20 to 30 feet. That's small in the world of trees. It's like saying an orca is small. That's small for a whale, but still really big for an animal. Thirty feet is a lot bigger than most people think when they plant something called a "small tree." Furthermore, folks don't really pay much attention to the part of the tree description that says the tree will get to be as wide as or wider than it is tall. The low, broad-spreading habit of the saucer magnolia makes it desirable, but it also means that it'll eat up half the average front yard. When people begin to realize this, about ten years after planting the tree, they usually respond by limbing up the tree. I don't like this solution because it defeats the nice spreading shape that the tree is meant to have. I also find that it results in water-sprout regrowth, and frequently the next-highest limbs will dip back down to the ground. (With most other trees, especially large-growing ones, limbing up works well.)

With a saucer magnolia, I just recommend that people keep removing grass so they

Figure 11.31 A. Removing a lateral that is too large will **B.** cause water sprouts to grow.

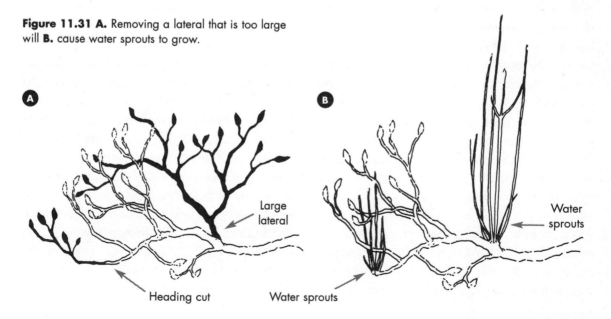

A

Large lateral

Heading cut

B

Water sprouts

Water sprouts

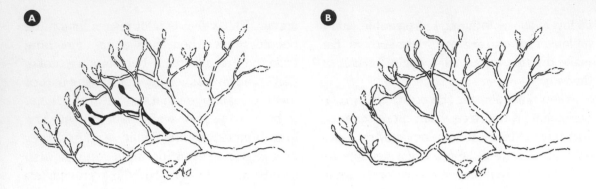

Figure 11.32 A. A few small, internal, well-made pruning cuts will **B.** not result in regrowth and water sprouts.

don't have to mow under the low-hanging limbs. And I advise planting a nice ground cover and spring bulbs in the bed. By the way, it is important to note that magnolias rarely transplant successfully—another reason to consider their site carefully.

Although it takes up a lot of room, I nonetheless consider the saucer magnolia a gardenworthy tree. Not only does it have an exquisite winter branch structure, it blooms with enormous pale purple flowers of heady fragrance. They are impressive without being gaudy. Even before they bloom, the elongating buds—like white candles standing on the branches—add to the intense excitement of oncoming spring. I love to watch them. And, to my knowledge, neither the saucer nor the star magnolia is plagued by any serious diseases, unlike many other flowering trees.

Later in summer, the magnolias set up some very interesting seed pods; the husk splits open to reveal a spiral of shiny orange pearls. I wonder if the formation has something to do with the fact that magnolias are one of the most ancient orders of plants. You might miss the pods if you are not looking. But the discovery and admiration of odd pods is an example of the rewards awaiting those who do their own maintenance. You get these little treats, if you are paying attention.

The saucer magnolia has large leaves, which add some contrast to the summer landscape. But better yet, those big leaves decompose through the winter, leaving a finely netted, leaf skeleton—lovely as lace. I don't get to bring those home either.

Evergreen or Southern Magnolia

Some people like the evergreen magnolia *(M. grandiflora)*, preferring evergreen plants to deciduous ones in general. The enormous green leaves of the evergreen magnolia have a contrasting feltlike brown backing that looks good in floral arrangements and wreaths. Broadleaf evergreen trees are relatively rare in our area. This accounts for the fact that an early explorer misnamed Magnolia Bluff in Seattle. The trees he saw lining the bluffs weren't magnolias, they were madronas *(Arbutus menziesii)*, our very own native broadleaf evergreen tree.

Like those of the saucer magnolia, the flowers of the evergreen magnolia are also big and fragrant, but they tend to bloom off and on, rather than putting on one big show. These trees get much taller than the saucer magnolia and therefore can be limbed up more successfully, if access is needed. However, it is preferable whenever possible to leave the lower limbs on this and all magnolias. Besides, if you limb them up all the flowers are overhead. This makes planting an evergreen magnolia down the hill, or below the second-story balcony (off to one side), a good idea.

I must confess I bear a grudge against evergreen magnolias. It's their leaves. They don't decompose—and they're slicker than ice. I worry about little old ladies slipping on them, and not-so-little or not-so-old maintenance gardener ladies too. This feature makes them a bad choice for sidewalk plantings and patios. Raking them up is like raking up shingles. And the limbs are weak, breaking under snow loads (except the 'St. Mary' and 'Victoria' varieties, perhaps). I have also seen a few trees get a virus disease that causes the leaves to die. It's not a big deal, but it's another strike against them.

On the other hand, I know many other gardeners who especially like the evergreen magnolias. It really is just a matter of personal preference. As you advance in the world of gardening, you become disenchanted with the most common species and more enamored of the rarer and often less showy varieties. My personal feeling is that the reason many, if not all, of the most popular plants are most popular is that they really are the best. I think if you lined up a bunch of those smarmy horticulturists who (for some inexplicable reason) had never seen a magnolia tree before, they would pick out these three as the best.

Star Magnolia

Now the star magnolia *(M. stellata)* is truly a small tree (when it grows up). The mature ones I know are about 10 by 15 feet. For the first decade or two the star magnolia will serve as a nice shrub. Its flowers resemble stars, with straplike white petals. It has the characteristic fuzzy buds, articulate branch structure, and the magnolia's penchant for throwing water sprouts when pruned. Like all the magnolias, it should be planted where it can reach maturity in height and width without restriction.

You can get into trouble limbing up star magnolias, because then you'll have to remove the water sprouts two or three times a year for eternity. (Boy, does that get old fast.) But I have seen star magnolias sold on standards as trees. A standard is a long straight trunk upon which the crown is grafted. These trees, as well as the shrub form of star magnolias, are available with either pink or white blooms.

Other Magnolias

Despite my preferences, you might care to know that horticulturists in our area will be more impressed by finding a cucumber magnolia with yellow flowers *(M. acuminata subcordata)*, a bigleaf magnolia *(M. macrophylla)* with fabulous 1–2½-foot leaves, or a Campbell's magnolia *(M. campbellii)* with flowers like water lilies on bare branches in March. There are many others. But rest assured, magnolias, no matter what variety, are never considered banal.

Summary

Magnolias are very touchy, and it doesn't take much pruning, even selective pruning, to set off the water-sprout response. Therefore, deadwood only. If you do prune, do so minimally, using small, internal thinning cuts whenever possible.

ORNAMENTAL CHERRY, CRABAPPLE, AND PURPLE-LEAF PLUM TREES (*Prunus and Malus*)

This spring I got a call from a lady who said, "I pruned my flowering plum tree according to the instructions in my pruning book. I took out all the crossing branches, the ones headed into the middle, and the water sprouts. There's nothing left, I think I may have killed it!" Although she may have, the more likely scenario is that it will explode into water-sprout regrowth over the course of the next year.

Plums (*Prunus* x *blireiana*, *P. cerasifera* 'Atropurpea' and other cultivars), crabapples (*Malus* spp.) and flowering cherries (*Prunus* spp.) suffer from a great deal of mal-pruning because they have fairly confusing, and to some, upsetting branch systems. They are also usually at a height that most pruners can get to (although height doesn't seem to stop people when they get a hankering to top their birches—the single most abused tree in the Seattle area). The branch patterns on plums, crabs, and cherries naturally cross back and forth. Andrea, my mentor, described it as "dancing branches." I think they look more like someone took the lid off a box of bunnies.

Don't

Watch out! The main reason these trees are difficult to prune is that they are extremely prone to water-sprout regrowth. Water sprouts are the straight, skinny, rapidly growing shoots that are the result of mal-pruning and other forms of stress. These trees just seem to have itchy buds. Walk past them with a pair of Felco pruners and they're likely to throw enough sprouts to turn your hair white. ("Oh, is that what happened?" I can hear someone saying.)

The other problem with plums and cherries (not crabs) is that they are horrible compartmentalizers. (Can I get a "Prunus with an absence of malus" joke in here somehow?) That is to say, they die back readily if branches are shortened (headed). When the jerk who owns the apartment building down by the Jack in the Box in my neighborhood topped five full-sized purple-leaf plums, two died stone-cold dead within the first two years. The rest grew back to exactly the same size (except now their winter branch pattern is ruined and they all have suckers growing from the graft union). I have even seen young cherry and plum trees die from numerous small heading cuts (less than 2 inches). The fact that these species are so sensitive makes me resist even the slightest bit of size reduction.

I remember buying my 'Mount Fuji' cherry many years ago. At first I longed for the branches to be lower and more horizontal. To my delight, I found that over time the limbs folded down and out. A few years later, I realized that they don't stop growing. The lower limbs kept lowering. Eventually one branch headed into the parking space. The one on the other side lowered into foot traffic. I headed one branch back selectively, cutting back to a largish side limb. The other one I cut off completely. This year the tree is near dead, mostly because of a virus (no inside leaves) and the brown rot (killing branches from the tip back). But I'm certain that the pruning hurt it as well.

It is not uncommon for homeowners with very old, broad-limbed cherry trees to ask to have them pruned back "just a little" to stop them from getting too wide. I never oblige. It's just too hard on a cherry tree, in my opinion, which is old at age forty (figure 11.33).

I was most unnerved when some grossly topped cherries (3-foot-diameter trunks, 1-foot topping cuts) that I pass on my way to the Center for Urban Horticulture survived, resprouted, and seemed to be doing fine. Two years later they were gone. I wish that plants responded more predictably to bad pruning, and did so within the first month. Would that trees had vocal cords too. Unfortunately, the death and dieback from topping, heading, and repeat-stripping is bad for trees in a statistical sort of way. Smoking cigarettes only kills some people (not all), and then only after a long period of time. The ill effects of bad pruning often take years to show up. By then no one connects the cause with the effect. The trees are dead and gone.

The Other Common Pruning Mistake

It is important to avoid stripping out the center of a plum, crab, or cherry. New gardeners frequently overprune in this way. If a little is good, a lot is better. But as in cutting hair, it is important to know when to quit. Overthinning is a little harder to forgive when done by experienced professionals, but it is extremely common. In particular, we had one such well-loved arborist here in Seattle. He was the darling, in fact, of some of the wealthier garden clubs. He routinely stripped out these trees to "accentuate" the branch pattern. We sarcastically called him Art the tree shaper. Of course the trees bloomed pathetically, and the tree owners were locked into the expensive re-removal of water sprouts every year, forever. He died a few years ago, but I still run across many examples of his work, living monuments to his ego and his misguided love of trees.

Figure 11.33 Resist size reduction in pruning: **A.** Water-sprout regrowth from "proper" crown reduction **B.** Dieback from heading-back "a little"

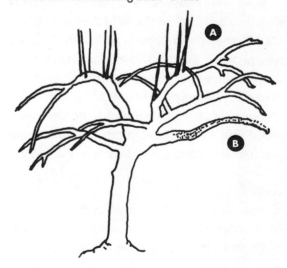

An entire subset of well-educated arborists in the San Francisco area have subscribed to this sort of overthinning; readers down there will have a hard time discerning those arborists who prune well from those who prune too well when talking to them or to their devoted customers. However, I can offer the following advice: With few exceptions, a properly pruned tree will not regrow into a forest of water sprouts the following spring. (The exceptions include elms, which tend to water-sprout no matter how lightly you prune them, and espaliered fruit trees.)

Deadwood

Ninety percent of your cuts should be dead branch, dead stub, and dead twig removal. Summer pruning will make it easier to spot the billions of tiny dead twigs in your cherry tree. I hope you have strong knees and a good aluminum three-point orchard ladder, because such a chore can take up to three hours on a large, old, neglected flowering cherry. But it is well worth the effort.

When I teach grounds crews how to prune we eventually get to the field demonstration, and afterwards a novice is apt to say, "I didn't realize what a big difference taking out the deadwood would make." And next year the job will take only a fraction of the time. For you new pruners, remember to do the deadwood first and to spend almost as much time placing and setting your ladder as pruning.

Live Wood:
Remember the Pruning Budget

Now let's move on to pruning live wood. It helps to think of plants as having a pruning budget, which you can spend any way you like. On crabs, cherries, and ornamental plums, the live-wood budget is small (because of problems of compartmentalization and water-sprout regrowth). For example, you can have three big cuts and ten small cuts, or twenty small cuts, or five large cuts, or any combination thereof; but remember you will *not* be allowed to remove *all* the crossing/rubbing, wrong-way branches. So consider carefully before you cut. Choose to remove those branches that will give you the greatest aesthetic improvement (see Figure 11.34). Look for the worst first.

Look for branches that actually touch each other (crossing/rubbing) but that have not grafted to each other (as sometimes happens). If they are not too big (more than 2 inches in diameter), maybe you can cut one out and leave the other, better-placed one. Usually you choose to leave the branch that heads out from the center, but not always. Especially on these trees, the branches' natural habit is to backtrack. I like the description of thinning out trees that says "Every space is filled, but with fewer branches." Try to restrict your cuts to true thinning cuts, taking a small lateral off a parent stem rather than making selective heading cuts that reduce a limb by cutting back to a lateral.

You get more aesthetic bang per buck by removing branches that crowd near the branch crotches. But be careful, it looks so good to take out some of the laterals that you might feel compelled to continue out the branch, leading to overthinning. It is also a common desire among new pruners to cut off all the small twiglets commonly found on cherry tree trunks and branches, to give them that clean look. But remember, these twiglets bloom in the spring and are quite pleasing. Leave as many as you can bear.

Pruning students are admonished not to stay too long in any one place, lest they over-prune. Keep moving, keep moving. When I consider an area of crowded branches, I first try out several possible cuts in my mind's eye. If I am at all in doubt, I don't prune; instead I leave it and move on to something I am confident should be pruned. This is another way to keep yourself from overthinning a tree.

Especially resist the temptation to remove branches at the upper crowns of crabapples in order to smooth out the tree's profile. It invariably causes an upsurge of water sprouts, which *really* ruins the outline. You'll

Figure 11.34 Correct pruning: Choose to remove branches that will give you the greatest aesthetic improvement. **A.** Dead stub **B.** Wrong way branches **C.** Suckers

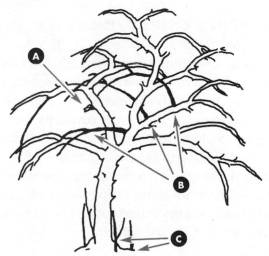

never get rid of them by repruning, and the tree will, in fact, become more labor intensive and unmanageable every year.

The best looking purple-leaf plum trees I've seen are ones that are very old and have never been pruned. Go in, take out "the dead," and leave the rest. Young plums have a lot of water sprout/sucker-like growth inside the crown. This is normal, and if you insist on removing it you will get to do more of it every year till you die. The other alternative is to leave those long skinny shoots and let them age, curve gently, and become graceful branches after ten years. Nonintervention is the best strategy.

Do, however, remove any and all true suckers—those that originate on the trunk, graft union (looks like a bulge), or roots. This is a common problem found on crabapples. These suckers will ruin the looks of your tree if allowed to remain. If the suckers originate below the graft union, they will grow up into large trees, overtaking the originally selected plant. Due to mower abuse, my local pizzeria now has three large, green-leafed, white-blossomed plum trees and only one of the original small, purple-leaf, pink-flowering plums that were planted on the parking strip.

Rehabilitative Pruning

I watch trees and landscapes over years, and I am constantly amazed at how well most of them recover, given half a chance. About four years ago, at a condominium I frequently drive by, the landscapers stripped out four purple-leaf plum trees as part of their grounds maintenance program. That spring, the trees shot back up with a ton of water sprouts thick as the hair on a dog's back. Over the next two years the sprouts turned back into branches about the diameter of my wrist. Once they reached the height of the previous tree, they began to arch out and put on side branches. I couldn't believe my eyes. Most of the lesser water sprouts remained puny or died off.

This example goes to show that after a tree has been tipped, topped, or stripped, the next course of action is to WAIT. Getting "on top of it" early will simply put your tree back into a spasm of regrowth (see Figure 11.35). In fact, it's probably best to wait three or four years to do any crown restoration. The exception is the removal of deadwood (stubs, twigs, and branches) as it occurs. After the tree has reached its original height, you may slowly, gently, and over the course of a few years thin out the crowded areas where several branches originate from the same point. Back at the condo complex, the trees reestablished without any help just in time for the next crew to sweep through and tip them all back (arghhhh!).

For a tree that has been clipped into a perfect globe, thin out the lower portions, trying to make the tree more uniformly branched. Grounds crews or condo owners who have inherited globed or umbrellaed trees may simply have to scowl and bear it as trees are resheared until they die (the tree or the person). Few people can endure the middle phase (waiting) in crown restoration. It reminds me of growing out a "perm" or a bad dye job.

Summary

Don't top these trees. Don't tip them or shape them into balls, boxes, or hamburgers. Don't clip your crabapple into a cute umbrella every year. Don't try to turn a fastigiate (skinny) cherry tree into a horizontal tree or cut it back into a diaper shape. Avoid shortening (heading-back) major limbs and overthinning. As a general rule of thumb, restrict yourself to pruning less than one-eighth of the living canopy in a year. If water sprouts return at the places you cut, you either overpruned or sliced into the branch collar. Don't restrip trees that have been malpruned in the past. I don't care what your old pruning book says.

Do thin lightly, and avoid pruning altogether if you can. Removing deadwood and dead stubs is always in order and doesn't count against the pruning budget. Take out a few of the worst crossing/rubbing and wrong-way branches. Clean out the branch crotches a bit. Take no more than an eighth of the live crown and put up with a lot that is "wrong."

WEEPING CHERRY (*Prunus subhirtella 'Pendula'*)

"It was a weeping cherry, now it's a crying shame!" So said my co-worker upon seeing a brutally headed weeping cherry tree. It was a double shame, since weeping plants clean up so nicely with a good pruning job. I am always pleased to see a weeping tree of any kind at the site of a pruning demonstration. They're great for giving people a clear idea of what can be done with thinning and without having to get out the ladder.

Figure 11.35 A. Original cherry tree **B.** Overthinned tree: Laterals are stripped. **C.** The cherry begins to water-sprout. **D.** Wait! Another year. **E.** About four years later: The new crown forms.

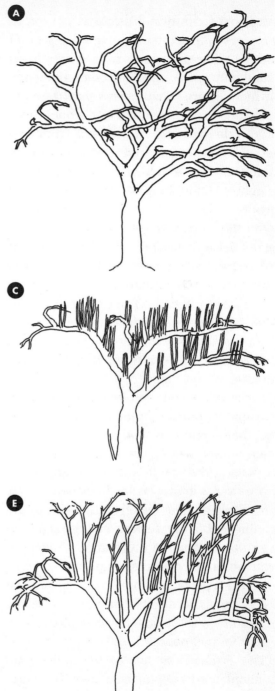

The Most Common Mistakes

The worst mistake is topping or any other general whacking done to a cherry tree. Genetically speaking, cherries are bad compartmentalizers. That means that they are more likely to rot out and/or die back from such rude pruning. Worse still, they are loaded with dormant buds that are just itching for an excuse to turn into a forest of the straight, wild-looking shoots called water sprouts.

Another common mistake is evenly shearing the branch ends off, like a hair trim. This isn't so hard on the tree's health, but it looks a lot like a "Moe" haircut, and it creates bunching at the ends. The preferred way to prune is to carefully cut each strand back to an out-facing bud or lateral branch. And stagger the cuts at differing lengths around the tree.

Yet another common error is tidying up the topmost portion of the crown by removing that errant branch that sticks up unpleasantly (see Figure 11.36). Next growing season the result will be the growth of two or three more errant branches (water sprouts) beginning exactly at the site of the pruning cut and growing very straight up from there. Remove those and . . . you get even more! So resist the temptation to make your tree a perfect umbrella. Those weeping cherry trees that are that way are genetically programmed to be so—for example, *P. sargentii* 'Snow Fountain'.

The errant branches of the more commonly planted weeping cherries will eventually droop down as the tree ages, evening itself out naturally. If you look at mature trees in your neighborhood, you will see that they are always a bit asymmetrical in their growth habit. It's how they increase in size.

It's likewise ill advised to try to stop a weeping beech from increasing in size. They don't water-sprout as vigorously as cherries, but like almost all trees, they too resist being kept down.

Suckers

Suckers from graft unions must be removed. Sometimes I drive by a big cherry or plum tree that has mostly white blossoms with a smattering of pinks lower down. The white belongs to the vigorous rootstock that broke free and has outgrown the chosen variety. It's a lot like the "Exorcist" story. Most plants have the weeping part sort of spliced onto the trunk, and you will see that graft union as a bulge at the top. Sometimes there is another bulge (graft union) between the trunk and the rootstock. Keeping your tree healthy, well watered, and properly pruned will help keep Mr. Hyde out of the picture. Should you spot a straight shoot from below that lower graft, saw it off promptly even if it requires a rather big cut.

Deadwood

Deadwood is the next thing you should search out. It's pretty easy to find on cherries. They are commonly and horribly afflicted on the west side of the Pacific Coast mountain ranges with two terrible diseases, blossom blight/brown rot (a fungus) and bacterial canker. Brown rot fills the trees with tiny dead twigs and causes the branches to grow even more kitty wampus than they do ordinarily. In the spring, the disease enters through the blossoms (which later hang on and look water-soaked) and the branch dies from the tip back. At the point where the disease is finally stopped by the tree, the next nearest bud or twig will grow out (usually at an unsightly 45-degree angle). Nearby and on many branches both large and small, you'll find sunken spots called cankers or lesions, which are another sign of disease (see Figure 11.37).

Bacterial canker (a bacterial disease) causes even larger cankers or lesions on the branches and trunk. It favors injured trees, like those that suffer from mal-pruning. If you follow "the rules" and cut out all diseased branches with lesions on your average cherry tree, you will destroy it! Pesticides, even when dutifully applied, are often ineffective. So it's best to just cut out all the little dead twigs (which can be very time consuming indeed, and is easiest when done in the summer), and rake up all the leaves in the fall on which the disease overwinters. But what a difference deadwooding makes! The ragged ugly mop turns into a lady's dainty parasol.

In the case of very small weeping cherries (easy to get to), the meticulous removal of dead twigs plus the increased air circulation can significantly reduce both diseases (I've eliminated brown rot on one client's patio tree). Larger, harder to get to cherries will still be chronically afflicted with diseases in wetter, warmer (warm to the fungi) climates. Pruning simply gives the tree a fighting

Figure 11.36 Young weeping cherry with errant branch **A.** Don't remove errant branch. **B.** Do remove lowest branches and ones hanging closest to the trunk. **C.** Errant branch folds down in time.

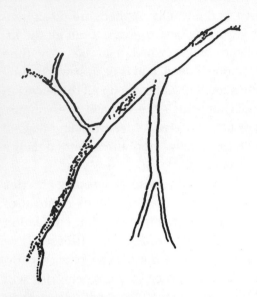

Figure 11.37 Dieback and lesions on a cherry tree

chance and makes it look better. I think of cherry trees as the sick kids of the plant world. There are so many cherry tree diseases (for all the cherry trees), in fact, that the Washington State Cooperative Extension publishes a little booklet titled "Why Cherry Trees Die" (publication number EB0668). It's good for both sides of the mountains and has great descriptions and photos. Contact your local county cooperative extension office if you want to order a copy (look for them in the blue pages, under "County").

Thinning
Thinning in general is the other pruning to be done. You see much improvement by thinning where all the branches meet up together at the top. There you will usually find several big dead stubs where the last pruner failed to cut them off completely. Carefully saw these out. Don't scar the bark

of nearby limbs or the trunk, or you will stimulate bothersome water sprouts.

Then remove a few of the lesser crossing or crowded branches. People always want to cut the top back, which, as mentioned above, may get you into deep trouble. Instead, go inside and remove the branches that are being shaded out underneath. Especially *target the branches that hang closest to the trunk* (see Figure 11.38). Follow them up to their larger parent stems and thin them off where they join it. Trust me, this process will make a huge difference.

Additional definition can be achieved by selectively heading some of the weeping branches that hang down, crossing into branches below. Follow the offender back to a good-sized lateral (at least half the diameter of the branch to be removed). Choose a lateral branch that is located on the upper side of the parent stem that is to be short-

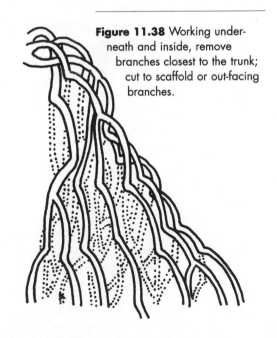

Figure 11.38 Working underneath and inside, remove branches closest to the trunk; cut to scaffold or out-facing branches.

ened. Look for one that heads out from the center of the plant, and make your cut there. This process can be used to raise the skirt, should it be trailing too low or on the ground.

Other Weeping (and Curly) Plants

These same general procedures apply to the other great weeping plants (you will find *pendulata* in their botanical names): weeping willows, beeches, spruces, pines, and birches (see Figure 11.39). Thinning will also help turn a wall of weeping blue Atlas cedar into a lovely beaded curtain. But don't attempt to thin out a weeping giant sequoia (it looks like a giant muppet); that one is best kept full bodied.

A good general thinning and deadwooding also does miracles for curly plants (they often have *contorta* in their names), such as Harry Lauder's walking stick (*Corylus avellana* "Contorta') and corkscrew willows. There are several plants that both curl and weep, such as Camperdown elm and some mulberry trees. They too will benefit from similar thinning.

Figure 11.39 Weeping birch

Summary

Take out the deadwood first. Then prune off some of the worst crossing/rubbing branches, but not all of them. Most pruning is done from under and inside the plant. Remove limbs that hang down closest to the trunk. Selectively head lower branches to upper, out-facing laterals. To lift the skirt, prune to out-facing buds or lateral branches of sufficient size. Go easy on the cherry trees because they water-sprout easily, removing no more than one-eighth of the live canopy, and ideally less.

Index

Japanese plum, 189
Julian's barberry, 80, 83
juniper
   crowding of, 70–71
   dead zone of, 69–70
   deadwooding of, 71–72
   description of, 69
   grab-and-snip method for, 71
   lowest limbs of, 70–71
   pruning of, 69, 72
   rehabilitative pruning of, 71
   removal of, 72
   shearing of, 69

K

kerria (*Kerria japonica*)
   creeping of, 81–82
   description of, 78, 80
kiwi, 149
Kolkwitzia amabilis. See beauty bush
kousa dogwood, 181

L

lace-cap hydrangeas, 92–94
lavender, 65–66
Lenten rose, 129
Leyland cypress, 121
lilac
   blooming of, 124
   crossing/rubbing branches, 122
   deadheading of, 123
   description of, 121
   leaning of, 123
   pruning of, 124
   radical renovation of, 123–24
   size of, 121
   suckers, 122–23
   summary of care for, 124
limbing-up, 13
lion's tailing, 14
Lonicera. See honeysuckle
loppers, 43–44

M

magnolia (*Magnolia*)
   Campbell's, 204

compartmentalization by, 200
description of, 199–200
evergreen, 202–3
M. acuminata subcordata, 203
M. campbellii, 204
M. grandiflora, 202–3
M. macrophylla, 203–4
M. stellata, 203
M. x soulangeana, 201
miscellaneous types of, 203–4
overthinning of, 200
pruning of, 200–201
rehabilitative pruning of, 200–201
saucer, 201–2
southern, 202–3
star, 203
Mahonia aquifolium. See Oregon grape
malpruning, vii–viii, 20, 25, 62, 179
Malus spp., 204
Matheny, Nelda P., 163
mildew
   on deciduous azaleas, 116
   on rhododendrons, 132
mock orange, 142
Moon shots, 51–52
Morris, James "Ciscoe," 102, 150–53
mounding-habit shrubs
   abelias. *See* abelias
   artemisia, 65–66
   boxwood. *See* boxwood
   broom, 68
   burning bush. *See* burning bush
   definition of, 50
   heathers, 65, *66*
   heaths, 65, *66*
   juniper. *See* juniper
   lavender, 65–66
   pruning of, 50
   senecio, 65–66
   spiraea. *See* spiraea
   types of, 50

N

Nandina domestica. See heavenly bamboo
1-Napthaleneacetate, 25, 122
node, 4–5, *5*

of magnolia, 200–201
of plum trees, 207
of spiraea, 74
rhododendrons
  arborizing of, 127
  bed size for, 125
  deciduous azalea. *See* deciduous azalea
  description of, 115, 125
  layering of, 131
  "leggy," 128–29
  mildew on, 132
  nicking of buds, 129–30, *132*
  pruning of, 125, *126*
  R. ponticum, 132
  R. thomsonii, 127
  radical renovation of, 127–28, *129*
  rootstock, 132–34
  selective reduction of, 126
  size reduction, 125–27
  spaghetti, 131–32, *133*
  transplanting of, 125–26, *127*
rockrose, 67–68
root mass, 19–20
rootstock roses, 96
rootstock suckers, 98–99
rose(s)
  climbing, 97, 149
  deadheading of, 100–101
  deadwooding of, 98
  diseases of, 100
  in Fall, 101
  hybrid tea. *See* hybrid tea roses
  pruning of, 98–100
  rootstock suckers, 98–99
  shrub-type, 97
  in Spring, 102
  time to buy, 97
  types of, 97
  where to cut, 99–100
  in Winter, 101–2
rose hips, 97, 100
Roundup, 159
runners, 155–56, 158

S

Salix spp., 163
saucer magnolia, 201–2
saw, pruning, 44–45
scaffold branches, 14
Schenk, George, 113
scion, 168
selective heading
  of cotoneaster, *112*
  cuts, *11*
  definition of, 11
  illustration of, *9*
  Japanese maple, 195–96
  of laurel, 117
  of photinia, 117
  of shrubs, 12–13
  of trees, 11–12
selective pruning, 13, 58, 65, 88, 107
senecio, 65–66
shearing
  of abelias, 51
  counterproductive uses of, 8–9
  description of, 6–7
  of evergreen azaleas, 61
  health effects of, 7–8
  high maintenance requirements of, 8
  inappropriate uses of, 7–9
  of juniper, 69
  natural beauty effects of, 9
  photinia, 117–18
  shrub size controlled by, 7, 13
  of spiraea, 74
  stress caused by, 7
  texture effects, 9
shell pruning, 192
Shigo, Dr. Alex, 13, 162–63
"shotgun" method of pruning, 82, *83*
shrubs
  English laurel as, 118–19
  mounting-habit. *See* mounting-habit shrubs
  overthinning of, 56
  photinia as, 118–19
  selective heading of, 12–13
  size of, shearing to control, 7, 13, 19